365 Daily Inspirations~ Ideas For Higher Living

By Kristin Pedderson

A daily collection of reflections designed to uplift, encourage, and transform your spiritual journey. Drawing from personal experiences and timeless wisdom, Kristin offers a year's worth of inspiring messages that guide readers toward a deeper connection with God.

Each day provides thoughtful insights, practical ideas, and empowering affirmations to help you live with intention, embrace positivity, and nurture your faith. Whether you're seeking encouragement, clarity, or a fresh perspective, this book will help you elevate your thinking and live with greater purpose and fulfillment. Let these inspirations ignite your spirit and lead you toward higher living—one day at a time.

A NorCal Press Publication

TABLE OF CONTENTS

INTRODUCTION

Welcome to *"365 Daily Inspirations ~ Ideas For Higher Living"* In the busyness of everyday life, it's easy to lose sight of what truly matters. We often find ourselves overwhelmed by responsibilities, challenges, and the constant stream of information. These writings serve as gentle reminders to pause, reflect, and reconnect with the deeper aspects of God, yourself, and your life.

Each day offers a fresh perspective and a simple, biblically-based idea to help you live a more intentional and meaningful life. My hope is that you will find comfort, motivation, and enlightenment as you read, guiding you toward a higher way of living. Whether you're seeking personal growth, inner peace, or a deeper connection with the world around you, this book offers a path to enrich your journey.

As you explore these pages, take a moment each day to absorb the message. I believe that by incorporating Godly wisdom into your life, you can experience abundant blessings and happiness. And finally, I pray that these inspirations will be a source of light and encouragement, helping you to navigate your days with grace and purpose.

DEDICATION

This dedication is a heartfelt tribute with awe and gratitude to my circle of friends who inspire me to reach higher on a daily basis, even as they are unaware of their great contribution. Your quiet strength, love, and unwavering support have been a source of light in my life. To each of you, thank you for being a reflection of God's grace and for encouraging me, often unknowingly, to pursue my highest potential. This book is a testament to the love and friendship we share, and I am forever grateful for the role you play in my journey.

Love, Kristin

JANUARY

January 1

The Better Way

For many, making wise decisions is extremely challenging. Choices can be difficult and life changing. And when we do not pay attention to Truth, we lack wisdom.

Jesus is The Way, the Truth and the life. And those who place their faith in Christ, have guidance when they seek it. Believers are never alone and consistently guided to choose the better way. And even when failing and making mistakes, the believer can hear the Holy Spirit.

Have you ever said to yourself "I won't do that again?" Perhaps you made a big mistake or a small snafu that in hindsight taught you a better way? We learn from failures. And after we've made enough mistakes, we get good at knowing the better way. It is always the still small voice that says, "do this" or "go this way", all for our benefit.

At times we feel unsupported through trials. However this is false, as Scripture tells us in Psalm 16:8, "I know the Lord is always with me. I will not be shaken, for He is right beside me." This tells us that we are not alone on our journey, and as we venture into new opportunities and vistas, we simply need to believe God is near and guiding our steps. Additionally, the Lord hears our prayers.

There are times, we must step out of our comfort zone, because faith without action is dead. And when we step out and try something new, we gain and grow effectively. We do not succumb to fear of failure, mistakes, or the idea that we are alone. We don't navigate through tough terrain on our own. We understand and believe that God is always near to us and providing wisdom.

Today, thoughtfully consider your path. Will God bless iniquity? No. If we think we are getting away with something—choosing a road that includes lying, stealing, cheating, or engaging in immorality (behavior that is morally wrong or outside society's standards of what is acceptable)—we can expect correction. And even though God is merciful and long-suffering, the truth remains: God wants the best for us. He desires us to take the high road in our lives.

The Lord will show you the better way when you invite Him in. He does not want you crying, deceived, or living in darkness. His desire for you is to be joyful, knowing that you are loved and valued. God's Love is unconditional. And even though you may mess things up, when you have a heart willing to confess your missteps, you are still on track to receive a flow of abundant blessings.

January 2

Eyes To See And Ears To Hear

We find happiness in the place where we find Truth. And our encounters shape us uniquely. Each person holds impactful experiences that can include every type of condition, trial, and temptation. We face joy and sorrow, pleasure and pain, distinctive in some sort of way. Further, it may appear on the surface that someone has a cookie cutter life, or nearly perfect. However, every person has a level of trouble and prior conditioning.

And it's true that people get angry with God when they have suffered difficult things. They can turn their back on the Holy Spirit's guidance and become very self-sufficient. But self sufficiency does not produce happiness. It does however produce strain, loneliness, and a lack of miracles.

When walls fall down, it can be devastating. And unfortunately, some walk with their eyes closed and rarely hear the higher direction of Love. Plenty do not hear and listen for God's voice. Perhaps they are too busy monitoring their inner dialog, that's been developed by conditioning or failure.

Regardless of where you have been or what you have gone through, you can be happy where you are today. The key is to have eyes to see and ears to hear. Being truly happy means being free to hear the truth of God's unconditional Love with honesty and humility. Listen and hear, and see, with eyes of Love. And God's Love moves us forward in ways that do not disappoint, as Grace abounds with hope.

Begin by envisioning yourself laying all your burdens at the foot of the Cross. Can you see it? Then, take a moment to listen and hear what God is saying to you. People may have their opinions—'You're too loud' or 'You're too quiet,' 'You're crazy,' or 'You're a big dreamer.' But there is a deeper Truth that whispers to the believer: 'You are greatly loved, just as you are.

January 3

Faith Beyond Doubt

There is an odd thing about believing and having faith, yet still having an inkling of doubt. It's the situation where in your heart of hearts, you believe, yet you still feel an inkling of doubt that something may fail or not be exactly as you have believed it to be.

Great strength to overcome obstacles and to see dreams come true, requires believing firmly without a doubt. It's like walking a tightrope that requires a single minded focus. However, being human and believing in the unseen can be difficult. It's as if we weave in and out of trusting God. So we must refresh our faith daily, to get back to the place of firm belief.

There is no way to remain balanced if we are constantly looking to the left or the right. Just as a ballet dancer finds their focal point to make precise turns, or an archer aims for their target with unwavering precision, we too need a single-minded focus on the Truth of Christ. This focus encompasses courage, sacrifice, gentleness, and a greater vision.

Scripture says in Colossians 1:11, "We also pray that you will be strengthened with all His glorious power, so that you will have all the endurance and patience you need."

When we focus on Jesus—embracing His mercy, forgiveness, and Grace daily—we become more established in the faith. Over time, this focus helps us experience less doubt and grow in belief, fostering a deeper reliance on God. If we aim to manifest greatness, we must keep life in its proper perspective. Rather than clinging to the things of this world, we should strive to live in a way that makes an eternal difference.

And plenty do not care about manifesting greatness. But what most people truly desire is peace. And true peace comes from firmly believing in the Lord who saves. The One who knows every hair on your head. The God who goes before you. The One who orders your steps.

So, if you are struggling with belief today and experiencing doubt, consider God's great Love for you. He sent Jesus as an example and cornerstone. Reflect on His life and how He endured the Cross, knowing that we would be the ones to benefit. You can pray: "Lord, help my unbelief. Help me to see clearly with eyes of faith." Amen.

January 4

Everything Beautiful In Time

A soul's path can be likened to a tapestry that appears beautiful on one side and on the other, a tangled mess. And although we do not know what is coming, facing forward, the picture displays a unique beauty. And while there are ugly things we must face and experience at times, God is at work in us, to make everything beautiful in its time.

Scripture says in Ecclesiastes 3:11, "He has made everything beautiful in its time. He has set eternity in the human heart; yet no one can fathom what God has done from beginning to end."

We all struggle with self-acceptance and loving others unconditionally from time to time. That's okay because the struggle often serves as a glue that holds all the parts of our lives together. When we keep our focus on walking in Love—toward God, ourselves, and our fellow man—every moment becomes a thread in a beautiful tapestry that unfolds over time. So, live in the moment, walk in Love, and always consider what Love would do in every circumstance.

Often, we become disappointed when things don't unfold the way we envision. We strive to bring our ideas to life, believing it's up to us to make things happen and change ourselves or others. However, the best way to see genuine progress is to take a hands-off approach. We don't need to impose our will on the lives of others or attempt to shape circumstances according to our preferences.

The Lord knows what each soul needs to grow. We need to trust God, who orders our steps. While we may not always like our circumstances, we must remember that they are temporary. It's not that we first loved Him, but that He first loved us. And when we understand that God's Love is in control, not ours, we can relax and trust the journey of the soul to unfold naturally.

Our journey through this temporary life belongs to the One who loves us and keeps us for all eternity. So, rejoice and be free. It's not up to you to do it all. Leave this beautiful work of art to the One who makes everything beautiful in its time.

January 5

This Grace Is Yours

Doing something you have not done before, requires a level of risk. And each of us has ideas, but for many, it's not easy to take a leap into something new. Change can be frightening, due to impacting factors especially of the unknown. But what is needed is faith with action.

Nothing great comes without risk and the possibility of failure. We learn the most about success and ourselves when we are brave enough to try something new. If we settle for the status quo, we place unnecessary limits on our lives. Unfortunately, many people play it safe and later regret not taking risks as life unfolds and time passes.

With many responsibilities, the high cost of living, and time constraints, chasing dreams and starting something new can be complicated. While these challenges are real, we don't have to settle, when pursuing the life we envision. We must move forward with the confidence that if it is God's will, the doors will open.

When there is a God-given dream, there is also a grace and precise timing where all the necessary elements come together. However, if we are slow to act on a new vision, we might miss the opportunity, and it may not come again. On the other hand, if we get ahead of God's timing, we might find ourselves in a dilemma.

Scripture tells us in James 2:19, 'Faith by itself, if it does not have works, is dead.' This means that while having vision and faith is important, without taking action, we may miss out on blessings and see little change. As you walk with the Lord today, trust that He will guide you in the way you should go. Pursue the dream in your heart with both faith and action.

This grace is yours. As a child of God, the Holy Spirit dwells within you and will guide you through every decision. Step out in faith and keep prayer at the center of your journey. As you share your heart with the Lord, trust that He will bring about the manifestation you need. It might look different from what you envisioned, but it will be perfect in its own way. The growth that comes from stepping out in faith is truly priceless.

January 6

Praise His Name

Are you feeling depressed today? Do you struggle with sadness? When these feelings arise, it's important to be proactive and praise the Lord. Call on the name of Jesus and shout praises to God, for there is power in His name. Praising God can actually bring healing.

Speak Truth from your mouth, because words have the power to change your circumstances. Even a simple song from a thankful heart can shift a feeling or a mood. Have you tried saying His name out loud yet? Praise the name of Jesus!

There is always hope for a new beginning and freedom from depression when we verbally give thanks and praise. Christ is a gift to humanity. He saves, heals, and teaches us how to walk in what truly matters. He is our healer, our "Great Physician."

Remember, in the beginning was the Word, and the Word was God. This shows the immense power of our words. If you constantly speak of being depressed or complain, it won't help you. Instead, find a quiet place to pray and shout praises to the Lord. Speak them out loud. When you feel depressed, defeated, or down, sing a song of praise. Use your voice for positive proclamations.

Seasons change and your life can change in a moment. We all go through difficult seasons. And as a cold winter brings a process of renewal for the earth, tough times can also renew our spirit. Therefore, be gentle with yourself as you go through and speak out loud: "This too shall pass."

Did you know that focusing inwardly can sometimes increase feelings of depression? When we allow our thoughts to become too self-absorbed, it can weigh us down even more. Instead, try shifting your perspective—believe in surprises and expect God to surprise you. One of the best ways to combat loneliness and depression is to reach out and help someone else. Look around and see how you can be a blessing to someone in need. By serving others, you'll find that your own burdens feel lighter and your heart grows fuller.

Lastly, go easy on yourself. This season might be challenging, but God's got you. Don't wait until it's too late to call on Him. Face your fears and call on the name of Jesus today. Remember, there is power in His name—so praise Him amid the storm.

January 7

The Heart That Speaks

Most of us have made choices we wish we could forget. But mistakes are valuable opportunities for growth. The goal is to learn from them and not continue in folly. When we leave this world, we aren't remembered solely for our accomplishments. If someone has a harsh tongue or hurts others emotionally or physically, those actions are remembered. People may forgive, but they rarely forget. This is why it's essential to heed the Scripture that encourages us to 'live a life beyond reproach.'

No one can deny that good and evil exists. So why would we think that we can be good and continue bringing evil into the world? It's true that no one is perfect, but we must be aware of the real situation between good and evil. Especially as mature adults.

Scripture tells us in Ephesians 4:29, "Do not let any unwholesome talk come out of your mouths, but only what is helpful for building others up according to their needs, that it may benefit those who listen."

If we want a better life, we need to put away perversity. In our youth, using swear words might seem adventurous or rebellious. But as we grow into adulthood, we need to let them go, because what we say not only affects others but also reflects the condition of our hearts. To turn away from what is evil, we must rely on the Holy Spirit to fill us and guide us toward what is right and good.

Do you desire great blessings and a long life? Then choose life. Everyone has things they are not proud of, but Scripture reveals that 'out of the mouth, the heart speaks.' This means that what we say reflects what is in our hearts. It is essential to recognize that our words are vitally important for the healing of both ourselves and our world. We cannot expect to be blessed when our hearts are filled with vile, rude language, and perversity.

What will people remember about you? Hopefully you'll be remembered for the good that you bring into the world. But if you are participating in expressing evil and especially to innocent ears, do not expect good results. Make yourself beyond reproach. Here you can choose to do the best you can to consider how your words and actions impact other people.

January 8

Guard Your Heart

When we value something, we protect it. We guard our devices and instruments carefully, ensuring they don't break if they drop. We use cases, screen protectors, and even lanyards, and sometimes we hide them in inconspicuous places. And just as we take measures to protect the material things we consider valuable, we must also guard and value our hearts.

When you are a loving person, you are open to vulnerabilities. This is why it's important to be observant and take time to see people for who they really are. When we initially meet others, there is little way to know the full spectrum and condition of their heart. Someone can appear good, honest and loving, yet they may hold hidden agendas.

So how do we truly know a person's heart? Scripture tells us that only God knows the heart. However, it also says, 'You shall know them by their fruit.' This means that a good indicator of a person's character is the fruit they produce—whether it is good and plentiful, or bad and lacking. We must remember that not everyone has the same inclinations or intentions.

Every heart has value, so we must prioritize listening to others. Understanding is essential, and we should not fear open communication. In fact, we should strive to be experts in it. True understanding begins with listening. Once we genuinely listen and understand, we can express ourselves in a loving way. The goal is to honor one another and address situations that work against kindness and the cultivation of good fruit in our lives.

Whatever the situation may be, when we walk guarding our heart, we are able to grow together. The ideal is to allow friendship and love to develop over time, without much expectation. And when people hurt or offend us, or when we hurt or offend others, we need not completely dispose of the relationship, unless it's obviously unhealthy. Instead, we can be quick to forgive, and not easily offended. We can imagine a protective case around our feelings.

We need mercy and wisdom. And as we guard our valuable hearts, we can look for the fruit of our lives to grow. We can stay in balance, with the understanding that every person is imperfect. And because we know people by their fruit, we can learn much by watching others to see what is being manifested into their lives. Proverbs 4:23 says, "Above all else, guard your heart; for out of it flows the issues of life."

January 9

God Orders Our Steps

It's easy to feel stuck on occasion. We have dreams and ideas that we'd like to see come to fruition. And for most of us, much is required each day. We may hold a job, need to pay bills and have families and loved ones that need our attention. However, when we have God inspired dreams, we can follow knowing that our steps are ordered by the Lord, one day at a time.

Some may entertain the thought, "Oh it'll be better when I have more money to work with" or "I'll do this, when the opportunity arises." Or you might say, "When I can afford to hire a team, I will begin." And with these, the dream gets put on hold and there is not much progress. For many, time passes and the pursuit of the dream dies. So we must be faithful to put one foot in front of the other and not wait for all the circumstances to be ideal.

The Lord knows what each of us needs in every instance. And without God in the center of our dreams, our greater purpose can become tainted. And there are fortunate ones who jump into an idea, with little difficulty, and make money at the onset. Also there are some with help from families or a support system. But oftentimes, especially in artistic expressions, the money doesn't always come so easily. And countless individuals begin a dream with the wrong motives and then fail to persevere. They spend plenty of time and money just to discover their ideas are not flourishing. Perhaps they were chasing the dollar or even fame?

Maybe you have been hoping for certain opportunities. However, personal growth comes not from getting what you want right away. There must be trust that whatever we're faced with and must go through, is for the highest good. And if opportunity knocks before we are ready to stand, we may not handle the situation with the level of maturity that is required to sustain the vision. Additionally, we may think that we know what's best for us, but we need to understand that the Creator of the Universe knows the deeper things that our soul needs.

What if we do have the ideal components as we try something new? It's possible that what we hope for may not always be in our best interest. Therefore, start by taking small steps toward your vision and make peace with the fact that, while we make plans, it is God who orders our steps. Consistent small efforts are often enough. And as you trust and allow God to reveal your life path for the greater good, you evolve into the whole person you were always meant to be.

January 10

Can I Do Over Please?

If you had the chance to do certain things over, would you? Most people would agree to change a few things if they could go around again. But often choices we are given, have a time stamp on them. There is a grace for the time and moment that we are in.

Maybe you let go of what you thought was the love of your life and they found someone new? Or another example might be that you missed the window for having children. Now it may be difficult to change the situation. Unfortunately, there is no going back or changing what has already occurred. And we do reap the consequences of our actions.

We must do the best that we can, with what we are given. And as long as we are alive, we have the opportunity to change our direction and venture into a new path for the better. We can begin where we are today and determine ourselves to make wiser choices. The goal is to walk with understanding, humility, forgiveness, and hope.

In Scripture, 2 Corinthians 5:18-20 says, "Anyone united with the Messiah gets a fresh start. And all this comes from God who settled the relationship between us and Him and then called us to settle our relationship with each other".

This is the goodness of God at work in our lives. And you may need to reassess your journey, so that every day counts for good. It's never too late, and smarter to turn and choose wisely. Especially when you realize you have made a less than stellar choice.

Are you feeling discouraged about your life and the choices you have made? Forgive yourself. Bring your heart to Jesus and leave your sorrow at the foot of the Cross. Invite the Lord to walk with you in a simple prayer. "Say God help me. Come into my heart and guide me for your good." Amen.

Also, ask God to show you the desires of your heart. Even if you are late to the game, and struggling, the Lord will help you to take the focus off what was lost. He will show you a new vision and what can be found. Only come as you are and believe. He delights in giving you the desires of your heart. And it's never too late to pick up the pieces where you left them.

January 11

Moments That Matter

We can get pretty distracted by the noise of daily life, and at times we may begin to lose our peace and focus. And just as every good relationship needs effort, we need to continually put effort into our thought life. We must take control of worry and release negativity.

Life is like art, and we put it all together by remembering the moments that have truly impacted us. And when times are tough, we can take care, to focus on the beauty that remains and matters. We do this by using all of our senses. For instance, we can use sounds, smells, beautiful pictures, and touch, to change our disposition and brighten our way. When we remember the times we made it through a situation, we are strengthened.

Do you remember the moment of your salvation? Or the times that you faced great fear and made it through? Perhaps a time when you were delivered from a crisis? Utilizing senses, makes it possible to slow down and re-create moments that strengthen us through difficult times. Consider the sound of passing trains or church bells in the distance. Or perhaps the sound of rustling horses or a bubbling brook. Whatever the case, our senses help us overcome difficulties. So remember the nuances that warm your heart and soul.

Obviously, we do not have the ability to control the future. But the present moment is now and how we choose to experience it, is up to us. When things are exciting and good, it's easy to feel encouraged. But when trouble rears its ugly head, we need not get stuck in negativity or fear. Instead we can choose to reflect on the beauty that has come before us.

Scripture says in Deuteronomy 6:12, "Be careful that you do not forget the Lord, who brought you out of Egypt, out of the land of slavery". This passage encourages us to remember what the Lord has done in our lives and how we have come into freedom. We're to remember the journey, the deliverances, the sights and sounds, the smells and the times that changed our lives for the better. And as we recall provisions made for us, our fears are eased.

Do you remember the first time you discovered that you could trust God? Or perhaps a realized feeling of undeniable Love? Remember the moments that matter. Remember you are covered by the blood of Jesus. And do not allow pain and difficulty to overcome your daily life.

January 12

Let God Carry You

Following the Lord's vision for your life can feel like an uphill climb. The path may be steep and sometimes it's as if you are placing your feet on steps or rocks that are unstable. But through the fire and the unknown, you can be sure that God will carry you.

When we take the time to pray and ask for guidance from God, He provides and goes before us. Additionally, we gain strength to walk in accordance with His will.

Climbing any ladder to reach the top can be frightening and traumatic. And most great achievements require great risk. This is because as we venture into new things we have never done before, we will face some fear. So we need to be careful not to fall on our face.

Consider your ways today and step carefully. The idea is to place your feet in the ideal position for the best results. And how can you be sure that you have your feet in the ideal position? By listening to the still small voice of the Lord within as your guide. When you take time to pray before setting out, you will move toward the desires of your heart. And you may not always see things happen the way you envision, or on your timetable, but you can trust that your steps are ordered.

And it's good to know that you do not need to do it all yourself. As you walk forward, the Holy Spirit works in your favor. And every step of faith reveals that progress rarely comes easy and anything worth keeping requires effort. So keep climbing upward toward new borders. Each rest brings consequence, and every step requires contemplation.

Your journey is rarely smooth or straight, so put your trust in the Lord to carry you. You are not alone as you move toward your dreams and destiny. God will bless your faith, as this journey is for His glory and purpose. Trust Him through all situations and discover the rewards that come when you place your faith in the One who leads the way, with no regrets moving forward.

January 13

Pride Before The Fall

Pride goes before the fall. And when we pay attention, we recognize when we get a lesson. Mostly, the hard way. So as much as possible, we need to listen to our inner thoughts and watch our efforts. We can avoid trouble by avoiding prideful actions.

In Scripture Proverbs 16:18-19 says, "Pride goes before destruction, And a haughty spirit before a fall. Better to be of a humble spirit with the lowly, than to divide the spoil with the proud."

So we can avoid trouble, when we choose to walk carefully. A good way to begin is to note your words and thoughts as you enter into situations. Perhaps you have been doing everything right and are now tempted to judge someone else. When you assume that you are above a matter, as a child of God, you will likely experience a spiritual reprimand or chastisement.

Additionally, our lives work better when we walk a humble path. It is good to have a sensitive heart. This is the way of humility, because when we are overconfident in our own security or greatness, perhaps puffed up thinking we know it all; or that something won't touch us, we are in trouble. So be on guard and take notice of an arrogant attitude.

Most people do what they do, without little introspection. But we can open our eyes to arrogance and pride. These characteristics are not good and can cause a mighty fall. And troubling results in any given situation, often work as a wakeup call. So consider your motives. The goal is to remain with integrity, while resisting the temptation toward self centeredness.

Remember to keep your heart in the right place. Everyone is frail and faulty. So walk in Love with guidance from the Holy Spirit for the best results. Our world can be treacherous, and pride will produce trouble. So, leave it behind. Pray and ask God to help you walk with a humble heart today and everyday. Pride is not the way of the Spirit filled man/woman. So let it go today.

'

January 14

Get Right With God

Do you feel distant from the Lord today? It's not too late to get right with God. Perhaps you have been a believer for some time, but lately feel as if you are not in step? Are you having difficulty hearing from God? Receiving Christ and walking with Him daily, is The Way that delivers the most joy in this life. And we gain strength for the journey, through repentance.

Scripture tells us in 1 John 1:9, "If we confess our sins, he is faithful and just to forgive our sins and purify us from all unrighteousness".

Are you missing the clarity that comes from honoring the Lord? Walking with God, we have a friend who shares in every blessing, along with every experience we endure. And it's easy to get caught up in day to day matters. We may think or believe we can do what we need to, on our own, without guidance that comes from the Holy Spirit. But this is not the best way.

Also, we are not all knowing. And our lives have meaning beyond this earthly realm. We enter into this world as a soul, and will leave as a soul. And it's true that our days are numbered. So to accept this path and live in this temporal state, we benefit greatly by acknowledging God.

When we walk in the Truth, we are blessed. So whatever stage of life you are in, and wherever you are, take the step of faith to invite Jesus Christ into your heart today. You may need to begin anew, to share your journey in a new way. In Christ, there is covering, peace and understanding, with guidance. He is a stable center for thriving through any storm or trial.

You may have already accepted Christ; however, today, you may feel far from the Lord. Come to know the height, depth, width, and length of the love of God in Christ Jesus for you. When you invite the Lord into the center of your heart as the cornerstone, you will find freedom in every circumstance. Knowing Christ and understanding what it means to be a follower of Christ will bring you comfort and victory when trials come.

Are you hurting today? Do you feel that God is far away? The Spirit of the Living God dwells in you. So get right with God. Consider repentance from self sufficiency or any particular lingering sin. There is no greater gift than the Grace of God, which offers forgiveness and clarity along with the peace that surpasses all understanding.

January 15

Talk About Love

It's smart to share the good things of God. Especially to bring attention to ways we can improve. However, we must pull the plank out of our own eye, by looking introspectively at ourselves, while not judging others. Additionally, when we are good friends, we care enough to bring about the best in ourselves, before correcting others, for the sake of Love.

Scripture tells us that "iron sharpens iron". This means that we grow by our interactions with one another. We will on occasion need to be corrected. And we will find ourselves making judgements. However, to be an overcomer and achieve wholeness, we primarily need to be forgiving and especially focus our attention on our own personal growth and correction.

When you see your neighbor in trouble, do you stop to help them? Or, if your brother, sister, or friend is self-destructing, should you not step in? When we value ourselves and others, we understand that a good conversation about love, health, and communication can bring thoughtful ideas and, most importantly, healing. As we bring something good to our loved ones' attention, we know that it is love at work through our concern. This is how we show we truly care.

A real friend will speak up when you are going in the wrong direction. So when a friend does not care enough to confront you regarding an important issue, there is a problem and they may not truly be your good friend. Additionally, it's true that some friends do not want to stir the pot. So they will go along with you when you are in trouble. This type of friendship is not for overcomers.

Also, if someone brings a matter to your attention and you take offense, there may be something deeper that needs to be addressed. A person walking in the way of humility and kindness would be able to say, "Thank you for your concern; I will consider what has been said." They do not respond with indifference, anger, or hostility.

Consider if a loved one is heading in the wrong direction or self-destructing. It may be time to step in for the sake of love. Love cares about people, and it's good to talk about hopes and dreams, concerns, and desires. Just remember that taking offense can be a sign of deeper trouble.

In Scripture, Colossians 3:13 says, "Make allowances for each other's faults, and forgive anyone who offends you. Remember, the Lord forgave you, so you must forgive others."

January 16

God Will Lead You

There are times for all of us, when big changes come. And as we go through, it can be frightening. We may need to adjust our experience to live better lives. Stepping out has its challenges, because so much is unknown. And every move of faith takes courage.

And when these passages come, we can feel sad or sorrowful. We may feel that a loss in some part of our lives is occurring. We've been accustomed to the way things are. Now, everything feels different. Also, we may not have a firm idea of which way to go. The future may appear scary, however, we must trust that our path is mapped out for a positive outcome.

Scripture says in Psalm 37:23, "The steps of a good man or woman are ordered by the Lord, and He delighteth in his way."

Trust is the best way forward. And even when we are not paying attention, God is ordering our steps and helping us. We must always remember that God is Love. And that He has a good plan for us. He knows the beginning from the end and will help us, in every situation.

The Lord's desire for you is not to be downtrodden. His love is amazing grace, and He knows what is best for you. If you struggle with believing or trusting, understand that your thoughts and mindset can affect the outcomes in your life. You may experience lack or a less-than-stellar outcome. And although we can't always foresee what changes are coming, we can choose to trust that God is working on our behalf for the highest good.

If you feel sad today, or are leaving something or someone behind, or feel lost, now is the time to have a good cry and bring your pain to the Lord in prayer. Remember, God will lead you in the way you are meant to go. He will lead you home. So, do not be afraid to feel your emotions. Trust that the Lord is guiding you toward a good outcome.

As believers in Christ, we understand that we go from Glory to Glory. And with this knowledge, we rejoice and trust that in every situation, we grow brighter by the Holy Spirit. Our surroundings may look different, and they may take time to get used to, but with each day, we grow to receive greater understanding, as we walk along The Way. Don't hesitate to share your heart openly with Him on the daily. He will lead you in the way that you are to go, for your benefit and good outcome.

January 17

Following God Brings Freedom

We all go through circumstances where we feel tried and tested. And even when we are pressed on every side and stressed to the point where our freedom seems in jeopardy, we must remember that God is in control. Following God is what truly brings freedom.

Being out of control is unsettling, and sometimes people may try to control our actions. Attempting to control another person is a form of manipulation, which can feel like a violation. While we may want to honor those in our lives who have poured into us, when their intentions seem to hold us back from fulfilling God's purpose or from living in the fullness of our destiny, we must remind ourselves who is really in charge.

As Scripture says in Galatians 5:1, 'It is for freedom that Christ has set us free. Stand firm, then, and do not let yourselves be burdened again by a yoke of slavery.'

When we are young and impressionable, we are vulnerable to following the crowd and others' ideas.

Parents and authority figures often play significant roles in guiding our early life decisions. However, as we mature, we need to break free from others' opinions and seek guidance from the Holy Spirit. This is how we discern what is truly best for us.

This may seem straightforward, but when you have experienced controlling people, breaking free and standing firm can be very challenging. Primarily because standing firm often leads to conflict. However, you must have the courage to follow God. And one of the biggest mistakes you can make is to ignore the guidance of the Holy Spirit and compromise the blessings God has for your life.

So, listen to the Lord's leading today and remember who is in control. Take time to pray and ask for strength. Receive freedom from the fear of confrontation. You can do it. God is in control.

January 18

Invasive Species

It is interesting how certain plants can dominate and become invasive species. They often start small and beautiful, yet they can overpower other plants that provide balance to the ecosystem. And it's not just plants that can be invasive; invasive species affect and exist in the ocean, among insects, and within populations of mammals and other animals. Like plants, as invasive animals, mammals, insects, and even humans grow, they overtake and disrupt the whole system, often leading to the extinction of others.

Invasive species can destroy and bring harm to the entire population. We should remember this when admiring an idea, politician, group, or anyone claiming to have the best interests of all at heart. People may seem magnificent and admirable at first, but wrong motives and a desire for power can consume and corrupt, much like an invasive species. As the ideas or actions of a person or group evolve, the balance and beauty of the entire system can fade away.

We need to see things for what they truly are, and we do this by clinging to the truth. Remember the Holocaust and consider leaders like President Putin. Think about the Taliban, Hamas, and others who have demonstrated evil throughout history. We must discern motives with integrity as our guide, and integrity must always be revered.

Humans are flawed, but those who can admit it and who value the truth are the children of God. Look for humility, humble hearts, and a contrite spirit that can repent when wrong. A few good indicators of healthy, loving people are those who admit their faults when they're wrong—people who are generous and helpful to the whole.

The world is our church, and as part of the Body of Christ, we need to remember Hebrews 12:1, which says, "Therefore, since we are surrounded by such a great cloud of witnesses, let us strip off every unnecessary weight and the sin that so easily ensnares us, and let us run with endurance the race that is set before us."

January 19

Are You A Renegade?

Paul wrote much of the New Testament and lived to be around 60 years old. At around 33, on the Damascus Road, he saw a bright light, fell to the ground, and was transformed from Saul to Paul. He heard a voice ask, "Why are you persecuting me?" Touched by God, he went on to write 1 Corinthians 13, regarding Love, among many other writings. He was changed in an instant, and his words have endured through the ages. All of this stemmed from one beam of light and an encounter with God. Paul was a renegade who taught unity. He emphasized that while we are not all the same in our beliefs and experiences, we are all one in Christ.

For many, these experiences still happen today. The moment we encounter a spiritual awakening, we are changed. We can't help but rejoice over everything new in our lives, and we are likely "on fire" for the Lord. Now, we are free because we understand that we are accepted and loved as we are. This free gift of salvation captivates, revealing a passion for The Truth.

And when we accept the promise of eternal life, we become beacons of light and hope for those around us. Before this rebirth, we likely experienced significant darkness in some form. We are familiar with the "other side," so it is a great relief when the washing away of sin and the fear of dying are removed. And as these fears dissipate, our trust in God grows.

Now, our lives reflect the light of Love as we enter the Kingdom by faith. Our understanding broadens with every breath because we are saved. Daily, we evolve to learn that this journey is not about our broken hearts. We have been renewed, with all things made new, for His purposes. Now the Lord guides our way, and we are never given more than we can handle in our earthly trials.

All of this is for the working of the Holy Spirit in the world, creatively. Are you compelled to serve the Lord before leaving Earth? Renegades find something meaningful to do for God. Are you ready to rise up and go, becoming selfless in serving your fellow man? Have you been reorganized by your higher power? The goal is always Love, unity, and peace. And every moment counts. Like Paul, every interaction and intention has a purpose, with Love at the center.

January 20

Purpose Fuels Passion

Finding a reason for doing something is a powerful driving force. When we truly discover what we are passionate about, the next step is to find purpose in our actions. Without purpose, we may still produce results, but eventually, our motivation tends to dwindle. Our actions may not progress far, and even if we continue doing what we enjoy, we might experience reduced stamina and focus. However, when purpose is at the heart of our dreams and desires, our impact becomes significant.

Passion stems from purpose, and being passionate about something makes life exciting and fulfilling. It provides a reason to get up and hit the ground running each day. And discovering something that you are passionate about is crucial for your happiness. While greatness comes to those who have a fervent desire to achieve high goals. Therefore, be passionate!

When we are passionate about something, it's natural to pray. Prayer is a powerful tool that leads and strengthens our way forward. Utilizing prayer, we become co-creators with the Lord, who gives us gifts, dreams, and visions. And as we translate desires held in our hearts, into physical reality, we find ways to serve humanity and are rewarded by our actions.

The daily ritual of manifesting purpose through prayer and practice, brings joy and fulfillment to our efforts. And maintaining a positive mental attitude is essential for becoming an expert achiever in any endeavor. Additionally, how we use our time is crucial. When passion and purpose are combined in doing what we love, every adversity brings a benefit, contributing to something greater in the present moment—both within ourselves and our dreams.

So, why do you pursue your dreams today? Is it to help a cause or someone in need? Perhaps to bring ease to those seeking solutions or to lift someone's spirit? These are meaningful reasons to engage in something you are passionate about. Having a good attitude is valuable, but without purpose, you may eventually run dry.

Today, find something you are passionate about and tap into its purpose. This is the way to experience rewards that make the journey enduring and impactful. When purpose aligns with passion, every step becomes meaningful, and the path ahead is filled with growth and fulfillment.

January 21

Trust In All Things

The Lord gives and He can take away. And until we learn to trust our important life matters to Him, we may have difficulty coming into the abundant life. We must follow and become obedient. The goal is to not rebel and do things to get ahead in our own ways. And when we do act foolishly, perhaps causing a real setback, we need to fix it. Correcting the issue is the best possible way to keep moving forward.

Do you realize that you can have much, and still not be happy? You may experience great prosperity, yet are not able to live an abundant life. The abundant life is a life that trusts God through everything. Whether abased or abounding. It is hearing from the Lord and following His lead. The abundant life is a state of obedience. And we will get the lessons until we get it right.

Simplicity has a joy and value beyond measure. When our state of mind is centered on the energy of Love, good comes forth like a bubbling brook. You can be in the direst of circumstances, yet, when you trust God going through matters, there is inner peace and calm. However, if we attempt to hold the line in our own strength, we are bound to come to the end of ourselves eventually. This type of self sufficiency is pride. And sooner or later we will reap what we sow.

Life presents ongoing lessons in humility. And each one of us at one time or another, will face some sort of health crisis. How we go through is a reflection of our dependence on God. Will we trust that the Lord is our healer? Will we have the faith required to move mountains of fear? Will we live in abundance while we are suffering? Can we believe and put into practice trusting God through all things? Even to the point of death? Do we believe that God has us in His hand?

Learning lessons the hard way is a path everyone takes to some degree. And experiencing life with fewer regrets is priceless. Trust God in all things today. Listen for the still, small voice that provides direction and gently nudges you to follow the right path. While everyone hopes to build wealth, scripture reminds us that it is the Lord who gives us the ability to do so. And when there is wealth without trust and purpose, the soul may perish.

January 22

Love At The Center

Are you mad at God? Perhaps angry at the pain you have suffered, or the challenges you face? Is God attempting to get your attention? Do you feel like fighting? Don't harden your heart when the going gets tough. Instead, choose to make peace with God and get to the root of the matter.

When angry at God, we can go for quite some time without realizing it. We may not even be able to pinpoint what it is we are angry about! However, the Lord is all knowing. And there is plenty of hurt and compromise in life. But having a hardened heart and being angry at God stems from unforgiveness of some wrong suffered. And perhaps there are many.

We all have been slighted somehow, at one time or another. And for countless individuals, it can be devastating. The issues we face and the brutality of this world are no joke. They are very real and not to be downplayed. But instead of putting up walls and cutting the Lord out of your life, the best alternative is to wrestle with God. If we continue on without dealing with hidden anger, personal issues will likely compound and trouble may increase.

When we have a hardened heart, we are holding on to the past. And it is not uncommon to put up protections, so that we do not have to face even more pain. But this is a detriment to our happiness, health and wellbeing. And it does not release us from pain, but in fact can cause even more pain in the long run. So as a remedy for the sake of letting go, we must place our hurt and unforgiveness at the foot of the Cross of Christ. Here we leave the injustices and the failings of others and ourselves. We may not forget, but we can forgive, for our sake.

Life will never go exactly as you expect. So, let go of the anger you feel toward the Lord, yourself, and others today. Reconciliation will benefit you in the long run, as it helps to uproot the bitterness that can grow if left unattended. Choose to trust the process and the lessons that come with it. By keeping Love at the center of your heart and partnering with God, you will experience a better, stronger, and happier outcome.

January 23

A Best Friend Like No Other

When you've been through the fire and experienced the goodness of God, there is a confidence and heartfelt appreciation for all the Lord has done and is. And in life, as we mature, we learn and grow accustomed to the loss of Earthly Love along with friendships, which can dissolve over time. Through it all, God is found to be a friend like no other, by faith. And because of this, we can draw nearer to God, where His Love is our primary relationship.

And having a best friend, the world becomes a little lighter. We appreciate the comradery and are thankful for the understanding that comes from our shared experience. This friendship opens us to receive blessings that come from connection. As God is your best friend, the giving and receiving increases, as you Love on Him and He loves on you.

How do you make God your best friend? You talk with Him in your spirit and share everything in your heart, daily. Just as you would a close friend that you converse with over the phone. He is always with you. Additionally, it is healthy to express anger and emotions that are not always pleasant. This is an intimate relationship. And not only is it a friendship, but it is the way that you are to work out your salvation, moment by moment.

Now most people believe in God, yet they are lacking the intimacy that comes from sharing their heart with the Lord everyday. Furthermore, they may have faith for things, yet miss what is required for enjoying real spiritual fellowship. The world can be distracting. And even though people believe, they often feel apart from God. Life moves along and deals its blows. The loss, pain, rejections, and physical difficulties can cause individuals to feel really alone.

However, having a best friend like no other, provides comfort that surpasses anything you may experience on Earth. There is strength that comes from this friendship that is based on trust. You can flourish in it. It's the security in knowing and believing that you are never alone and always with the One who has your beginning and your end in all things.

Therefore, take it easy today and share your heart. Talk to the Lord and tune in to what He wants to say to you. Trust Him. The journey will be lighter, and The Way more pleasurable.

January 24

Boldness With Confidence

It was a bold man or woman who ate the first oyster! What were they thinking? They were confident that whether they lived or died, or went sick or euphoric, that they could do it. And their boldness paid off, to the point where many people today now enjoy oysters.

Boldness requires stepping out into something new. And boldness is needed to be a great achiever. Further, boldness is the first step and the place that requires our will, perseverance and strength. There may be opposition. However, the follow up is confidence. There must be confidence in the follow through, after a bold move.

Confidence is the steady ability to keep going in that which we believe. It is not allowing anyone or anything to knock us off the path we determine to follow. And true confidence especially comes from knowing who we are in Christ. We are not always strong in ourselves and there are times that we don't feel like we have all the goods.

However, when we rely on God and His righteousness, and receive this, we have what it takes.

Do you believe that the Lord is with you? Understanding that we are the righteousness of God in Christ, produces boldness *and* confidence. This righteousness is not based on our own merits or actions but is imputed through the redemptive work of Christ at the cross. We are justified and blameless through the lens of Christ's righteousness. Righteous in the eyes of God. And living as the righteousness of God, requires us to align our thoughts, actions, and values with the teachings of Jesus. In this great Love, we are made whole.

When you are a faith-filled believer, there will always be naysayers. Many will criticize your bold actions, and because you are unique and courageous, some may feel intimidated by your confidence—perhaps even wishing they had the same. But remember, opposition makes you strong. Don't be discouraged when resistance and criticism come your way. Fight through, knowing the Lord is by your side. Pray, keep your confidence high, and press on.

People may try to tear you down, but the Lord will build you up. No good thing will God withhold from those who walk uprightly. So, when you pursue greatness or venture into something new, do it with Christ at the center. Be bold, be brave, and have confidence in who God made you to be.

January 25

Wrestle If You Need To

Countless people struggle with frustration, as they face what comes their way each day. And matters can be trying. Especially when we have expectations about things that should be in our best interest. We may believe that we know how things will be better for us. But situations do not always go the way that we expect they will. Issues bring us to the edge of our seat, where we feel exhausted. And often our patience gets tested, along with our peace of mind.

Peace and comfort are desirable, yet when troubles compound, we feel out of control. Solutions may appear out of reach. Additionally, we may hold on to anger within our circumstances. And because confrontation can be unpleasant, sometimes, we go about our business without facing our circumstances. Situations get stuffed under the rug, to be cleared up later. Surely they will rise to the surface again. And unfortunately, we must wrestle with things again when they do.

When we resist God's will and choose to go our own way, we really don't get very far. And there is no avoiding that which will come to us. Everything circles back around in time. We may doubt or not believe. However, God wants us to trust Him. And when we don't, we miss out on guidance, and resolution, along with shared experiences with a loving God.

The Lord desires to reveal His great Love in your life. In Genesis 32:22-32, Jacob wrestled with God in his frustration. He went all night, attempting to overpower and fight a situation that was clearly bigger than he was. Eventually, he stopped fighting and requested God to bless him. Finally, he was changed. And remember, Christ did not fight God. Ever. He asked for the cup to be removed, if it was the Lord's will. But He had no resistance to what the Lord wanted to do in His life. We need to be more like this.

Sometimes we resist forgiveness for ourselves and those around us. We hold on to things that we should let go of quickly. Often, we resist trusting in difficult circumstances and imagine that we can handle things ourselves. This is not the best way for the highest good.

Today remember, it is healthy to wrestle with God when resolution is needed. Come to Him with all matters and lay everything out in prayer. If there is a need to express anger, that's ok. Just let it out so that your heart can be made pure again. There is power in being in agreement with this great intelligence. God has the better way.

January 26

Because He First Loved Us

Over time we become who we are meant to be, by the grace of God. And we see His hand working in our lives. We don't do it all ourselves and we need circumstances to force us to maneuver. We have free will and can use it, however, it is not in our best interest to go without being attuned to the Lord's will. If not, we often find the results teach us what not to do.

Simply, we need assistance to change ourselves. And knowing the Lord is working in our lives, and changing us bit by bit, is a relief when we have a propensity toward perfection. If we are perfectionists, when we strive and miss the mark, we can feel defeated and blame ourselves. In contrast, when trusting in the Lord, we do not need to harbor feelings of inadequacy or blame.

Scripture says in 1 John 4:10, "This is Love: not that we loved God, but that He first loved us and sent his Son as an atoning sacrifice for our sins."

God first loved us, and because of this, we must believe that the Lord is always working on our behalf. His Love comes before our love for Him. When we experience this love firsthand in our lives, our faith grows, and with it, wisdom and ability. While proclaiming victory is important, we must remember that it is not by our own strength, but by His work within us. God is bringing His great love to fruition, pouring it out upon us in ways that we can truly see and feel.

And as the Lord pours into our lives, we are more inclined to do our best to honor Him. There is a desire to please Him. And if we've had difficulty trusting God over the course of our lives, it can be challenging to have faith. We may be rebellious and doubt that God is really around to support us. And even though we believe in God, we may be unsure that matters of obedience are truly important. However, obedience to the Lord is the most important thing, for our own happiness.

So strive to become the best version of yourself today, and do your best to obey what God is asking you to do. God is omnipresent and understands your weakness. And as you grow from glory to glory, proclaim victory, but walk with care. Always remember that God will get the glory. Stand firm and know that He will do it. It may take some time, but this victory is for you.

January 27

The Journey

Embarking on a road trip is perceived as a physical journey. A chance to explore new landscapes and create lasting memories. However, beyond the scenic routes and roadside attractions, a road trip can be a profound spiritual experience. The open road provides a unique canvas for self-discovery and contemplation. It offers valuable lessons that extend far beyond the destination.

Road trips provide us with an opportunity to face our fears and learn to trust. As we navigate the open road, it's an ideal time to pray and express gratitude for the experience. With the inherent risks involved, it feels natural to ask God for protection and a safe arrival at our destination. Embracing the present moment on a road trip brings a flood of inspiration. We notice the signs around us—messages on the backs of trucks and billboards, some political, many inspirational. The constant change in scenery, combined with the hum of the engine and the rhythmic flow of the road, keeps us anchored in the here and now.

We often experience a heightened sense of awareness during road trips. The unpredictable journey, with its unexpected detours, weather changes, and roadside surprises, teaches us to release the need for absolute control and trust God with the uncertainties that life brings. On the road, the meditative atmosphere invites us to find peace in the silence. In the absence of constant noise, we are given the space for introspection, self-reflection, and a deeper connection with both God and our inner thoughts and feelings.

Road trips can help us to discover profound spiritual lessons that enrich our lives and broaden our perspectives. Here we are overcoming challenges. We may be navigating unfamiliar paths or facing unexpected setbacks. However, these experiences serve as reminders of the importance of gratitude. When we give thanks to God for the adventure and journey itself, and the lessons learned, our way is a spiritual practice that transforms the mundane.

So go with God today on your journey, and embrace the present moment. Let go of control. And as you navigate both the highways and the inner landscapes of your soul, remember that you are never alone. God goes with you. Do not be afraid. The journey is a destination worth savoring.

January 28

Rest A While

An important part of succeeding requires knowing how to rest and take our hands off the wheel. For high achievers, this can be a challenge. And any great achievement will have big challenges. So knowing when and how to rest, can help to rejuvenate and counter failure along the way.

Dreams take time to come true. And sacrificing hours for family, or building a brand, are factors that build character and test each person individually. And with any dream or endeavor, perseverance is required. When we are energized, it is easier to engage with a sense of purpose. However, doing the hard things we dislike can be stressful. There may be times we feel like we want to quit. Instead, we need to see difficulty as a marker, to rest awhile and then keep going.

Matthew 11:28 says, "Come to me, all who labor and are heavy laden, and I will give you rest."

This scripture is comforting when we are worn. And whether or not you do what you love daily, or perhaps show up to some mundane task to keep the bills paid, it's essential to rest and savor your down time. It's important to know that resting periods are valuable times, spent toward accomplishing goals. At rest, we can quiet the mind, and share our heart and matters with the Lord.

Maybe you are a student with extensive classes and tests to complete. Stepping away from the tasks at hand can help you experience clarity and avoid mind boggle. And in fitness, rest is required for muscle recovery. Additionally, rest is required for the spirit. We need time to renew and grow stronger. So rest and step away today. Turn everything off for a time.

Remember to come to the Lord as your rest. Climbing a mountain is hard work. It's easier to keep going when you see rewards and positive outcomes. But when you don't see results the way you imagined, don't give up, as some would. Quiet your mind and have a plan to relax. Perhaps eat some delicious food, or grab a movie. It does not take a lot of money to rest well. But it does require freedom from distraction of phone calls, messages, and other people.

Scripture tells us that on the seventh day the Lord rested. He created the Earth and everything in it in six days. So follow this lead and give the best you have to everything. Come to the Lord and rest.

January 29

Strive For Excellence

What we do and how we handle both the insignificant and important tasks we encounter daily reveal much about who we are and where we're headed. It's often in the small, everyday moments that we find the greatest joy. Even in times of poverty, trouble, or suffering, practicing 'excellence' in our words and deeds creates a positive impact both within us and around us. Striving for excellence is a way of saying, 'I care.'

Scripture says in Acts 17:28, "For in Him we live and move and have our being."

Striving for excellence is a form of spiritual warfare. Walking in excellence is a reflection of inner competence and brings enthusiasm and satisfaction to your spirit. It's the language of Love. When your words and actions align in any circumstance, you are giving your best. This isn't about perfection but simply about pursuing excellence.

In contrast, approaching matters with mediocrity often pulls us toward our fallen nature. Even when your strength is low and your will feels weak, staying committed to excellence—by doing both simple and difficult things with quality and distinction—brings great reward.

Excellence is contagious, where one effort leads to another. It creates champions. So if you desire to be a champion, strive for excellence. You can do this in every small task—whether cleaning the house, going to work, or driving the kids to school. Striving for excellence reflects your state of mind.

Countless people run on autopilot, not paying attention to their daily actions. However, excellence is for those on the upward climb. Thankfully, it's not about perfection but about walking in the Spirit of Love. When you practice excellence in all you do, you begin to feel excellent. You'll notice more energy, enthusiasm, happiness, and contentment in both the little and big things as you make this a daily practice.

January 30

A Commitment To Commitment

To experience greater happiness and success, we need to have our actions line up with our words. And being a committed person, means perseverance with a commitment to integrity. This is how to truly experience blessings and favor, and all the goodness life offers.

And plenty of people lack a commitment to integrity. An example of this is when we say that we will do something, and then we don't. When we cannot keep our word; we let others down, as well as ourselves. Additionally we need to be committed to our goals and tasks toward our dreams. This is primarily a discipline so that the path is fulfilled. If you say to yourself that you are going to the gym four days a week, and then you don't go, you are breaking trust with the Holy Spirit. But when you follow through, you remain on course for obtaining greater outcomes.

Now no one is perfect, and integrity is a lifelong challenge, because in one instance, you may find you are able to have your words line up with your actions, no problem. However, in another moment, you may miss the mark. It's an ongoing practice and something to always strive for. And as we get better at it, we succeed greatly in our ways and especially with God.

Being a committed individual requires perseverance through the low times. This includes the hard times, the boring stuff and the lonely days or nights where work is required to achieve abundance in all things. Seems like a no-brainer right? To be a committed person means that we do not place our trust in our feelings, because there will be times, we do not feel like doing the work. We must be able to overcome feelings and push forward, to follow through with our commitment.

Persevere today. And when you mess up, just say so. Simply bring it to the Lord in prayer and receive grace to move on and get it right the next time. The more you evolve in this area, the more power God provides for His glory. Be content knowing you have a committed heart.

January 31

The Difference

Breaking through barriers and experiencing "the difference" requires getting really good at being fearless and taking healthy risks. When you are brave enough to do this, you will become more resilient and confident in all aspects of your life. The status quo will never do.

And being a difference maker requires courage to face reality. Do you feel bored or stagnant? Are you living in a state of disinterest or lethargy? Have you lost hope that things will ever change? Could it be that everyday tasks have become mundane? Are you seeing any progress in your work life? It may be time to do something different.

People who take healthy risks are true leaders. And in business, it is necessary to step out and grow to outsmart the competition. No matter the outcome, taking a risk is good for the sake of building skills to improve your chances of achieving future goals. And being fearless helps you to evolve.

Taking risks to achieve something requires facing the fear of uncertainty, but it's crucial to have peace about your choices. When in doubt, hold out. Always ensure your physical safety as you step forward. Whether you're asking someone out on a date or embarking on a five-week adventure across the country with your dog, taking chances requires putting yourself out there. In these moments, we become one with the Holy Spirit. As we lean on the still small voice of the Lord for guidance, we grow to trust that God always has our best interest at heart.

Are you ready to be fearless and experience the difference? Being fearless and taking healthy risks, will make you feel very alive. And when you succeed and experience good outcomes, even through challenges along the way, there will be ecstasy.

Being fearless brings clarity and a heightened sense of awareness. So be a difference maker today, and discover strength and confidence you never knew you had. Life becomes exciting, fresh, and new when you live in the moment, moving forward toward everything good. Your dreams and daily adventures will flourish as you walk with God on your journey of discovery.

FEBRUARY

February 1

Our God The Great Physician

If you're struggling today, seek the Lord, to release the pain. He is the great physician. He knows what you need and can heal you, when you believe. Additionally, the only way out is through. So if you struggle, keep walking forward in faith, because everything changes eventually.

The Lord is able to heal you physically, emotionally or both, when you believe. And the One who breathes life into every living thing, desires for you to be whole. You can receive strength when you bring your sins and missteps, past, present, and future, to the cross of Christ.

Every person faces challenging situations, and the pain we feel is often very real. We live, we die, and we endure trials, tribulations, and health concerns. This is part of the human condition. However, we have a choice: to go through these experiences with increased strength and victory, by believing, or not. It's essential to know who you are as a child of the Most High God, the Creator of the Universe. When you learn what God's Word says about you, you will experience greater healing, wisdom, and energy.

And plenty of people encounter what they refer to as miracles. Some are transformed in a moment, while for others, healing takes time. So, there is certainly a reason to pray. Because communion with God brings wholeness. God's ways are not our ways and we must keep an open mind and use prayer, to obtain guidance and direction toward the best possible outcome and course of action for our healing.

We may not always be healed immediately or in the way we think we should be. And while we may still face problems, our minds can be renewed with the strength to endure the storms. Does that make you unreasonable or delusional? No. But you understand that there is a force of evil that seeks to steal, kill, and destroy. By holding on to the Word of God, you gain Truth and greater clarity. With humility and wisdom, you will see better outcomes. When our thoughts and energy are aligned with the promises of God, we become all the stronger for it.

February 2

Are You A Spiritual Warrior?

Most people believe that respect is earned. Yet, everyone is worthy of respect. And when people disrespect each other, it is devaluing and a breach of Love. The result is a chain reaction of negativity toward human kindness. So, as open-hearted souls, we must recognize the importance of respecting each other through situations.

And countless individuals have suffered trauma. Even multiple traumas. Many are broken. Because of this, disrespect runs rampant in our society. We need to flip the script. And if we are truthful, we can see that we don't know what someone is going through, or where they have been. We do not know the root causes of a person's behavior. So having mercy and empathy is necessary.

Many have been greatly discarded and dishonored, due to pride and selfish ambition. We notice blatant disrespect on social media and at TV stations around the world. We see it in our leaders. These are the politicians and journalists who are supposed to be the example. It's in the city streets, between races, religions, sexualities, and the elderly.

However, true respect goes beyond tolerance. It embraces understanding with appreciation for the unique perspective another person brings. Respect forms the foundation of harmonious and meaningful relationships. Situations may appear to be a mystery. However, when we attempt to look from God's perspective, the veil is lifted. We understand that respect begins in us.

To be the change, and to truly respect people, we must love well. It starts within us. In a respectful interaction, people actively listen to one another, while valuing diverse experiences and viewpoints. Humility is required. We need not be quick to judge or condemn. Instead, we need to understand that people heal when treated respectfully.

We can do better. No one is perfect, therefore, we must be in a loving way. When we teach respect by honoring others, we will see fewer people fall through the cracks. This is the way of the Spiritual Warrior. To actively listen, while being slow to anger and to speak the Truth in Love.

February 3

Real And Lasting Change

Sometimes we feel as if no one understands our experience. We go through trials and can feel very alone. And these are the times, we might fall into the wrong situations and temptations to seek relief. Or, we may have expectations for other people to make us feel better.

We may not always realize how vulnerable we are. When we listen to someone who doesn't have our best interests at heart, we can be led into danger. Many people turn to methods found on YouTube or other platforms, which can lead them astray. Some may instruct us to do this or that, but what we truly need is for our soul to be transformed in a more permanent way. Nothing can replace bringing our concerns to the Lord, who always has our best interests at heart. If we seek real and lasting change, we must trust and walk with the Holy Spirit as we share our concerns.

Scripture says in 1 Peter 5:7, "So throw all your anxiety onto Him, because He cares about you."

There is nothing quite like a friend who shows up and offers a shoulder to cry on and relief for what ails you at the right time. And when we share our circumstances with God, the Lord hears our prayers and goes before us. As we listen to the Holy Spirit's direction, we are better able to discern what is being said. All of this happens deep within the spirit for real and lasting change.

God knows what you need. And as we cast our care on the Lord, we receive peace. Therefore, we must do our part in coming to Him in our condition. What is needed is a comprehension of His Love. You must believe that your steps are ordered by the Lord. He knows The Way forward for you and will comfort you when you put your trust in Him.

Many people are given platforms and microphones and are telling others, "this is the solution" and "this is what you need to do". But do they have your best interest at heart? They may not know you and your particular situation. However, God knows. And He alone can bring real and lasting change to your life today. Place your heart in His hands and lay it all out for the peace you seek.

February 4

Don't Lose Sight Of The Vision

Visualization is a powerful tool for success in any field. We need to imagine the possibilities and see ourselves in the places we aspire to be. So, don't lose sight of your vision—it's important to honor your ideas and not discard the view.

Your dreams are enticing suggestions that bring life and a sense of purpose to your journey. And dreams are especially exciting at the beginning. Along the way, they can be both thrilling and frightening. However, after pursuing your dreams for some time, you will either be encouraged to keep going, or you may become discouraged and rest on your laurels.

Scripture says in Habakkuk 2:3, "For the vision is yet for an appointed time, but in the end it shall speak, and will not lie: though it tarry, wait for it; because it will surely come, it will not tarry."

This tells us that when God gives a dream, He will do it and bring it to pass. We only need to remember that the vision is for an appointed time. And when the road gets rough, we must remember that God's timing is perfect and there will always be hills and valleys to walk through.

And when it appears as if nothing is developing according to our plans, it can be difficult to step forward. We may feel as if we are waiting and waiting for what should be. When this happens, we may question ourselves and wonder if the dream was really a God given dream after all. And if we start to believe the doubts, we may begin to lose hope. Perhaps the idea was clear at the onset, but now it feels like a faded vision. If this happens, don't give up. This is how we die spiritually.

When we neglect to push through, we may have regrets later. Whether you are starting out, or you have held your dream in your heart for some time, without faith and vision to push through, your dream may perish. Please don't listen to the enemy and believe that what you have imagined to be possible, is not. It is essential to keep going and press through, when deception comes against you.

Start fresh with what you can do to energize the situation and face the pain you feel through prayer. Do not become disheartened. Instead, focus on God's purposes and don't lose sight of the vision and dream. Consider how you can create something new. These are your heart's desires.

February 5

When All Appears Lost

There are times, when all may appear lost before being found. And when these moments come, usually, all that is desired, is a bit of good news. A smidgen of hope for something wonderful to happen. Yet, hope can feel absent and hard to find.

Do you feel forgotten or forsaken today? Personal matters may have been building for some time, leaving you scratching your head and asking why. You resolve to push through, but in truth, your intuition and understanding are likely your best guide. You may speculate earnestly, but ultimately, no one has the answers.

When all appears lost, trusting God is all that there is left to do. This is where something wonderful happens. Here, we catch a glimpse of the Creator at work. We begin to have the clarity to see from a distance. To see with the Lord's eyes in our situation.

Yes, we are staying the faithful course, but what choice do we have? When all feels lost and you struggle to take another step, trust that God sees you. The Lord has not forgotten you. He would never forget His beloved. It takes courage to stand and wait on the Lord. And it takes bravery to wear a smile, when it feels like you are dying inside.

Don't lose hope. Rest assured that something will be found today. And keep believing that God is working on your behalf. Wait for the Lord to birth a new thing. And when the going gets tough, hopeful people can be either irritating or inspiring. And nothing feels so sad as to assume you have been skipped over or forgotten. Your pain may be great, but something wonderful is about to happen. God's love will provide. He will bring about something new in your life.

Scripture says in Isaiah 43:19, "See, I am doing a new thing! Now it springs up; do you not perceive it? I am making a way in the wilderness and streams in the wasteland."

February 6

Change Will Have Its Way

Most of us have something we would change about ourselves if we could. Some of us work at it for a time, only to know defeat. And just as our influences and habits develop day by day, we are also gradually changed, step by step, inwardly, so that we become better outwardly.

And from the time we are born, until we die, we are changing. The seasons renew themselves, and we're also being renewed. So change will have its way with us, eventually. And while some may believe it's not important to change, if we want to live, we must evolve and change.

Perhaps, we desire to improve how we speak with other people. Or we commit to change our daily habits, such as the food we eat, the beverages we drink, or our exercise regimen. We may feel a need to dedicate more time to spiritual practice and learning. Or improve our intimate life. Yes, we often try to change ourselves in various ways. And these are all good things to strive for. However, without God working on our behalf, most efforts are short lived.

Scripture says in John 15:2, "Every branch in me that does not bear fruit, He takes away; and every branch that bears fruit, He prunes, so that it may bear more fruit."

It can be very difficult to believe for lasting change. Many people give up. But one thing is true; we are beings that grow. And rooted deep in our depths, is a propensity to change, which helps us to become better people and to bear more fruit. This is the work of God.

So, just like the vine, we are being pruned. And that which no longer serves us, will be cut off. And many only experience a portion of what God has for them. Mainly because they do not bring their issues to the Cross to receive full possibility. This is likely because root causes are too painful to address. But facing root issues is powerful, healthy, and possible.

Thankfully, we are not the same person as we were five years ago. Hopefully in hindsight we notice that we have become more refined, even tempered and truthful. And as 2 Corinthians 3:18 says, "We all, with unveiled faces, beholding as in a mirror, the glory of the Lord, are being transformed into the same image from glory to glory. For this comes from the Lord who is the Spirit."

February 7

Are You A Spiritual Wild Child?

To be a spiritual wild child, one must attach to God and not people. Here, needs are met with greater abundance. In addition, there is a flow that embraces change with a heightened sense of awareness. A wild child does not hesitate to stand alone. And a wild child is committed to learn from every experience.

Being a wild child means being free to try new things, independent of what others think. There's something liberating about not being confined by laws or rules. While we do follow laws, we don't live by them, and at times, we all break them. Rules are in place for our benefit, but we occasionally break them too—perhaps to find our boundaries and gain a deeper understanding.

A spiritual wild child will face opposition because they don't conform to the status quo. They are less codependent and more interdependent. Their path is unique, and they rarely follow the crowd. They learn primarily through action, by making mistakes and experiencing failures.

A spiritual wild child will touch the edge of knowing what God is doing. So do not think about playing it safe. Instead comprehend your worthiness and become who you are intended to be. Culture may try to influence you with limits, because socially, we are conditioned to believe that we should be this way or that way. But to uniquely follow your heart, especially the will of God for your life, is one of the greatest gifts to possess.

Without the courage to try something new, you won't experience the personal growth necessary to reach your destiny. So embrace the wild child within and don't miss out on important soulful healing. God is Love. And as long as you stay committed to walking as Jesus walked, by attaching to the Lord with a childlike trust, you can be wild and free, to learn and grow, and know God.

February 8

Obedience - It Don't Come Easy

Every person has a self-will. And the word obedience, for some, can cause a cringe. We want to do things in our own way and are primarily concerned about ourselves. But just as a parent protects their child, we need to recognize that God has our best interest at the center of our walk. And He desires for our lives to be greatly fulfilled.

When we come to the Lord Jesus Christ, we learn a new way of being and are destined to inherit the many blessings of the abundant life. This path requires a commitment to the Truth and it rarely comes easy. And most people think that they know the best way forward, so the idea of obedience and learning to trust God, can cause some distress.

Are you a defiant one? We are all at times defiant and rebellious by nature. Some more than others. And our unique circumstances create who we are and our level of rebellion. For the extremely self-willed, it can be a painful process to get the lesson.

Furthermore, we grow through outcomes, and when the Lord whispers and directs us to do something, and we do not; we reap negative results. A familiar example would be to remember when you were small and told not to touch the hot stove. Hopefully you listened. However, some children learned the hard way. The result was getting burned.

Jonah ran from God and the call that he was given, to tell the Ninevites of their impending doom. Jonah was rebellious and stubborn and later found himself in the belly of a whale. Thankfully, to be spit out. And after running for some time, Jonah finally began to obey the leading of the Holy Spirit. Grudgingly, he became obedient.

Scripture tells us that God chastises those He loves. This learning can be a painful process. But after repetition, we come to understand and choose what is right. And like any good father, the Lord expects us to obey. And as we grow, we comprehend that rebellion is no longer a smart choice. We learn that obedience to the Father extends our joy, for living our best life.

If you are being taught the hard way today, don't let it get you down. Instead, see it for what it is. Turn and repent and walk uprightly. It's important to grasp that if you want the favor of God in your life, you need to understand what the Lord is saying. God always has your best interest and will bless your obedience.

February 9

An Attitude Of Gratitude

An attitude of gratitude is cultivated over time. It often begins when we are rescued or provided for in unique ways. And when amazing things happen, we become more aware and appreciative, recognizing these moments as surprises we don't take lightly or for granted.

Gratitude makes all the difference. A thankful heart is both confident and trusting, which is a wonderful place to be. It's important to be grateful not just for the big blessings, but for every small provision—and even for the challenges we face. When things don't go our way, recalling every blessing, large and small, makes the journey more joyful.

Over time, we become increasingly aware of God's presence. We recognize that He guides, directs, protects, and blesses us wherever we go. His generosity touches our hearts, even amid deeply painful situations, fostering an even greater attitude of gratitude—one that empowers us to embrace bigger challenges and adventures.

And a complete attitude of gratitude is powerful, carrying us forward. While people generally rely on their self-will, learning dependence on God takes time. We can be thankful when we first receive salvation and discover our calling, but as we go through life's experiences, our gratitude deepens. We come to recognize God's favor in all things—from the smallest grace to the greatest successes.

As we navigate life's significant matters, we realize that the more we see God's provision, the more our appreciation for His goodness grows. Gratitude becomes natural, and this reliance on God strengthens. We come to see Him as our source, and ourselves as His dependent children.

February 10

The Winners Walk

As we climb the proverbial ladder, we advance upward toward the fullness of who we are meant to be. Nothing is as vital as our freedom on this Winner's Walk. We come into our own, each of us bringing a unique vision to everything we do.

And today, we ascend this earthly journey with sharp focus. Hopefully, the contributions we make to society are purposeful and used for good. At every crossing, experience becomes our guide, and we carry those lessons forward. This training is crucial. Like a horse wearing blinders, we avoid looking to the left or right. We stay focused on the path ahead, sidestepping distractions to remain committed to our purpose.

Now, we confidently move forward, discerning the trials and tears along The Way. The past is gone, and we let go of the heavy burdens we no longer need to carry. We have grown in ways that keep us light on our feet. In maturity, we stand firm in our faith.

As we move forward, we release what no longer serves us and head in a new direction. We remember to lay aside every weight and the sin that so easily entangles. Like an Olympian, we run the race set before us, focusing on what truly matters.

We are onto bigger and better things. And on this Winner's Walk, we see the big picture. The choice is ours as we determine to successfully reach our destiny with a sense of completion. In this race, all the runners run, but only one receives the prize. So, we run in a way that we may obtain it.

Are you focused today? Are you committed to bringing good into your circle, benefiting those around you in lasting ways? Do you hold onto hope with faith when the road darkens? Are you determined to never give up? If so, you are a winner on the Winner's Walk. And the Lord sees you.

As Scripture reads in Genesis 16:13, "I have now seen the One who sees me." El Roi—He is the God who sees.

February 11

Proceed With Caution

Love requires movement and effort. And joy comes from encouraging and helping those around us. When we truly love people, we will be givers. Certainly, not selfish with our actions.

Discernment is the ability to judge well. It is spiritual guidance. And the Lord knows what's best for every individual. There may be times when we are inspired to show up for someone, while it is not necessarily in the person's best interest. Therefore, we must learn to discern where and when to give. Should we give to the panhandler at the street corner? Or perhaps a society like the Red Cross or Salvation Army? What about our neighbor? Perhaps we click something on the internet to help starving children. Whatever the case may be, there are times when we desire to help, only to find ourselves faced with personal trouble. So, learning to have intuitive boundaries is ideal.

Caring for others and their wellbeing is challenging. We want what's best, yet we do not want to enable souls. And one thing is for sure, we learn through trial and error. Taking time to pray thoughtfully about what is required in a situation is important. Because our ideas of what someone might need at any given moment, may not be what they need at all.

Using discernment, both the giver and receiver can experience positive results. And it's been said that you cannot out-give God. And even when giving causes difficulties, any act of generosity will produce something positive. Yes, we need to grant help to our fellow man. But we need to use wisdom in doing so. We may not be able to give monetary blessings, but there are always ways to bless people. Your time is valuable, and so is any social support or sharing of material possessions.

In Scripture, 2 Corinthians 9:6-8 reveals, "Each of you should give what you have decided in your heart to give, not reluctantly or under compulsion, for God loves a cheerful giver. And God is able to bless you abundantly, so that in all things at all times, having all that you need, you will abound in every good work."

The goal is always for the highest good. Therefore, remember to be generous today and say this: "Today I do my best to pay attention to what is in the best interest of another."

February 12

Casting Down Imaginations

When we have a dream or vision that comes from God, we have peace about our path and destiny. We do not know how things will transpire, but we do know that God moves us forward to reach the fulfillment of our heart's desire. And following our dreams there is a level of excitement. Therefore it is not unusual that we risk security for liberty, as we trust with childlike faith.

And because the entire journey requires creativity, it's not strange for us to imagine how things may come to be. We have ideas about possibilities and may try to predict the results. This is because we feel powerful when we are in the "know". But imaginations can be a stronghold. Additionally, we may attempt to hold imaginations for the sake of mental safety.

When we have things figured out, we feel better. However, as we develop, we discern that our imagination may not necessarily be God's plan for our lives. Yes, we use imagination for creativity toward our goals, but we do not want to put our imaginations about how things will emerge, before God's perfect will. God is in control, and what we are doing is unique.

So let us not be tied to imaginations. These can hinder, as we innocently create scenarios and situations that may not be a part of the path we are to take. Some examples might be, when we think that we know who we will marry, or where we might flourish in business. Perhaps we have ideas about our bandmates, our brothers or sisters too. And as much as our imaginations and ideas may be good ideas, they may not be God's will for us.

In Scripture 2 Corinthians 10:5 says, "Casting down imaginations, and every high thing that exalts itself against the knowledge of God, while bringing into captivity every thought to the obedience of Christ."

What this means is that we are to stay in the moment and bring every thought to the Lord. Let us take one day at a time as we reach for our dreams. And let us remain humble and recognize each day as a gift, where our path transpires directly in relation to our level of faith. Let us cast down imaginations to trust and remember, that it is the Lord who orders our steps.

February 13

God Is Our Supply

What really matters to you? Material wealth? Good relationships? Having achievements that put the spotlight on you? Maybe there is a need for emotional support or healing? Perhaps provision for necessities? Or maybe simply having good health, is what is most important to you.

Whatever the case may be, when we ask God, He answers. He has promised to meet our needs with what is required. However, we must understand the difference between wanting and needing. Most of us have a plan of action for things, but as we move forward, it's important to ask: Is this something I want, or something I truly need?

We live in a culture of instant gratification and generally do not enjoy waiting. We put it out there and expect a return immediately. But God's timing is different from ours. And because the Lord is powerful and above all comprehension, we must take our hands off the wheel and learn to trust His perfect timing in all things, especially in having our needs met.

And letting go can be difficult. Without trust, we struggle. It's common that most of us like to do things in our own strength. However, when we let go, we see God work in our favor. Soon we discover that we get what we need. Further, it is rewarding when we come through with a better result or opportunity than what we had in mind originally for ourselves.

Scripture tells us in Philippians 4:19, "And my God shall supply all your needs according to His riches and glory in Christ Jesus".

God's glorious riches in Christ Jesus are centered in Truth. And the Lord is our provision. So after we have done all that we can, we need to stand and let God shine forth His goodness. He will meet our needs in unique ways, where He gets the Glory.

Finally, true riches are not a matter of what we control. Instead, they include having a peaceful soul. And the accumulation of things can cause great burdens. So we must consider the idea that God knows what we need to be happy. Are you attuned to hearing?

February 14

Live For Love

People may not always be all we hope they would be. And the world will break our hearts. However, we do not give up on Love. We essentially live for Love. And whether we are in relationship with another person, or not, our heavenly Father cares for us deeply.

We are the beloved of God. And God is Love. Now it can be rather difficult to comprehend this, when we consistently suffer loss, and pain. Therefore, we need to remind ourselves of the goodness of God. We need to do all that we can to keep our hearts right, and not become insecure as if we are lacking in this great Love. We stay filled up, by remembering God's great gift and the many times the Lord has made a way, where it seemed there was no way.

Scripture tells us in Romans 5:6, "For at just the right time, while we were still powerless, Christ died for the ungodly."

Therefore, when we truly believe in Love, we can comprehend Christ. He was Love manifested in the flesh. And Romans 5:7-8 follows by saying, "Very rarely will anyone die for a righteous person, though for a good person one might possibly dare to die. But God demonstrates His Love for us in this: that while we were still sinners, Christ died for us."

At any stage of life, the road forward is a mystery. And it is easy to feel alone. But Christ came to fill the empty place in our lives and heart, from the time we start out, to when we are old. Christ understands every difficult thing we face, because He went through our human suffering.

Love can be painful. It is also filled with pleasing elation. However, if we are not able to comprehend the Love of God before we "fall in Love" with another person, we are sure to experience difficulty. We need to Love ourselves as God first Loved us.

Remember today that God loves you. And everything begins and ends with the following Truth: "For God so loved the world that He sent His only begotten Son, that whosoever believes in Him, shall not perish but shall have eternal life." (John 3:16)

February 15

See With Eyes Of Love

Most of us know someone who has perished from Covid 19, RSV, flu or some other virus. These are dangerous diseases that seek to destroy the weak and vulnerable, as well as the unsuspecting. And vaccines and mask mandates have divided many around the globe.

But let us not forget that there is a force in this world that seeks to destroy, and a force that works all things for our good. We do not want to focus on what divides us, including what we think is right or wrong about a situation. The thing that matters is that people recognize there is danger.

What if each person walked in Love? What if we took the time to seek the will of God in every moment? Do you think the world would be better for it? Be aware that as a virus spreads, so does Love. And just as evil can grow, so can Love. So, we need to remember that when someone wants to fight, Love is the answer. Is this possible in our world today?

We need to honor God, especially to avoid destruction. We live in a volatile society where many believe they are right and think they have all the answers. But what if people were humble and embraced humility? What if we listened more than we judged, and prayed more than we spoke? Our world would benefit, because Love sets people free.

Having humility doesn't mean living a diminished life. On the contrary, our lives become more vibrant and enriched as we receive daily refreshment from God and the Holy Spirit. We carry the breath of life within us, which nourishes and strengthens our soul, allowing everything to grow healthier.

See with eyes of Love today, and be filled with the Holy Spirit. Be slow to anger, and quick to listen. And when you go into your private place, pray for the good of all mankind. Life is but a breath. For now, we know in part, but one day we will know fully.

February 16

Are You Free Today?

There is strength in personal freedom. And true freedom leads in the way of triumph. Have you noticed that people who are free, tend to upset those who are not? If you are free from condemnation and culture, people want what you have!

And Christ appointed freedom, comprehends respect. Every race, color, and creed, in every culture and religion, are the foundation of humanity. We are a living masterpiece, intended to Love one another. And Love must be our number one goal. So it is with practice, that we are consistent in our consideration of others.

However, people frequently feel better about themselves when they are agreed with. And there are many who want others to do what they believe they should do. So, when God is leading a person in something distinct, there will always be a level of division and difficulty. Someone will not be getting their way. Regardless, we need to follow God's lead.

When we ask, "What is Love?", we simply look at what Love is not. A person walking in Love will not take advantage of another. Or use their freedom to overpower. Love is not proud, or easily angered. It does not need its own way; it is not envious, and it keeps no record of wrongs. Love does not delight in evil, but rejoices in Truth.

So Love brings freedom. And it's true that plenty who are in bondage, struggle. However, dependence on God is how we gain resilience to face issues that guide in ways that unite us. Additionally, freedom in Christ means to follow God and not man. It means to speak up and venture out to discover the fullness of joy. It is leading by example with a humble approach.

We need our spirits filled up, to express Love in all things. Are you free today? Remember to take time to pray today and move forward. When we hold Christ in the center, and apply a cornerstone of consistent repentance, we have an unmatched level of clarity. And as we seek God's face, we are built up and strengthened to do the hard things that require great courage.

February 17

Are We There Yet?

Most of us have heard the expression "one day at a time". And in the Lord's prayer, we are instructed by Jesus to pray, "give us this day our daily bread". So, not getting ahead of ourselves and taking the journey one day at a time, is an ideal way to take life.

There are moments when the road toward the fruition of our ideas can be quite difficult. The waiting is not always easy, as the Lord often provides only a limited view of the journey—perhaps so we do not become overwhelmed and give up. Whatever the case, we may find ourselves wondering: Will we arrive in time to see the manifestation of our heart's desires?

Life is but a breath, and we need to finish strong. With any God-given dream, our purpose always involves others. Our ideas about how things should unfold are often quite different from how they will actually transpire. Yet, God's will shall inevitably come to pass. And there is always more happening than what meets the eye.

We are co-creators, doing our best to listen and act. However, God does not play with our emotions—He creates a masterpiece, guiding us toward becoming our ideal selves. Are you tired of waiting and wondering when your dreams will finally manifest? Perhaps you feel stuck in a situation that seems unfruitful. Don't be dismayed—God will bring forth your best fruit. Continue to stand for love and keep moving forward, one step at a time.

Have you noticed that many people saved by grace and the precious blood of Jesus Christ never seem to retire? They keep going, continuing to create and pursue what they love well into their senior years. Their fulfillment surpasses anything the world has to offer.

Reflect on how far you've come, and resist the urge to be impatient today. Trust and be thankful for where you are now. You have come so far. Praise the Lord each day going forward, and trust Him to bring beauty and wholeness into your life. He will do it, one day at a time.

February 18

Life Is A Highway

Life is a highway, and when we see the marks of burnt rubber on the asphalt, we recognize the moments of sudden stops and urgent braking along the journey. These streaks are a significant sign. This is where the stopping started. In hopes of avoiding some sort of accident or collision.

Each of us are influenced by culture and our upbringing and experiences. And as we travel the highway of our life's journey, there are choices to make. We might avoid disaster, or we may encounter it. One thing is for sure, there will be scars.

This is where the rubber meets the road. And countless people are unhappy and believe it's just part of life. Many do not recognize they are burdened by their choices. And as a person ages, the weight of one's choices can grow heavy. Each of us will face the outcome of our ways.

Many run unaware of the sin that ensnares them, and their fears only compound. People naturally avoid pain, often trying to shield themselves from further hurt. Countless individuals come from broken homes and families already disadvantaged and suffering from trauma. And where there is fear, avoidance, and confusion, love is displaced.

To move forward in freedom from burdens and barriers, we must embrace the importance of repentance. This is how the scars of our journey are erased. It's necessary to revisit the place where our choices were made and bring them to the foot of the Cross. There, our scars are confronted head-on and erased completely.

When we avoid facing our scars, darkness can creep in, threatening to extinguish joy and hope. In contrast, there is freedom when no underlying subconscious sin weighs us down. So if you've lost your joy or the spring in your step, go back and retrace the road you've traveled.

Pray to the Lord, saying, "I am sorry for this transgression; please forgive me." True joy and freedom come from not having to bear the weight of sin. You can also say, "I'm sorry for not choosing Love and for missing the mark." Tears may come, and it's okay to welcome them. It's a simple process, knowing that joy follows on this road to peace.

February 19

Disposition Makes The Difference

When we do not see much progression toward the desires of our heart, while in the midst of watching other people get blessed, the waiting can be very difficult and even painful. However, there are countless stories in God's Word that reveal the Lord lifting the most inconceivable people to glory, because of His great Love and Grace.

Consider a woman who wants to be pregnant, and she can't. Or someone who desires marriage while others are marrying and posting pictures on social media of their joy and happiness. Maybe it's a desire to own a home or car. Each person has circumstances. And whatever the case may be, envy can cause problems in us and with those around us that we love and do life with. So it's important to release feelings of dissatisfaction, impatience, and frustration.

It's no fun to feel neglected or rejected, forgotten, and even misunderstood. And it's true that when other people get blessed in ways we desire, we often focus on ourselves and the fact that we're not seeing the results we envision or even expect. It may be that we are being treated unfairly. But it's important to remember that we live in a world of opposites. And our disposition makes all the difference. As we honor God, He honors us.

Scripture says, "the last shall be first, and the first shall be last." So, in other words, being in last place, and the one who is disregarded and unfairly treated, sets the stage for greater things to come within God's favor. It is our attitude going through matters that is important.

We may not always understand what's going on in us and with the people around us. However, the Lord knows what we need, even before we ask. Focus on this and count your blessings while you go through any difficulty. Commit to simplicity and be thankful.

Your disposition makes all of the difference. And the Lord is just and His timing is perfect. Every person receives a share of blessings and trials. So choose peace, while waiting for the desires of your heart to manifest. Don't give up when you feel disregarded. Instead, keep believing in dreams, visions, and ideas, because with each new day, there is the possibility of a new vision.

February 20

The Value In People

Every person has value and merits understanding. And when people put walls up and go silent without communicating what they are feeling, it can surely hurt. Plenty walk away and "ghost" without an explanation. This is disrespectful and not the way to be.

If abuse is involved, it's crucial to sever ties quietly. However, when there is no abuse and people are functional for the sake of the greater good, the best approach is always to walk in Love. This means caring about feelings and choosing to be kind by expressing our truth and communicating openly. We can offer closure and grace because every person holds worth and value in our lives.

Plenty of us have experienced the loss of a close friend at some time. The years of happy moments and shared heartbreaks are now a memory. There is silence where there once was chatter. And the impact of this can be devastating and difficult to overcome. But as we grow in maturity, we understand that loss is a normal part of life. We need to keep going and strive to take the high road.

People change, and this challenges our relationships. There may be those who walk away, but that does not make them any less valuable to God. Furthermore, we are never truly in control, and when someone fears losing control, they may act out, or leave in silence. Whatever the case may be, we need to be compassionate. We must be brave and value our brothers and sisters greatly.

God will never go silent. The Lord will always be your protection and sustainer. And if someone ghosts you and doesn't reply to your texts or calls, the reality is, that there is something going on with them. Accepting rejection for the sake of peace with God, is above all, the most important thing. So pray for people and wish them well. And do your best to express Love in all situations.

Even in difficult and unpleasant times, God knows your heart and will meet your needs in the new season. We never know when we will be called home, so remain true to Love. Doing the right thing, even when it is hard, brings great rewards. There is no reason to fear the future, for God will take care of you. You are of great value to Him, and your pure heart before Him is what is most beautiful and endearing.

February 21

Are You Worried Today?

Worry is repetitive negative thoughts and emotions, perceived in an uncontrollable manner. It is a state of anxiety and uncertainty over actual or potential problems. And it's certainly not difficult to get stuck in worry, with the many concerns that affect our daily life. However, worry is not good for us and we need to let it go, as soon as we realize we are in it.

Nations are at war and inflation is causing prices to rise in every area. With costs up, some can not even make a living wage. Many work two or three jobs. Add to that, health matters and family concerns and it's easy to understand the propensity toward worry. People have big day-to-day challenges. However, worry is fear-based thinking. When worry escalates, it can lead to self-harm or cause us to take our troubles out on others.

Worry causes stress in the body and it does not solve any problems. When we worry, we are troubled. For this reason, when we notice worry creeping in, it's time to cast our care on the Lord. And as we share our concerns with God, we will likely feel emotion and a level of pain being released. Letting go is a relief, but for many, feeling pain is not easy or desirable.

Are you experiencing worry today? When worry begins to rise, it's time to sit down and pray. Cast your care on the Lord, for He cares for you. (1 Peter 5:7) And remember you are loved immensely by the Most High God. You belong to Him and He has your best interest.

The Lord will make a way that is intended ideally for you. So please do not hesitate to face your fear and release any worry today. This is where the healing flows and the Universe opens up to you. No matter what you may be facing, you can have peace and confidence going through, when you place complete trust in God. And as you let go of controlling thoughts, turning over all of your concerns to the Lord, you receive the clarity to walk on, knowing that God will provide.

February 22

The Beginning Of Wisdom

An encounter with God is an experience that awakens our senses and demonstrates synchronistic, supernatural developments. And when we have these, we are not quick to test the Lord and go against His goodness. We have personally experienced His great intelligence at work and comprehend that the Creator understands more than we do.

Everything is always changing on our living planet. However, there is an order to things. So having our thoughts and actions in order, is wise. And it's through experiences, including falls, missteps and conflict, that we evolve and grow. Hopefully our errors are not big wanderings that cause great pain as we mature. Having reverence for life itself, along with our fellow man, and especially the Creator (God), amidst the evil we see, is needed.

And we can see the weight of abusive power in our world. Many do not fear the Lord. Instead they pursue ego driven and destructive behaviors that affect others. Countless people die. Spirits are crushed. And we see all of this as nations rise against nations. We see the places where tyrants' rule. It appears to be a lack of order. However, there is an intellect that reveals itself, and an enduring light that shines through darkness.

Scripture tells us that the fear of the Lord is the beginning of wisdom. So what this means is that, as we come to know and honor God, (who is Love) we grasp that choosing Love in all things is wise and also for the highest good. By honoring God, we grow in wisdom. And the Creator is living wisdom, breathing life into us and providing more insight than what we have, in our ordinary minds. We do not have to have all the answers now. However, choosing to honor God and let Him lead the way, produces wisdom for lasting beauty in our hearts.

Jesus spoke about hell often. And judgment. He said there will be consequences. He also said that every person will confront their choices. Do evil-doers consider that they may face their actions when their time is up? Is everybody offered a wake-up call? Foolish and disastrous moves do not produce lasting results that are revered and respected.

Today, be an example by choosing to honor God with your actions. We may not understand why there is so much suffering in the world, but perhaps it is to teach us how to love. By examining history, we can learn what to avoid. And honoring God is the beginning of wisdom.

February 23

Love Is Understanding

War—what is it good for? Why must we fight? Why aren't we more empathetic? If every person were compassionate, the world would be wonderful. Yet, we've always had warrior souls, learning the necessity of self-defense while realizing that nothing is guaranteed. And difficult people will always be around. So, what are we to learn from this? That evil must be overcome?

When Jesus taught the Lord's Prayer, He said, "On Earth as it is in Heaven," meaning we should bring about Heaven's purpose on Earth. Are we praying for God to use us to fulfill His will? We should avoid foolish paths of destruction or misery and instead engage in introspection to understand our motivations better.

Micah 6:8 states, "He has shown you, O mortal, what is good. And what does the Lord require of you? To act justly, to love mercy, and to walk humbly with your God."

This Scripture tells us what is essential to our focus daily: choosing humility over hatred, moving beyond fear, and placing complete trust in God. We are called to be humble, just, kind, and loving—also empathetic, communicative, and attentive. This pleases God.

Since the beginning of time, Love and hate have influenced us. We must recognize our role in this dynamic and make our choice. Each of us faces challenges, but Love begins within. And to walk in victory daily, we must choose empathy, which is also mercy. Remember, there is a battle for the soul, and our choices will determine our success or failure.

In Deuteronomy 30:19, God says, "I set before you life and death; choose life."

We need to choose life to overcome the world and resist evil desires. Understanding our motives in every situation is powerful, with mercy being fundamental. We must extend grace to one another and to ourselves while embracing Love in all things.

February 24

Do You Have Hope Today?

Many people go through their day, with little belief that their prayers are being heard. For some, hope for a positive outcome, through difficulties is scarce. However, there is comfort in choosing hope. And although it may be difficult to find hope as we look around, we need to be proactive and remember to consider how far we have come. We must remember to have a song of deliverance on our lips and especially to keep hope alive.

When you have hope, you are better able to receive guidance for future provision. And matters in the world, with many pending problems, can elicit a sense of doom. Some often try to anesthetize themselves and go through with numb feelings. This makes the journey more difficult. With little hope, there is depression, which steals away joy. So, the more hope we have, the more strength we'll have. This is very true when we face significant trials. Especially where we see people perishing and injustice transpiring.

It is not wise to hope in the things of this world. Instead, we need to have hope in the Lord and His will for our lives. We need to comprehend Christ and what He came to accomplish. Because believing in Christ, offers hope with the understanding that our steps are ordered precisely. We are exactly where we need to be to fulfill our purpose. This is our hope that will not fail.

Christ is Love personified. Through Him, we are never alone in our trials. He gave His life to show that we can overcome any difficulty we face. No one else provides what Christ offers, nor is there another teacher who exemplifies this path of sacrificial Love. Believing in Christ for salvation is the Hope of Heaven.

When you close your eyes, focus on what you hope for and do not be afraid. Fight the good fight of faith and put your hope in the Lord today. Do all you can, to learn about Love. And even when you have been hoping for a very long time for something, without seeing it come to pass, don't give up. There is purpose here. And the Lord will lead you through.

February 25

The Direction Of Dreams

Chasing a dream can feel a lot like being on a roller coaster ride with many ups and downs. The path is always the least expected. One moment we go one way, and then the next, we are moving into a new thing. And while the direction we're going at times is subtle, we often navigate and discover ideas by surprise. And these can seem miraculous.

For instance; we might encounter a person who has a significant connection, or we may stumble on a message that leads us to try something different. Whatever the case may be, when we believe in something big and difficult to attain on our own, we do not need to go to extremes. Instead, we must be patient and always keep a sense of balance.

When you dream for something new, it's likely you will pray and ask the Lord to bring it to pass. And where there are big dreams, there are usually big prayers. These petitions help us through ideas that seem impossible to accomplish on our own. And the way we go, is the most amazing bit. Full of surprise, purpose and wonder.

And stepping out to chase your dream, requires the courage to face your fear. This provides a real adrenaline rush, because dreaming and believing is exciting. However, when hitting the gate running, there needs to be stability with steadiness. A quiet faith. You may be thrilled, but you do not need to rise high and then sink low. This is out of balance and can cause stress to the body and affect your health. Also, you might lose some clarity and not be at your full potential. You may experience missed opportunities that negatively impact your path.

Keep your energy in check daily as you navigate the range of emotions that pursuing a dream brings. At first, you may feel exhilarated and full of faith, but as time goes by and ordinary life sets in, discouragement might follow. Nevertheless, persevere and keep God at the center. By doing so, you'll discover a world of opportunity that guides you with balance and helps you go the distance.

Scripture says in Matthew 7:7, "Ask and it will be given to you; seek and you will find; knock and the door will be opened to you."

Dreams really do come true and you can uncover all that God has for you, as you seek and follow faithfully. Keep moving in the direction of your dreams. And never give up. When the Lord is in the center, The Way forward will appear.

February 26

Who You Are In Christ

Understanding Christ and what He did at the Cross, reveals this great Love that God has for you. And walking with Christ means having your best friend by your side through every situation. In Christ, we go through experiences with increased vitality and victory. And we may even notice miracles with contentment.

When we come to salvation, having our sins erased brings relief and marks the first step toward release. Next, the Holy Spirit begins working within us to transform us. By keeping our focus on Jesus and His power to transform, heal, and sustain us, our hearts are forever changed and our minds are renewed. This is why we can go the distance.

When you know who you are in Christ, you have a direct line of communication with God. You embrace truthfulness and value integrity. Having truly received this great Love at your core, you gain confidence. The veil has been lifted, leaving no reason to hesitate in your fellowship with the Lord. With courage, nothing stands in your way.

And understanding the Word of God and what scripture says about you, provides freedom to not let the sin part distract. You are forgiven. And knowing who you are in Christ, means that you take on His righteousness and do not rely on your own strength and will.

Humbly receive what Christ provides today. And remember the importance of holding God's Word in your heart. With the Word living inside of you, you will be able to contradict any lies or confusion. And when issues come that challenge you, simply ask yourself, "What would Jesus do?".

Don't worry what the world or someone else thinks or says about you. This is foolishness. There is no reason to live in confusion or disorder. You must know who you are in Christ. Say this: "I am the righteousness of God in Christ Jesus".

February 27

Do Not Be Destroyed By Evil

When we embrace a born again experience, we are far from perfect. In fact we are more than likely broken and in need of recovery. And even with all of the recovery in the world, there are inadequacies that consistently afflict and dissuade us from the ideal. But God understands our weakness and leads us in His Love. And from the moment that we accept the Truth and receive Christ as Lord, we become Children of God, and are being changed.

Scripture says in Jeremiah 32:27, "I am the Lord your God, is there anything too hard for me?"

We are a rebellious people, and pride is one of the greatest causes of destruction. Many are consumed with self-importance, self-will, and the pursuit of power. Countless individuals resist God, often out of fear of failure. Yet, eventually, evil catches up and taints a life. Many are destroyed by evil because they deny God's Truth and the need for repentance. They keep pushing their sin and struggles under the rug and continue on, but it is their souls that are at risk.

Further, people generally do not like being corrected. But correction comes to those who are open and willing to grow. God can change a life. And although it may not happen in an instant, you can be sure that He who began a good work in you, will continue step by step, day by day.

Scripture also tells us in Luke 10:19, "I have given you authority to trample on snakes and scorpions and to overcome all the power of the enemy; nothing will harm you."

As we develop and evolve with Love in the center of our being, we can know that we have power by the Holy Spirit, to overcome evil desires and danger. Also, when we believe in the importance of following Christ over self and make it our priority, we progress toward the better way. Daily we are impacted by the power of Love working in us. And when evil arises, and we face difficulties, and temptations, we have recovery, protection, strength and safety for our souls.

February 28

Before I Formed You

"Before I formed you in the womb, I knew you", says the Lord. And what a relief this is to know, especially when we experience doubts and apprehensions about ourselves.

Each of us would likely prefer to be made up of only the "good parts" of our parents or the ideal we imagine. But, unfortunately, that's not the case. We see both the beauty and the flaws within ourselves. Yet, God shows us compassion and understanding. He loves us immensely, just as we are. Therefore, we must learn to readily accept His grace and Love.

Humans tend to see the negative, more often than the positive. And personal dilemmas and compromises can bring a negative self perception. Shame is a transgressor that can censure repeatedly. And shame comes to most people at one time or another. It is a complex emotion that commonly strikes those who struggle with personal mistakes, moral transgressions, societal expectations, and interpersonal relationships.

And coming through these things is difficult, to say the least. People who carry shame, might include those who have made regrettable decisions. Those who have violated their own values, or faced judgment and criticism from others. And understanding and addressing shame requires empathy, compassion, and support. And God's love through Christ, allows us to confront pain without fear. By fostering a safe environment for healing, shame is transformed into growth.

It's comforting to know that God sees you and understands. He loves you, especially when you feel inadequate and accepts you the way that you are. Even in weakness. He knows all the details of your life. Especially when you fail and mess up. He knew you before you were born.

Scripture says in Jeremiah 29:11, "For I know the plans I have for you," declares the LORD, "plans to prosper you and not to harm you, plans to give you hope and a future."

God is Love, and He reveals what we need to grow. Each of us will, at times, say and do things that steal our joy and power. Yet, God's unfailing Love endures to guide us along 'The Way.' Moreover, it's a profound realization to understand that God is actually pleased with us. When we approach Him with a contrite heart and sincerely repent, it brings joy to the Lord.

February 29

A Crown Of Glory

People aspire to be Kings and Queens. We long to feel special, and for our lives to have meaning. We strive to create greatness in whatever ways we can. Most of us want to leave a legacy and seek validation in certain aspects of ourselves.

It all comes down to what we truly value. But there comes a day, if we are wise, when we realize that the things of this world do not bring lasting glory. We may chase financial security or admiration, but these are not crowns of glory. What does bring lasting glory is every moment we choose to Love.

Love chooses between submission and assertion in different situations. At times, this can be relatively easy, but at other times, very difficult. It is during the difficult moments that we are truly tested. We must stay attuned to the leading of the Holy Spirit in all things. Yes, we will miss the mark at times, but hopefully, with each test we pass and in every interaction, our crown of glory continues to grow.

Knowing when and how the Lord is leading is paramount. There are always multiple factors that go into every decision. Therefore, as we place matters on the scales of wisdom, we ask "What would Jesus do?" This is how we gain a better understanding of how Love operates. In the end of things, we do not want temporary praise or admiration. Especially from people who are faulty in their own right. Our desire should be to please God. Because God has the highest good for our lives.

So are you having trouble with a relationship today? Submit to your partner in Love. This is where blessings flow. Let the Lord crown you, and do not let your ego lead you astray. Do you need to have more opportunities in the career or a dream you desire? Assert yourself gently with Love leading, and see how God will bless you, to wear a crown of glory.

No one knows what the Lord is telling you to do. So do not be afraid of people. Instead listen and obey. And each time you follow through, you become more attuned at hearing and following the path of Love, to wear a lasting crown of glory.

MARCH

March 1

Become A Prayer Warrior

It takes faith and determination to make change that affects our life for the better. We may awaken to a new day and recognize that we need to choose an improved way of living. Maybe we are striving to eat healthier, or to quit a bad habit like smoking. Perhaps we need to become better at listening. Regardless, there is room for improvement and lessons to be learned.

Choosing a new path requires discipline and consistent practice. And making the right choices demands strength, especially when faced with temptation. Most change takes time, and being a prayer warrior helps immensely. When seeking transformation, it's essential to be prayerful, to receive the power of the Holy Spirit to stand firm and resist falling back into old habits.

The Apostle Paul wrote to the Christians in Ephesus, in Ephesians 3:16: 'I pray that He may grant you, according to the riches of His glory, to be strengthened with power in your inner being through His Spirit."

We are creatures of habit, accustomed to familiarity. And praying fervent prayers helps us to break free of conditioning and habits. So, we must continue to ask, and keep knocking, to climb out of that which no longer serves us. The process of lasting change is not usually a one and done matter. For this reason, we need to consistently stay the course.

Scripture says in 1 Thessalonians 5:16-18, "Rejoice always, pray without ceasing, and give thanks in all circumstances; for this is the will of God in Christ Jesus for you."

There is nothing like having the Holy Spirit living within you, providing power for new challenges and goals. It's an incredible feeling to know that God is with you and won't let you go. Even if you slip up, don't dwell on your mistakes. Instead, repent, get back up, and face each challenge one by one. Your satisfaction will grow as you persevere and refuse to give up.

Striving for excellence is rewarding. And we do well to put our prayers on repeat! When we give our best to become mature in the Lord, we grow in ways that open doors to greater opportunities.

March 2

Priceless Beauty

Life is a gift, and there is an order to everything we see. And when it appears the world is falling apart around you, don't despair. Instead, choose to remember the things that are lovely and beautiful. Because beauty is our priceless strength, in a dark world.

When we focus our minds too long on the things that frighten us, we lose our joy. And there is no use dwelling on that which we do not understand. We do not need to let our mind wander and struggle to make sense of certain things. We won't have all the answers. Instead, we need to place complete trust in God and His purposes for our lives.

You've heard it said that beauty begins within? This is true. And when we bring every thought into the captivity of Christ, life becomes manageable and lovely. When we see with pure eyes of Love, we possess more compassion for ourselves and others. So please, do not let the world steal this splendor. There is a beautiful mystery at work in you. And when you focus on the beauty of God's Word and His Love, you will have your heart in the right place, to go through in victory.

When the Titanic was pierced and the ship was going down, the people danced and celebrated. They loved and savored the moment, until their very last breath. Now this is an extreme example, but a worthy mental picture we need to consider. That even when everything around appears to be adrift, and when trouble comes in like a lion, we should consider the lilies. Additionally, through loss and sorrow, our hearts are opened. And by heartbreak, we further develop the ability to genuinely care for one another.

So today, choose to remember the beauty that Christ brings. He offers freedom, and you can be assured of salvation while becoming a light to those in need. If you've been facing darkness in your life, invite the Lord into your heart with a simple, private prayer. Stay humble and take a moment to say, 'Forgive me, Lord.' You can also ask, 'Show me the way forward,' or 'Lord, restore beauty to my life and to my eyes.' In Jesus' name, Amen.

March 3

When One Door Closes - Rejoice!

It's tempting to be disappointed when something that we think is good for us, does not come to pass. It may be a job opportunity, a relationship, or perhaps an educational pursuit. And even though we do not see our vision manifest the way we hope or imagine, we don't lose hope. Instead, we rejoice knowing that something suitable to our needs is on the way.

Every day we can choose a good life. We must not complain or be disheartened. Instead we need to enjoy every moment and the adventure. Life is a breath and our time on Earth is limited. It's not wise to waste one day in regret over what did not happen. And when one door closes, it may be a disappointment, however, experience teaches us that when the door is closed and something does not work out, it is likely for our benefit and protection. Perhaps a grace from trouble.

With wisdom comes understanding. And what do we learn as we go through life's challenges? We discover that the more we endure, the better we become at letting go of control. In hindsight, we also realize that the doors that opened for us were solid opportunities.

We need to seek the highest good, to live full lives. And keeping our standards high and recognizing when we may be wasting time with the wrong people, or at a job we do not love is important. When we are frustrated, we are going in the wrong direction. Frustration is a key indicator of choices that hinder us from God's best. So rejoice today and remember who is in charge. Pray and put God first and know that your steps are ordered by the Lord. Follow Him.

When you let God take the lead, you'll accomplish more than you imagined. Along the way, there will be wonderful surprises and great things happening, even amidst the ups and downs. Though the road may get rocky, don't be discouraged. Instead, rejoice and trust God with childlike faith—something good is on the horizon. Embrace the possibilities and rejoice!

March 4

The Right Side Of Life

We cannot serve two masters, and it's true that we evolve toward what we focus on. Since both good and evil exist in the world, it's essential that we choose a side. Our hidden motives play a crucial role, and if we're not careful, evil can creep in and take root. It often begins with insecurity, greed, or a desire for power in a world where we may feel powerless—this is also how addictions start. The aim of this soul-killing process is to rob us of our effectiveness, our ability to live a blessed life, and to fulfill God's will. Sadly, many are lost in the process. Furthermore, when we drift through life without much thought about our direction, we can fall into traps and realize we've severely missed the mark. So, choose whom you will serve, for you cannot serve two masters.

Evil is a powerful and deceptive force in the world. Traits such as psychopathy, egoism, sadism, and narcissism are often associated with an evil condition, as individuals with these traits tend to put their own interests first—often to the detriment of others. Many justify their actions in ways that remove any sense of guilt or shame. These personality disorders often begin subtly and grow when left unchallenged. Selfishness, too, is an evil condition that can destroy and divide people.

There comes a time when we must choose to fight for Love. We must become vigilant in watching our steps and examining our motives. We are in a time where it matters more than ever whose side we are on. James 4:7 says, 'Submit yourselves to God. Resist the devil, and he will flee from you.' It's not just about resisting evil but also about submitting to God. Daily, we need to take up our cross, seek to walk in Love, and invite the Holy Spirit to guide us.

Have you given your heart to the Lord? If you're feeling bitterness or negativity, it's a sign that something deeper needs to be addressed. You may feel pulled in many directions, but the goal is to find Love, peace, and joy in the Holy Spirit. It takes effort to break old habits and change our ways. Confronting our motives requires honesty, but it's a worthwhile process. So today, choose whom you will serve, for you cannot serve two masters.

March 5

A Better World

When evil rears its ugly head, the good must rise in opposition. Humanity is stronger in unity, as one people. Yes, we are all in this together, especially as we overcome evil with good.

It would be excellent if we had Universal Love, but we are not there yet. We may try and get along with those who do not agree with us. But as we look deeper, we recognize that there are spiritual forces at work. What is real, is the battle for your soul.

Scripture says in Ephesians 6:12, "For our struggle is not against flesh and blood, but against the rulers, against the authorities, against the powers of this dark world and against the spiritual forces of evil in the heavenly realms."

If the seven deadly sins are envy, gluttony, greed, lust, pride, sloth, and wrath, we must remain vigilant to these notions within ourselves. Envy represents a complex dissatisfaction, while wrath manifests as extreme anger or rage. Pride involves narcissistic tendencies and deep pleasure in one's own achievements. If we are not attentive, we might become deceived and infected by these detrimental states of being.

In Deuteronomy 30:19 Scripture says, "This day I call the heavens and the earth as witnesses against you that I have set before you, life and death, blessings, and curses. Now choose life, so that you and your children may live".

In this scripture, we are asked to choose, and choosing is an internal process. This is why Christ is so essential. The Truth starts within each of us, and He is our cornerstone. When we walk with the Lord, we bring everything to Him—every good thing, every concern, and every shortcoming and failing. We must lay these before Him and continue moving toward the light.

Peace begins in you. And sin grows when not confronted and brought into the light. It might begin small, but it can manifest and cause problems later. So lay it all at the foot of the Cross and walk in a way that leads to wholeness. Choose life and choose Love. This is our entire purpose for living. To overcome evil with good. And if we want a better world, we need to be better people. Honest people. We need to understand the big picture. And not be afraid of being broken for the sake of being made whole. Choosing to serve Christ is an important step to a better world. So don't be afraid to look inward with honesty and choose life. This is how to overcome.

March 6

In God's Sight

You are beautiful in God's sight. And chances are, you have experienced self-esteem issues at one time or another. Both sexes are greatly affected, and the struggle is real, in unique ways and with significant challenges. However, doubting yourself does not serve well.

Men are often seen as fighters and warriors, expected to embody integrity and strength despite experiencing violence. Every boy, at some point, faces challenges related to conflict, race, sex, and power struggles, along with the expectation to lead. Unfortunately, some are left to navigate these issues on their own until they discover that true leadership involves being a caring servant rather than a dominating ruler.

Women contend with not being treated equally. And men are often preferred over women for employment and pay, although equally qualified. Some women are oppressed and regarded as possessions, to the point of requiring permission to go out and be who they are. In some Middle Eastern countries, women are mostly hidden, with few rights and little education. Add to that, sexual abuse, rape, incest, and the reality of predators.

So, both men and women face danger in different ways. And with all this pressure on the sexes, what we have, are plenty of people struggling with self-esteem. However, when people truly understand their worth, life goes better, and goodness prevails.

Psalm 139:13-14 says, "For You formed my inward parts; and covered me in my mother's womb.I will praise You, for I am fearfully and wonderfully made; Marvelous are Your works, and that my soul knows very well."

You are beautiful in God's sight—loved and accepted completely, just as you are. Have confidence in the Lord and His great Love for you each day. Never forget your identity as a child of God. Be aware that there is a negative voice trying to undermine your self-worth. In difficult situations, choose to do what's right by walking in Love, as this positively impacts your self-esteem. Make the right choice as often as possible to bring out the good. And when you miss the mark, embrace confession and get back on track, knowing that you are beautiful in God's sight.

March 7

Every Moment Precious

Every moment is precious, and your time on Earth with the people you love is a gift. When we're young, we often don't recognize this fully, as we're focused on becoming who we are through work, education, social circles, and hobbies. However, as we grow and evolve, we hopefully develop a deeper appreciation for life and come to recognize the significance of each moment.

And as we age, we tend to savor our time in ways that are more meaningful. Many who have experienced life-threatening situations, like health issues and loss of loved ones, often have a better appreciation for every moment. They know first-hand the limitations of time. Surely, we do not want to go through troubling matters to recognize the importance of each moment.

Sometimes we revisit places we've been, trying to relive special moments and recreate the feelings we had when they first occurred. We remember the times and people we were with, but attempts to re-create these experiences often fall flat. This is because we cannot replicate moments exactly as they happened. For most, the second or third attempt is never quite like the first. In hindsight, we recognize the significance of these moments, understanding that they have passed and will not come again.

Are you missing a moment today and longing for some experience that once made you happy? Stay in the present moment and value the situations and people that are around you now. When you do, you will not feel as if you are missing out on anything.

Please do not take the goodness of God for granted. As believers, we know that God goes before us, so remember to be thankful. When you feel a need for something more, look around and find ways to help others. This is a sure path to a higher quality of life. A self-centered lifestyle offers no true value. Instead, focus on the blessings you have and the people who surround you.

March 8

Let Mercy Flow

Most of us do not consider the idea that we need mercy each day. But we do. This is because every person is faulty and not without sin. We do our best, but inevitably, we miss the mark. And to appreciate our freedom, and not be hindered by past mistakes, we must recall God's great Love toward us. He has redeemed us and set us free. We've been forgiven and are loved beyond measure. For this reason, daily, we must receive mercy and offer mercy freely to others.

People sometimes do things that deeply hurt us, and it's natural to feel anger. However, holding a grudge or retaliating only brings more trouble upon ourselves. We don't want to become hardened or find ourselves growing bitter over time, nor do we need regrets. This is not the way to endure or to exit our existence.

Consider how we can expect to receive mercy if we are not willing to give it. Most people are doing the best they can, influenced by their past and current stressors. Therefore, we should be slow to judge or dismiss others, especially those who seek resolution and restoration. Instead, we can lead by example and guide others toward goodness. This requires a high level of self-respect and excellent communication skills. While we shouldn't tolerate continual disrespect, we can express ourselves lovingly and kindly, without condemning others.

The Lord desires unity between people. And the only way to have this is to work through things. We teach others how we want to be treated. And if we are unforgiving and cutting people off, especially those who desire a relationship, along with peace and harmony, then we are not walking in Love. We are also not helping others to learn to do better. And this can cause more pain.

Jesus said in Matthew 9:13, "I desire mercy and not sacrifice. For I have not come to call the righteous, but sinners."

We need to extend mercy while maintaining boundaries, understanding that everyone will let us down at some point—no one is perfect. Consider being merciful to those who have hurt you. Forgive them, but also expect a better way forward. Some genuinely want to grow and improve, while others may not. Regardless, we can forgive and lead by example, allowing mercy to flow.

March 9

Let Love Lead

Plenty struggle with taking responsibility for their actions. And countless look to blame other people, not considering the part they play in situations. But Love requires us to look at the position we take, along with our motives in matters. We are responsible for our role with others and every outcome. So, our participation should be our focus.

There will always be conflict in life. Most people are influenced by their past, along with what they believe to be true today. And disputes happen between friends, families, business associates, and nations. Conflict arises because each of us is unique and has filters and different ways of seeing things. So, we need to understand our role in matters.

When we take responsibility for our actions, we contribute to making the world a better place. Conflict isn't necessarily negative; rather, it can be like a light shining in the darkness, guiding us toward resolution. In the midst of conflict, we should ask ourselves, 'What is God trying to say?'

Jesus asks in Luke 6:41, "Why do you look at the speck of sawdust in your brother's eye and pay no attention to the plank in your own eye?"

It's common and tempting to point the finger at another person when disagreements happen. We may place judgment on the conflicting party. But when we do, we are not truly awake. Instead, we need to see our part in every issue with honesty. This requires a humble approach. There is something we need to learn. And every conflict brings the opportunity for growth.

Being fully mature to walk in Love, requires each of us to recognize our contribution in situations. Always take responsibility for your actions, missteps, and disagreements. Can you see where you have been wrong? When clear, it is easy to see our role in matters. And our desire should be toward maturity and the evolution of our soul.

If we choose not to take responsibility for our actions, instead opting to judge, dissect, or blame others, we hinder our progress toward Love. On the contrary, we remain stuck and may have to repeat the lesson until we learn it. True peace begins when we let Love guide our actions.

March 10

Shining As Stars

Those who are wise, shall shine like the brightness of the firmament and those who turn many to righteousness like the stars forever and ever. (Daniel 12:3)

One thing is certain: in our own strength, we don't have everything we need. We may strive to do good in the world, but our disposition isn't always perfect. People often desire power and glory, and pride can lead us astray. As believers, we recognize that true goodness comes from God. We understand that our flesh is weak, and any good we accomplish is a result of our reliance on the Lord and the Holy Spirit working within us.

And wisdom grants us the ability to see our mistakes and correct them. We achieve not by might, nor by power, but by the Holy Spirit. And being aware of our weaknesses, we rest in knowing that God's strength is made perfect in weakness. And wisdom allows us to receive criticism without being offended. We know who we are, and who lives in us. With wisdom, we can better see with God's eyes and not eyes of insecurity or judgment. We can freely choose whether to receive criticism and improve, or let it go and move on from that which does not serve us.

We are not perfect, but we are being perfected. So, there is no need for deception, or a proud and haughty spirit. When someone criticizes you, or how you do something, there is no reason to get tripped up. Instead, simply consider any truth in the occurrence, in order to become better. You can choose to accept or reject the criticism.

Are you walking in wisdom today? Wisdom is a journey marked by balance and grace, guiding us toward righteousness through our dependence on the Lord. It reveals our need for a Savior and the truth that we are sinners in need of redemption.

To lead by example, we must make the right choices with a humble heart. Righteousness is not earned through our deeds or actions but through what Christ has done for us. He died so that we might live and be forgiven, enabling us to forgive others and receive God's wisdom directly.

March 11

A Living Epistle

Our lives and actions tell a story. They reveal to the outside world what is happening inside of us. And hopefully the person you were yesterday, is not the same person you are today. It is healthy and good for Love to shine brighter within, day by day and step by step.

Scripture tells us in 2 Corinthians 3:2, "You are our epistle, written in our hearts, known and read by all men."

As a living epistle, your conduct, character, and actions should reflect the principles of Christ, including love, compassion, integrity, and righteousness. Living epistles reveal their stories to the people they interact with daily. Your outward life showcases your inward growth as you mature. Ideally, over time, you will have evolved to become more temperate, generous, and kind.

And people who rely on God become beautiful through their experiences and the lessons they learn. This is true success. And being the ideal living epistle, means that we demonstrate the fruit of the Spirit, which is Love, Joy, Peace, Patience, Kindness, Gentleness and Self Control. Our lives serve as a testimony that offers a practical example of what it means to follow Jesus.

Achieving consistency takes practice. Many of us grow up amidst dysfunction and challenges, where troubles and sufferings forge us through the fire. And as we navigate these difficulties, we become better at hearing God's voice more clearly. Additionally, the temptations of life are numerous. While pleasure may satisfy temporarily, over time, we often find ourselves back where we started, facing a level of dissatisfaction.

There is great value in the transforming power of Christ for living a rewarding life. The true reward is wholeness, which brings genuine satisfaction. Over time, we learn to release our attempts to control matters and let go of the past, moving forward toward what brings us contentment. This is crucial because, as we mature in our relationship with God, we model a better way of being that positively impacts our entire environment. As living epistles, we reflect the goodness of God.

March 12

Amazing Grace

This world is not our home, although it may feel as if it is at times. We can become very comfortable. But we are transient beings who are carried from one glory to the next. And we may think that we are in control, but truthfully, we are not in control.

And we see this when issues arise, and trouble comes. We may have to move or change our employment. Perhaps we experience a loss or separation from loved ones. Eventually every person will face matters that are out of their control. And through it all, there is a letting go.

Time and experience teach us that our security is not in the things of this world, but in the One who loves us enough, to send His Son, and show us "The Way". The more we grow in wisdom, the more we recognize God's great Love and care for us. He leads us by still waters and restores our soul, as we walk through the wilderness of this world.

Wouldn't it be wonderful if this world were our true home? Perhaps, but there are significant challenges here. While Earth is full of beauty and magnificence, we are also fragile. We face health issues and aging that lead us to places we'd rather avoid. We grapple with war and conflict, and many struggle daily for essentials like food and water.

However, as we contemplate our journey through this world, we can find solace in accepting and flowing with our circumstances. We are merely passing through. The best we can do each day is to embrace the good and the beautiful, which are truly priceless. And remember, with faith, that God holds us in the palm of His hand. We are His beloved.

So do not allow yourself to be hardened, tainted, or troubled by the things of this world. Instead, keep your heart open to every experience—joy, pain, sorrow, and laughter. Hold loosely to everything. There's no need to possess anyone or material things as you pass through this life.

Travel the road with God, following Christ who exemplified bravery, humility, service, salvation, and purpose. Trust is key to a fulfilling journey. Jesus demonstrated the purpose of serving others, encouraging us to help the poor and love the least of our brothers and sisters. This example of Love is a pure gift from God for our daily journey.

March 13

Getting High On Hope

People attending gospel revivals in the 1970s and 80s exhibited a joyous response to Christ and the promise of eternal life. Countless individuals gathered in celebration to contemplate Jesus' forgiveness and the hope of heaven. Traveling preachers like Billy Graham and others delivered messages of hope accompanied by uplifting songs.

To outsiders, these revivals might have seemed unusual, with faith healings, speaking in tongues, and altar calls for salvation and prayer. Yet for those in attendance, these gatherings were transformative. People brought their concerns, and the atmosphere was electric—attendees were often on their feet, caught up in the power of the moment. The experience was characterized by dancing, singing, weeping, and receiving spiritual renewal.

And these events were refreshing for the faithful and awe-inspiring for newcomers. There was a palpable energy, with people rising to their feet and lifting their hands in songs of salvation. The light of the revival was so intense that it frightened those unfamiliar with it, as they struggled to understand the phenomenon.

Today, many charismatic church services share this vibrancy. They are brightly lit, energetic, and dynamic, filled with enthusiastic attendees celebrating life through inspirational messages and spiritual music. In contrast, people also flock to nightclubs, concerts, and sporting events to dance, sing, and celebrate, seeking a temporary escape from daily struggles. But do these experiences offer the same "high on hope" as contemporary churches and the revivals?

Facing fear and embracing hope in our troubled world is crucial. It's beneficial to be bold and to seek hope in Jesus Christ. Engaging in activities that bring joy and connection is valuable, whether in a church or elsewhere. So, rather than judging those who choose the church, embrace the positive message, and celebrate life. Life goes by quickly, and you are a beloved child of God, accepted just as you are, however unique you may be.

March 14

No Hypocrisy In Christ

People often confuse religion with a personal relationship with Jesus Christ, but the two are significantly different. Religion is a man-made practice that involves faith, but also encompasses rules and rituals aimed at earning salvation and being welcomed into heaven. In contrast, following Christ represents freedom from religious constraints. It is a direct relationship with God.

And religion is not what Jesus taught. In fact, He opposed the religious leaders of His time, criticizing their practices. Jesus set people free by accepting them as they were. And following Christ is about experiential knowledge of Divinity, not merely adhering to dogma, beliefs, or intellectual interpretations. It involves humbling ourselves and inviting the Lord into our lives, regardless of our circumstances.

Scripture in James 1:27 states that the religion God accepts as pure and faultless is "to look after orphans and widows in their distress, and to keep oneself from being polluted by the world."

The Cross of Calvary is for those who recognize their need for redemption and restoration. It is for souls who can let go of pride to receive the gift of forgiveness that Christ offers. While change can be painful, suffering is a part of life. And Christ demonstrates courage in enduring injustice and suffering for the sake of Love. His example provides healing and comfort for those who suffer.

Scripture also tells us in Psalm 34:18, "The Lord is near to the brokenhearted and saves those who are crushed in spirit."

Religious people may have expectations of others, but followers of Christ are simply called to be. Accepting Christ's sacrifice for our sins in our fallen state enables us, as children of God, to let go of the heavy burdens we often carry. When we come to Christ, our past is erased, and a new life begins. This personal relationship is where the Holy Spirit reveals the Truth of God's Love.

Jesus is your friend, not a judge to condemn you. He is a patient Father and teacher who gently guides, speaking to our hearts daily. Through prayer and fellowship, we become overcomers and are never alone. Aware of our faults and Christ's sacrifice for us, we meet Him in our lowest moments. There is no hypocrisy in being loved by God—only a loving and active relationship.

March 15

Faith Born Out Of Desperation

Tough times come to each of us. And those challenged the most, tend to grow in prosperous ways. These individuals, when tried, know how to adjust their sails, and get the boat moving. They flourish, when pressed on every side.

And desperation is a good driver. Because, when a person is desperate, especially for survival, they begin to think outside of the box. And although it may be painful, the pressure of desperation cuts, to create new understanding, discoveries, inner strength and resilience. This is where we step into something new. And every person must first trust that they can.

Desperation can feel like a dry land where days are stagnant, and life's complex. These experiences stretch our faith and force us to overcome complacent tendencies. And for sure, we want to be growing in soulful places because we are alive. So it helps to refresh our vision with new ideas.

Are you missing out on building in important ways? Being desperate for change or an unmet need, can bring you to where belief is born. In contrast, when a person is comfortable or just doing enough to get by, they may not be challenged. They may have money and opportunity and settle for the status quo.

When it seems like all options have run out and you feel trapped, it's actually the beginning of something new! Embrace that feeling and push through. Avoid rushing into impulsive actions out of desperation. Instead, recognize that desperation can be a birthing ground for miracles. This is where exciting life changes are born.

Are you desperate for something new? For the wise, desperation leads to prayer. You may ask, "What more can I do?" Go with God, and He will go with you. Trust that in seeking Him, new possibilities will unfold, often in ways you never imagined.

March 16

The Abundant Life

There may be seasons where it can be hard to believe that good things are coming around the bend. Especially when you have been waiting for something for a very long time. But we need to be patient and keep our hope high, because God's timetable is not the same as our timetable. Additionally, the Lord may see a different approach and result than we envision for ourselves.

If we are alive, there is more in store for our good outcome. And although life has an abundance of daily challenges and struggles, small blessings are everywhere. Is it taking longer for you today, to see your ideas manifest? It can be a real struggle to hold on.

In 1 Corinthians 2:9, Scripture says, "Eye has not seen, nor ear heard, nor have entered into the heart of man, the things which God has prepared for those who love Him".

And big dreams have big ideas. Many dreamers experience repeated failures and challenges, both financially and personally. Faithful believers step out and try just about everything, often taking matters into their own hands. This occurs especially after waiting a long while and seeing little progress or change. And when we have not seen the fruition of God's promises in our lives after a long time of waiting, we can become impatient and tempted to give up.

But we should not give up. We do well to wait in faith and watch for intervention. Because as long as we're in the land of the living, God has more in store. Just look around and see how you fit into the scheme of things. Hold fast to His promises through hard times of waiting. And bring your petitions to the Lord in prayer. Rest assured, that He has a plan for your blessing and that there is nothing too hard for Him.

Remember that His ways are not your ways. So let go of any strongholds, or outcomes you may have in mind and allow God to manifest the results. This is where you will see that God makes everything beautiful in His time. When you let go, and let God work, you will grow stronger in faith. And grasping the light of Love everlasting, we are partakers in this great eternal Grace. You can be at peace knowing that Christ is "The Way, The Truth and The Life."

March 17

Love Moves Us Along

What can we truly hold on to? Perhaps family? At least until they are gone. Maybe we can hold on to our friends? We are blessed if we have a few good friends who stick with us for distances. But truly the only One we can hold on to is the Lord.

Life moves us along. And Love is the only thing that lasts forever and is eternal. While the people in our lives are precious, changes come, and friendships evolve as loved ones go on before us. For this reason, we especially do not need to hold on to the past. When it's time to change, we do not want to miss the good things coming our way for the future.

In this world, we can expect to be scattered. We may feel part of a crowd one day, traveling along together for some time. We become very familiar with the people we do life with. But then a shift comes and we find ourselves scattered. And although it may feel lonely or sad at the onset, this scattering is not a bad thing. It is a part of the Sojourner's way, because we are meant to live free. We are pilgrims on a journey. Not to be held back from possibility.

Your life and path is for the evolution of your soul. And it's true that we grow through the twists and turns, and winds of change. So when we let go of circumstances and outcomes, along with attachments to people, to graciously accept change, we flourish in our earthly adventure. We are much more open to the present moment. And this is where our future needs are ideally met.

It can be intimidating to go forward on your own. But God in His great Love, cares for you and knows just what you need. You may notice people going their way. They may move or start a new family. Perhaps someone passes away, and you begin to feel abandoned in places you were once partnered. It can feel as if you are alone. But you are never alone.

Love moves us along. And the people you Love and trust may become scattered, but rest assured, these experiences and feelings come to everyone eventually. God will never abandon you. You entered this world as a lone soul and will leave that way. You can live a victorious life today by placing all of your trust in the One who leads "The Way".

March 18

Edit Your Filmstrip

No one knows the hour or the day they will die. It is the moment when life's journey transitions into eternity—a mystery for all. Yet, many have heard stories of near-death experiences, where individuals describe a phenomenon akin to watching a film strip, seeing their life flash before them.

People in crises often express having a visual passage and a time of reflection. At this point, memories flood their mind, shaping their thoughts and ideas. These recollections—both good and bad—arise, perhaps ingrained deeply in the soul, where our experiences and choices are revealed.

Nearing the end of our earthly existence without confronting our shortcomings can be detrimental. Though daunting, no one wants to leave this life with unresolved doubts or regrets. Resolution is key. Therefore, it's essential to consider the idea of altering our life review before it's too late. But how do we do this?

The first step is getting right with God, and this requires complete honesty. Jesus said, "I Am the Way, the Truth, and the Life." Accepting Christ as the One who gave His life to redeem our soul is foundational. We must invite the Lord into our hearts. And if fear stands in the way, we must recognize that facing it is the best approach. Running away only leads to darkness, but standing at the crossroad with Christ brings light. Don't wait.

The second step is having the courage to dig deeper. We must revisit places in our minds where we've made poor choices, hurt others, or even harmed ourselves. As we recall these moments, it's important to reflect on our motivations. Understanding why we acted as we did—whether out of fear, pain, or confusion—helps us move toward healing. At the Cross, we receive forgiveness, and our missteps are forgotten, remembered no more.

Finally, the third step is letting go of that which no longer serves us. As we receive God's refreshing grace, we experience a deep and lasting peace. No longer will we allow situations to rob us of this peace. The soul begins to glow with the light of true inner peace.

While we cannot know everything now, if we do experience a "film strip" or life review at the end, wouldn't it be wonderful for it to be beautiful—free of guilt and shame? Of course, it would. So don't wait. Take action now, edit your film strip, and clear "The Way."

March 19

A Vibrant And Interesting Journey

When we have been conditioned to believe wrong things about ourselves, it can be difficult to know what makes us feel alive. And if we have lived a life of oppression, we may struggle to be who we truly are. But we have one life to live. Therefore, we need to lay aside the past and move into the future with freedom to experience a vibrant and interesting journey.

We do not want to stay stuck or remain broken, so forgiveness is the answer. And we do not know what causes people to do the things that they do. So whatever we have had to endure, we must overcome by seeking the Truth in Love. Additionally, healing wounds and hurts that have been with us for some time, can feel much like reliving the trauma. So, a shift is required. Not an angry shift, but a loving shift. We may feel angry that part of our life was affected negatively, but anger does not help us to move forward in freedom.

The wounded heart is often home to a prisoner, and shame is a destabilizer that most people carry to some degree. It is crucial to release any wounds and the shame within our soul because shame, buried in the subconscious, affects everything we do in our conscious lives.

Shame is the opposite of vibrancy. It can cause us to resist healthy relationships, miss great job opportunities, or even act in ways that hurt others. Furthermore, it can lead to destructive behaviors, such as overeating, substance abuse, or self-harm. Those deeply burdened by shame may even contemplate suicide or inflict harm on themselves. And to live a vibrant and fulfilling life, we must do the difficult but necessary work of confronting and healing from these wounds.

The process is accelerated when we are willing to honestly examine the times we've compromised ourselves, as well as moments where others' actions have caused us to adopt false beliefs about who we are. We must take responsibility for our own "rubbish" and own our journey toward healing. We honor ourselves by speaking the Truth in Love. Every step of growth is rooted in forgiveness, made possible by receiving what Christ did on the cross to set us free.

When we fully uncover our issues and bring them to a place of transparency—the place where there is no veil, only the cornerstone of truth— all matters are finished, to be remembered no more. This is the path to restoration and the key to living a vibrant and interesting journey.

March 20

Shake It Up!

When we do the same thing day after day, and have a routine that rarely changes, we can miss out on valuable growth. We may be uncomfortable or even fearful of any variation in our lives. However, variation helps to encourage a fresh inspiration and attitude. And it's true that many people come to love a good routine. But personal development primarily comes through change. So, it's important to shake things up now and then.

Often, we do not know how to do this, however, a great place to start is to speak out a desire, and then have the integrity to follow through. We might speak out something different, yet because we have not done it before, we may be hesitant to step out and even tempted to back down. But we need to follow through on our words, to do what we said we would do. This is how we receive added blessings while also experiencing a rewarding journey.

And even though it may feel strange or foreign at first, there is no reason to hesitate to do something new. Perhaps you are setting out on a road trip or riding a bike to work versus driving a car. Maybe you'd like to take a volunteer position at a local hospital part time. Whatever the case may be, it's normal to experience a level of fear when you first set out.

So go forward and do not be afraid. Realize that your words are powerful. And when you line up what you say with what you do, you enter a level of excellence that can and will bring many blessings. Start by speaking about what you dream of doing, and then do it. Don't be afraid. Only keep the Lord in prayer as you face your fears. You can shake things up.

Be committed to the integrity of your word and take a moment today to consider how you can actively change your circumstances. The "shaking" or challenges you face can be beneficial in leading you toward a fulfilling life. Additionally, self-preservation and protection won't serve those who truly desire an abundant life. This is because there's always a degree of risk involved in opening ourselves up to receive. So, step out of your comfort zone, and live your best life.

March 21

The End Of Folly

After living for some time, you may notice certain feelings, and ask yourself, what does it all mean? You may wonder, where do I stand today? And where is my heart? And if taking an assessment, you may wonder, where was Love good in my life? And where did Love flow?

These are important questions to ask, as understanding brings a sense of peace. You have reached the end of folly and arrived at maturity. Now, you realize that Love has always been present for you, and it is good toward you. Today, you understand who you are and what you truly need. This Love is now demonstrated through you. You have come full circle, and the evidence is seen in how you treat others and yourself.

You have arrived gracefully, and reaching the end of folly, you reach the end of confusion, insecurity, doubt, and fear. You have come to the end of feeling as if you are not enough or never will be enough. You know longer compromise in order to be accepted by others.

And after you have had enough tries and experience with relationships, what remains is the greatest Love you have ever encountered. This is the great Love of God. And with this understanding comes the recognition that anything less, would never be satisfactory.

Now, at the end of folly, the only way to truly love is with another who has also reached the end of their folly. This is the one who can fully impress love upon you, as both hearts have been humbled by the lessons of life. Together, you can experience a love that is grounded in wisdom, free from the illusions of past mistakes, and centered in truth.

The world can be a treacherous place for the loving heart. You may have had plenty of attempts to understand Love. But the reward is in the give and take, and all the tries, just to find out how well you are loved. You're at the end of folly and the beginning of wisdom. This is the place where True Love abounds. It is the end of folly.

March 22

Life One Day At A Time

As life progresses, we learn that our outcomes have much to do with many unknown circumstances. There may be family matters, health issues, romantic endeavors, along with sustenance requirements, like work and housing that directly affect our individual results.

Because the journey is unknown, we must learn to take one day at a time. This is a good place to be, as it's here we realize the Lord meets our needs. Our issues are resolved with the best possible outcomes in each moment as we trust God. We can anticipate goodness for our souls, knowing that today is all that is promised.

And trust is essential in approaching each day one step at a time. Tomorrow will bring its own circumstances. Taking life one day at a time doesn't mean we are not proactive or that we procrastinate. Instead, it means we're at peace with not having all the answers, trusting the process to unfold daily while maintaining our calm.

We must shift our thoughts and will from dwelling in the future or past to living in the now, where we can fully experience the freedom that letting go provides. As we embrace life one day at a time, the surprises become sweeter, knowing that God's plan is good. There is also a deep sense of liberation that comes from trusting the Lord for a good outcome. It's not always easy, but sometimes we simply have no other choice. As children of God, we belong to Him, and He always has our best interest at heart, working for our highest good.

Are you trusting God in your current circumstances? When you trust, with the kind of faith a child has in their parents, you'll find yourself happier and more free to enjoy life with clarity. So, discover unwavering faith and trust. And when things don't go as expected, don't be shocked or distressed—let go of your own expectations, but always trust that God will lead you in Love.

March 23

The Armor Of God

When the rain is pouring, and the water runs deep, we wear rubber soled shoes to protect our feet. And as we step outside, they keep us from getting washed up and washed out. And like rubber soled shoes, wearing the Armor of God is protection from danger.

The Armor of God includes the Sword of the Spirit, which is the Word of God (Scripture), the Breastplate of Righteousness (Christ within us), the Shield of Faith, the Belt of Truth, and the Shoes of Peace. When we put on this armor, our path is divinely protected.

Daily, we need help, especially when problems come. And when the water rises, the Lord hears our prayers and is an ever present help in times of trouble. We do not want to step out into any circumstances, without first getting down to basics. We need covering.

So today, as you walk through the muck and mire of various trials, you can envision yourself wearing the Armor Of God. Put on the Armor of God to be built up and preserved from harm. This protection is flexible and strong and the shielding moves precisely as you do. Bending when you bend and stretching when you stretch, to pass through matters.

We can be bold when wearing the Armor of God, so don't be afraid to make a big splash! Our deliverance is revealed in many ways, and God's Love is real and tangible. There's an exuberance in His presence, knowing He watches over us. As we move from glory to glory, our hearts are warmed by His Love—both flexible and strong, surrounding us every step of the way.

So remember to pray and envision the full Armor of God covering you in your human condition. Put on the Sword of the Spirit, the Breastplate of Righteousness, the Shield of Faith, the Belt of Truth and the Shoes of Peace. With these you have everything you need to go fully into the world and experience an abundant life.

March 24

Make Your Petitions Clear

Do you catch yourself wishing for things? Wishing that this or that would happen? Wishes often lack strength and true faith—they're like watery longings without much backbone. So, when you catch yourself wishing, try turning it into a real prayer request: "Lord, if it is Your will, I desire for [insert your desire here] to come to pass.

Wishing for the desires of your heart without fully trusting in God is a recipe for disappointment. We need to align ourselves with understanding God's will for our lives. When we realize that God knows our needs and delights in granting the desires of our heart, it becomes easier to align with His purposes and trust His timing.

Wishing often involves desiring something that may not or likely won't happen. When we don't receive what we wish for, it can lead to feelings of unhappiness or even resentment, especially toward those who seem to have what we desire. However, Scripture reminds us, "I will do it, says the Lord." When seeking a new direction or heart's desire, we must trust in the Lord to provide. So, instead of wishing today, try praying bold prayers before taking action, and believe that if it's God's will for your life, He will make it happen.

Do you have trouble sticking to your decisions or listening to your heart and following through? Think of the things you enjoy doing the most, as a basis for all additional blessings. Also, it's important to be grateful while embracing simplicity. This is a good place to be, because mostly after a good amount of striving, eventually, we learn to live quietly and to enjoy what we are doing.

Make your petitions clear today and trust the Lord to fulfill them. Avoid superstition and instead be brave and full of faith! Explore new possibilities by going deeper. When we honor God, we honor ourselves and become better partners and friends. Integrity provides an advantage, so maintain confidence, stay rooted in the Truth, and pray bold prayers. If you find yourself merely wishing, take the opportunity to reflect and go deeper.

March 25

Where True Freedom Begins

When we understand the goodness of God, we are far better able to see through the darkness in our world. And walking with the Lord provides strength for the journey. So invite the Lord into your daily life and circumstances, to gain wisdom and obtain supernatural grace and provision.

Without the Lord and His leading, we miss out on the higher things that come from communing with Love. This awareness guides and directs and blesses us uniquely. And if we choose to ignore this great intelligence, we negate a valuable relationship with a power greater than ourselves.

Scripture says in James 4:8, "Draw near to me and I will draw near to you".

When we choose to go through daily life without acknowledging God, our vision is limited. We may have education and experience, but with our eyes alone, our view is constrained. We need to engage in daily fellowship, which strengthens us spiritually. And it takes participation on our part for growth to occur. The best way to do this is by active participation, achieved through prayer, studying, and memorizing Scripture, which builds up our inner self.

The highest calling is an invitation for everyone to live for Love. To embrace this calling, we must place Love at the center of our lives. Remember that God is Love, and as we draw near to Him, He draws near to us. By growing in strength, wisdom, and purpose, we can experience a better life. This is true hope in a fallen world.

Today, as you draw near to God, you can gain insightful education and understanding that makes your journey fruitful and fulfilling. The Truth is accessible to every wise person, regardless of their walk of life, career path, or educational pursuit. When Love is at the center, true freedom is found.

March 26

Hold On To The Truth

We might know someone for a long time and then suddenly encounter something unexpected about them. The same possibility exists within each of us. Much of what lies beneath the surface of people is hidden deep within the subconscious, known only to God.

To better understand the state of a person's heart, we can observe the fruit of their lives. While people's actions may surprise us, anticipating surprises can help us remain open and adaptable. Embracing this openness through the twists and turns of relationships is a healthy way to navigate our interactions with others.

This earthly journey is about releasing everything opposed to Love—lies, fear, and selfish motivations. We must be willing to face the Truth. Are you in the refiner's fire? When each person comes to this realization, the world will change for the better, and we will grow in Love. The darkness within every soul will diminish, making the world a much better place.

Human beings are composed of good and evil desires and motives. And as the subconscious rises to the conscious, there may be hidden fears and motivations we see and notice. Therefore we must hold Truth as our Cornerstone. And in secret places, we definitely need clearing. Evil if not confronted, will compound and overtake, leading to a beleaguered state of being.

Most people withhold some Truth to spare others from pain, fearing the reactions they might provoke. Ironically, this often leads to the very pain they sought to avoid. In contrast, embracing Truth opens the door to understanding and Love. This is why Christ as our Cornerstone is so crucial. We need the clarity that Christ provides to move forward and grow in Love. Without daily repentance in Christ, there is no release from our sin nature.

People may surprise you, and you might surprise yourself as well. And when we are truly awake, we recognize our need for Jesus, who is the Truth, the Way, and the Life. As long as you are sincere and have a contrite heart, you can receive the mercy needed to move forward toward a higher Love. God will be there to lead you through.

March 27

Love Prefers Others

Winning in life and seeing dreams realized; is about going through the tough times with a good ear, the Truth, and a Love reply. This is because, at its core, Love is about connection and empathy. It thrives on the ability to understand and share in the experiences of others, which fosters a deep sense of compassion and care.

Every day, we are confronted with choices. One thing is certain: the world needs more Love. Love encourages others to discover their own abilities and opinions. It is never selfish. Love is a choice, and we can choose to walk in Love through our responses and reactions. Walking in Love is a spiritual practice that reveals exactly who we are and where we stand.

While it may seem counterintuitive in a world often driven by self-interest, Love flourishes when directed outward rather than inward. This preference for others over oneself stems from the very nature of Love itself. True freedom requires us to prioritize others in situations over our own desires. Choosing others is a testament to the depth of one's Love.

When Love takes root, we prioritize the well-being and happiness of those we cherish. This is not driven by obligation or expectation but emerges organically from the profound bond formed by Love. It requires humility, selflessness, and a willingness to set aside our own desires for the benefit of others. Prioritizing others demonstrates a commitment to nurturing and preserving the bonds of Love, even in the face of adversity.

Love always brings a sense of fulfillment and joy that transcends personal gratification. The act of giving and making sacrifices for the sake of others, for most, is a source of profound satisfaction and purpose. In this way, Love enriches both the giver and the recipient, creating a symbiotic relationship based on mutual care and support.

When shared generously and unconditionally, Love flourishes. By prioritizing the well-being and happiness of others, Love becomes a transformative force that enriches not only our own lives but also the lives of those around us. Love transcends the ego and fosters interconnectedness and unity, which is essential for creating a more compassionate and empathetic society.

March 28

Christ In The Center

Experiences define and make us. And even though we are born pure and pristine, we grow to learn new behaviors from parents, teachers, coaches, churches, the media, and whoever influences our life. Additionally, by looking around, we form our own views and opinions. And each is born with personality, where experiences, good and bad, work together, to create behaviors that are the backbone of our lives.

And every interaction, event, and decision has contributed to the formation of who you are. From the time you are born, you are immersed in this constant stream that shapes and molds your thoughts, emotions, and actions. Positive experiences reinforce desirable behaviors, while negative ones often lead to coping mechanisms or defensive strategies. These patterns influence how you navigate and interact with others.

We are dynamic and ever-evolving, continuously shaped by new experiences. As we encounter challenges and opportunities, we adapt and grow. Sometimes, we find ourselves stuck in coping mode, but these experiences serve as guideposts and catalysts for personal growth. They push us to explore new horizons, challenge old assumptions, and embrace change.

But how do we grow past negative experiences when things have not been so good? The key is to commit our way to the Truth. The Truth serves as the Cornerstone for clarity. We must come to understand the height, depth, width, and length of the Love of God in Christ Jesus, who demonstrated The Way. His direction leads us beyond earthly pursuits to deeper insights and perspectives that realign our beliefs.

With Christ at the center, we move beyond mere conditioning to transform our perceptions. This transformation enriches the tapestry of our lives. By embracing the diversity of our path in Christ, we cultivate resilience, empathy, and wisdom. Our defining moments come full circle with Christ in the center, guiding us as we evolve in Love toward our destiny.

March 29

Overcome Loneliness With Love

Loneliness is sometimes misunderstood as a condition of physical solitude. However, loneliness is not the mere absence of company. It's an emotional landscape where one feels disconnected, unappreciated, and misunderstood, even in the midst of a crowd.

And solitude can be cherished, while loneliness is unwelcomed. It's like being adrift in a sea of humanity, with no beacon to guide or companionship to anchor. And even though loneliness tries to weave its tendrils into the consciousness, it does hold promise for growth.

When we are lonely, even in the presence of loved ones, relationships can feel hollow. Add to that, vulnerability, rejection, or simply not being understood. All of these can intensify the feeling of being alone, exacerbating the sense of alienation. But there is no need to live this way. You are loved and accepted, just as you are. And God will never reject you.

In loneliness, the mind can become a battleground of extreme emotional pain, unmet needs and unrealized desires. What's the solution? God in us. Because in reality, we are all here solely on a spiritual journey. Some embrace their spirit beyond this world along with life's limitations. Others focus primarily on their worldly experience within the Universe. And there are those who look outside of themselves, and compare their lives and experiences to others. However, by looking inward, we embrace our soul and the heart as "One".

Loneliness can be overcome by friendship with God. And no one truly knows or understands the heart, but the One who it belongs to. If we are not in tune to this Love, God living in us, we are lost. Without the Lord to guide and commune with, we are missing a beautiful centerpiece that holds everything in the Universe together.

We are born individually and will leave this world individually. When we choose to walk with the Lord and fully experience our emotions, loneliness loses its power over us. We must confront our pain and fears honestly, rather than avoiding or suppressing them. Empowerment comes from holding fast to the Truth of God's Love. So, hold on to Love and let go of loneliness today.

March 30

The Art Form Of Love

Love is the most profound human experience, and can be seen as an art form in itself. And like any art, it requires skill, creativity, dedication, and deep understanding. Love transcends mere emotion, and is a complex interplay of thoughts, feelings, and actions that can be honed and refined over time. And Love requires a mastery of empathy and communication.

And this journey of discovery and transformation offers endless possibilities for growth, connection, and fulfillment. And much like an artist perfecting their craft, understanding needs, desires, and fears, requires emotional intelligence akin to an artist's ability to interpret the nuances of their subject. We become experts as seekers, when we "walk in Love", as an art form.

And walking in Love requires the ability to weather storms, navigate conflicts, and embrace imperfections. Effective communication becomes the brushstroke that shapes the canvas of our relationships, fostering connection and intimacy. In Love, we must continually adapt and grow, finding beauty in the process of learning and evolving together.

Love always prefers others, and Scripture teaches us that God is Love. When God is our anchor, we follow a unique path that requires patience and resilience. We must trust that our personal freedom is a gift, refraining from judgment and choosing only to bless. We let go of expectations toward others, becoming listeners who give space for people to express themselves.

When we walk in Love, we embrace our differences and paint the story of our lives, as a masterpiece of connection and belonging. Are you an artist? Do you need to hone your skills? Tap into the source of this art form called Love and learn to walk in it. You can become an example by reshaping your relationships with intention, creativity, and passion. And as you walk with the Lord on a daily basis, you will recognize the places that need refinement.

March 31

Living In A State Of Grace

Every day brings us to new levels of awareness and enlightenment through consciousness. Many believe they can control and shape situations, leading them to attach to specific ideas and outcomes—only to be disappointed. However, Scripture reminds us in Proverbs 19:9, "Man makes his plans, but God orders his steps." And living in a state of grace means holding our plans lightly, trusting in God's direction.

Grace is a miraculous gift of life force energy, where serendipity happens, proving that destiny exists. And living in a state of grace means being in harmonious alignment with God, self and others. Grace transcends mere contentment or happiness and embodies a profound sense of peace, acceptance, and gratitude as God demonstrates His Love for us.

And being saved by grace, we savor life, because our chains have been lifted and they are gone. We understand that Christ's sacrifice has set us free and now there is pleasure and joy in everyday experiences, both simple and great. We are filled with gratitude for the gift of God's unmerited favor and unconditional Love and have received blessing upon blessing. And now, living in a state of grace involves letting go of our need to control matters. It means that we are not burdened by regrets of the past or anxieties about the future.

Our time here is significant, and when we approach each moment with an open heart and mind, we welcome what arises with compassion, understanding, and a sense of acceptance and surrender. By grace, we navigate life's challenges with resilience and calmness. We know we are forgiven, and because of this, we freely forgive others, releasing grudges, judgments, and resentments. We keep an open heart, a humble spirit, and a reverence for our existence.

Living in a state of grace, we come to understand that attaching ourselves to specific ideas and outcomes often leads to disappointment. Instead, we are brave, trusting God through all things. We carry wisdom on the journey, striving to make sound choices under the guidance of the Holy Spirit. There is balance in this give and take and Love is always present, ready to lift us higher.

APRIL

April 1

Let Love Flow

Because every person is going through things, we must hold on to the idea of not being easily offended. We need to "let it go" and let Love flow.

If you have struggled with healthy relationships, it might be difficult to open up and walk in Love, which requires humility and self-examination. This isn't about putting yourself down or feeling inadequate but about understanding what isn't working in your life. Self-awareness allows you to make better choices moving forward. Remember, what may seem small to you could be significant to someone else, and what appears to be a reasonable request from your perspective may feel out of line to another. We are all unique in how we perceive things.

When we are still growing, much of what we experience is beyond our control. We may lose someone and be thrust into unfamiliar territory, forced to navigate change without full understanding. Or perhaps we were victimized by someone's actions or encountered a predator with harmful intentions. Regardless, there is a force that seeks to steal from us and create chaos. This force manifests through people, principalities, and powers, spreading lies and keeping us in bondage, limiting our potential. It is crucial to recognize that this power is at work in the world, alongside the power of Love. Therefore, we must cultivate discernment as we grow.

Being able to consider criticism without taking offense is a powerful state of mind. Listening to what others say and choosing whether to accept or release it is a sign of maturity. Are you feeling trapped today? As adults, healing from past trauma often requires us to examine the role we play in situations. Taking responsibility is key: understanding where we may have missed the signs, failed to stand up for ourselves, or didn't halt a disturbance. If we were truly powerless, we need to acknowledge that and extend forgiveness to both ourselves and others.

In every encounter, it's wise to ask: "What can I learn from this?" and "What is my role in this situation?" People will disappoint us, and each person sees things differently. By recognizing this, we can more easily let go of offense. We don't have to be easily offended. It helps to try seeing both sides, asking, "What would Jesus do?" and putting ourselves in another's shoes—because to fail to do so is unloving and selfish.

April 2

Press Through The Pain

Healing comes when we press through the pain.
Whether it's emotional or physical healing, we must
understand that our healing may not happen overnight, or
be on our timetable.

Have you noticed how some people remain vibrant and
whole well into their later years? This may have more to
do with belief than anything else. Jesus is often called the
"Great Physician" because of the healing Christ offers to
every soul that believes. In Christ, we find restoration for
our souls, which in turn brings healing to both mind and
body.

There is power in every thought. So we need to first
believe that we are being made whole. Furthermore, we
do not want to own something that does not belong to us.
Because every cell in our body and mind listens, we do
not use words like "my" condition or "I" or "our" for
anything we are facing, but instead, we say "this"
condition or "that issue".

Also, when we pray and believe, we may have difficulty discerning that any improvement is happening in us. Situations did not occur overnight, so they will likely take some time to reverse. But rest assured, the changes are in place. It's necessary to look at every ounce of pain and every bit of trial, as a step in the direction of restoration. We are to embrace the healing process with every thought and action that needs to take place toward our recovery.

Now it's true that we are aging and our bodies are slowly returning to dust. But we do not need to buy into the idea that we are dying to speed things up. Instead, we must keep our thoughts on wellness and healing for the entire journey. This is how we live long and hold on to as much wholeness and energy as possible. It's essential not to be defeated.

Healing requires faith, and that is why many call it "faith healing". You must believe beyond a shadow of a doubt. And when doing so, do not hesitate to lay hands on areas that may hurt, while believing and praying. This heals with God's energy. And when it's emotional healing that is needed, do not hesitate to bring the subject to the Lord in prayer and allow tears to wash you clean. Tears have cleansing components both physical and mental.

Rest assured that healing is possible and miracles can happen. Simply invite the Lord Jesus Christ into your heart, and pray in His name. There is power in the name of Jesus. Just say His name and see for yourself. Believe today that you are whole or at least being made whole.

April 3

Love At Work

Love is the seed you sow, and your life is a gift to share. And loneliness is a state of mind that touches everyone at some point. It can be a powerful spiritual attack, often leading to feelings of depression and making life difficult. Today, more people experience loneliness than ever before. That's why it's important to recognize loneliness for what it is and adjust our sails accordingly. Instead of focusing on being lonely, we can take action to break the stronghold of loneliness.

There are times in life when we may feel solitary, and as we grow older, loneliness can become debilitating. That's why it's best to address it early on. We do well to create a plan to stave it off by proactively changing our thoughts. As we shift our thinking, our actions will naturally follow, helping to reshape our experience. We should not allow destructive patterns to take root. Instead, we can find healthy solutions to avoid sinking into dark feelings. Recognizing loneliness as a state of mind allows us to prepare and implement positive, pre-planned solutions.

We often recognize, defensively, what we need to do, but being proactive means stepping out and building relationships while we can. It's important to think ahead. When participating in groups, we must remember that while we are part of a community, we remain individuals with unique voices. We should contribute for the good of the group while maintaining our independence and flourishing within it. As we honor Love, our relationships grow.

Scripture says in Hebrews 10:25, "not giving up meeting together, as some are in the habit of doing, but encouraging one another—and all the more as you see the Day approaching."

This Scripture emphasizes the need for community. For believers, this often means church. Others may find community in cultural or interest-based groups. Musicians gather with other musicians, knitters join knitting clubs, and outdoorsmen share their passion for hunting, fishing, or camping. There are always opportunities to engage and be encouraged.

The key is to avoid getting stuck in your head, allowing negativity or the lie of loneliness to take hold. Overcoming loneliness strengthens the spirit. So, step out today and remember that you are never alone when God is with you. When you're with others, focus on being a good listener and a blessing. By stepping out and paying it forward, you can be good to someone in need, or a friend.

April 4

Live For Love!

You may think that because you have been doing the proper and loving thing for some time, that you have reached some sort of aspiration, and now you feel a sense of accomplishment.

In one way, you have achieved the objective of living for Love. You've grown in self-control and understanding. But the work never stops. And the reward comes at the end of paths taken. So, it's good not to rest on your laurels and think somehow bliss is achieved.

As long as you are in the land of the living, always choose to do the right and loving thing, in every situation. In a world where darkness exists, kindness and Love are powerful forces. There is a reward in store, and it's up to you to make a difference. So, don't stop, and don't give up. Continue doing the right thing, even when you feel overwhelmed or hopeless. Even when you grow weary of showing kindness and Love in the face of oppression or neglect, keep going. Perseverance matters.

Each day when you awaken, remember to live for Love. This is the true purpose of life. We don't live to chase material things, seek popularity, or compete with our brothers and sisters. We live for Love—to uplift and connect with those around us. We live to follow The Way that heals and to ease the burdens of others who may be overwhelmed by their journey. So, keep living for Love.

If you feel tired, take time to rest. Show yourself abundant Love and Grace. Be encouraged, knowing that your steps are ordered by the Lord. None of us knows the day or hour when we will leave this Earth, so guard your heart and renounce selfishness and wrong thinking. You've got this!

Today and every day that follows, may you succeed in every way as you live for Love. This is the ultimate purpose of your path. In moments of doubt, simply ask, "What would Jesus do?" And remember the words from 1 Corinthians 13:4-7:

"Love is patient, love is kind. It does not envy, it does not boast, it is not proud. It does not dishonor others, it is not self-seeking, it is not easily angered, it keeps no record of wrongs. Love does not delight in evil but rejoices with the truth. It always protects, always trusts, always hopes, always perseveres."

April 5

Bold As Love

When you are a bold person, you are bound to come up against opposition. And when there are new paths, you can be sure that they will not be achieved by being timid or thin skinned. You must be bold anytime there is a desire to impact others, with your heart's desires.

When we are bold, there is no time to care what people think. When we are bold, we can speak our truth, express our needs and desires and connect with others on a deeper level. And boldness enables us to build authentic relationships. One of the most significant benefits of boldness is the ability to say no. When we are bold, we set boundaries, stand up for ourselves, and say no to things that don't align with our values or goals.

Yet still as we encourage others and ourselves, from time to time, we will experience pressure. This is the resistance that pushes up against those who reach out. And world issues can influence. So continue to be bold and be yourself. And if you are drawn to self-consciousness, remember that the battle is truly in the mind.

Social Media is a fun tool that connects people. These platforms affect every person uniquely. And each participant has their opinion, hurdles, and their truth to face and overcome. What are you bringing into the world? Is it positive and will it help someone else be better?

The world needs more powerful voices for victory. Let God's light shine brightly through you today. You were born into the world for such a time as this—to live an amazing life and walk your path with confidence, unburdened by others' opinions.

Are you living with purpose for what endures? Don't let the fear of judgment hold you back from fulfilling your calling. We answer to the Lord, so how we act and what we do truly matters. You may reach one person or thousands through your efforts, but the goal is to help others along their journey.

Every time we help someone else, we also receive the support we need to overcome obstacles and achieve our own dreams.

.

April 6

The Value Of People And Time

The beauty of this world is in our exceptional differences. And each of us brings something exclusive to offer. We hold the purpose to contribute and leave a lasting remnant for the world. And we are most pliable at manifesting results that have a lasting impact, when we are focused on loving people, while being planted in the house of the Lord.

Psalm 92:13 reminds us, "Those who are planted in the house of the Lord shall flourish in the courts of our God." And flourishing in God's courts means living a life of abundance, prosperity, and spiritual fulfillment in His presence—a state of growth, well-being, and faith.

And as we reflect on the broken places and the hurting people we love, something beautiful unfolds in every interaction. We begin to understand the true value of people and time. When we value time, every second becomes an opportunity to make someone's life better.

We can understand people more clearly, when we become good listeners. And there are some who enjoy groups and large gatherings, while others prefer one on one connections. Both are valuable. What matters most is being fully present with each person in your sphere of influence. This is how to inspire, motivate, and connect with the individual in mind.

There is no fear in love, so don't shy away from deeper connections or desolate moments. In the stillness, when time seems to stop and you feel alone, there is value. These are moments to reflect on the beauty and growth in and around you.

When you value both people and time, you become the best version of yourself. Age is irrelevant; each moment offers a new beginning, a fresh opportunity to create love and move toward your destiny. So today and every day, never dismiss people or time. Respect both deeply, for every person and every moment presents an opportunity to create love that leads to a fulfilling future.

April 7

Wisdom - A Great Gift

Life's too short to keep making foolish choices. So we need to pray for wisdom from God for our circumstances. The last thing anyone needs is more pain or sorrow. Life gives enough of these and it's best not to add to them, by being thoughtless in our actions and deeds.

When we walk with God in His infinite wisdom, we make better choices. We are not perfect, but we do have a higher vision and clarity as we keep our eyes on Him. And when we seek the wisdom of God first, daily, even when we do slip up and make wrong choices, they likely are not as significant and pain inducing. These types of mistakes tend to be gentle reminders that we need more of God daily.

Scripture tells us, "I set before you life and death. Choose life!" This Word can be helpful in determining the best way forward when making a difficult choice. We can ask ourselves; will this choice be wise? Will it bring life? Is this choice smart over the long term?

The Spirit is willing, but the flesh is weak. And when we are not listening to the Holy Spirit, by humbling ourselves and coming to God in prayer with our concerns, we get into trouble. We do not want to be desiring something that is not good for us. And even though humans learn mostly from mistakes, there comes a day when it is no longer necessary to go through the pain of a mistake to get the lesson. The choice is clear. And we choose accordingly.

Wisdom is a great gift. And a wise person will pray for wisdom. Wisdom does not come from reading books or going to any school. Wisdom is different from knowledge. Wisdom is learned by experience. And it is poured out spiritually in the individual who seeks it.

Our world is a messy place. And wisdom from God is always about choosing the loving path. Could you imagine if everyone prayed for God's wisdom in things? Also, remember that God is Love. When you follow the path that brings more Love to your world, you are on the right track.

April 8

The End Of The Line

It seems that God often brings us to the edge of what we are waiting for. We reach the end of the line, or our wits' end, where we feel we just can't take it anymore. At times, it may feel like all is lost, and help won't come through. We might even fear falling through the cracks.

But God's timing is not our timing, and the purpose of waiting is to grow in trusting the Lord of the Universe to meet our needs. He is never early and never late. After enduring many trials, we come to realize that we can make it through successfully—sometimes just by the skin of our teeth. Through these challenges, we become better at trusting in the midst of difficulty.

Perhaps you are sitting on the edge of something problematic and wondering, how to get through this trouble or quandary? You may feel anxious and curiously contemplate why faith is so difficult. Maybe you are frightened about the future. But what does fear and worry do? Nothing, except cause stress to the body, while making matters worse.

We will all go through difficult things from time to time. And help often comes when we are at the end of our rope. Therefore, we need to rise above and trust God's timing. We do not need to be frightened. Instead, we can be full of faith. And you may have plenty of experience in times past, where things worked out in your favor, and now you understand firsthand the deliverance of making it through. God has always made a way for you, where there seemed to be no way.

Finally, having years added to your life is a blessing. But with years, more faith and inner resolve is needed, to go the distance. Thankfully, God meets our needs one day at a time. He provides manna for the day. And trusting means that we understand that we will always be cared for, and all of the waiting is for our good outcome.

If you are waiting today and are struggling, cling to the Word of God. Remember the promise in Isaiah 40:31, which says, "Those who wait on the Lord shall renew their strength; they shall mount up with wings like eagles, they shall run and not be weary, they shall walk and not faint."

April 9

The Goodness Of God

Life is about growth. And as we continually grow, it is wise to invite progress into our consciousness. And when we request the things of God, which are Truth and Love, patience, kindness, longsuffering, gentleness and self control, we notice that we go from glory to glory, to become more Christ-like, every step of The Way. This is real growth.

And being committed to personal growth requires a level of character. There must be a willingness to seek Truth toward the highest good. Furthermore, charisma is not character. And committing to a path of enlightenment requires an openness to all that Love is.

Love is patient and kind, it does not envy or boast, it is not proud, rude or easily angered. And with Love there is an abundance of blessing, and grace that unfolds daily. Therefore, inviting goodness into our consciousness, requires cultivating a mindset of integrity, gratitude, kindness, compassion, and thoughtfulness.

Please do not waste an hour of your time running from the Truth. And do not take any experience for granted. Come to know your freedom, and do not be afraid to face any pain. This is the place where you will see and understand all that is working toward your demise. This place of pain is a birthing place, where new beginnings arise with opportunity for fulfillment.

Perhaps you didn't receive all you longed for while growing up, or maybe kindness and love weren't modeled in a way you could fully understand. Do not despair. Instead, practice compassion toward yourself and others by engaging in daily acts of kindness, empathy, and—most importantly—forgiveness in all things.

Jesus is known as the Comforter. And when you commit to the Truth, you will find comfort for your soul. So pour your heart out to Him, and you will notice a new light shining through. It will be worth every step and ounce of pain. Because when God heals and leads in a new direction, there is no stopping the goodness of God.

April 10

You Haven't Changed A Bit!

Have you ever encountered someone after a long time, and they say, 'You haven't changed a bit!'? While this might be a compliment about your physical appearance, hopefully, after talking, it's clear that you have changed.

Have you grown over time? Perhaps you've become more refined? If we aren't changing for the better and becoming better people, we aren't truly walking with the living God. God is like a refiner's fire, continually shaping our spirit, so that daily, our inner beauty shines brighter.

True beauty stems from within, and your eyes shine brightly with love inside. Are you more beautiful today than you were last year? Or perhaps you are someone that others handle with kid gloves? Do people tiptoe around you, hesitant to express their true feelings because you are easily offended? Do you struggle with holding grudges or with forgiveness? If so, there is more refining to be done to fully become who you're destined to be as a child of God.

When we walk with the Lord, we go from glory to glory. And rarely do people evolve from past relationships until they are willing to take responsibility for their part in matters. So when there is blame toward another person, there is a record that is placed on repeat. A person may grow outwardly, but they may be wasting time when it comes to growth inwardly.

To cultivate good friendships, we must first be good friends. It is to our great benefit to learn about mercy, forgiveness, and taking things lightly. Each step we take can be a lesson in kindness toward ourselves and others. When our daily actions are guided by Love, we experience a more abundant life that bears good fruit.

Do you find yourself falling into traps and experiencing negative results? Have you noticed why? The key to personal growth is taking responsibility for your actions. If we neglect to consider our role in situations, how can we improve? We must reflect on where we've missed the mark and strive to change for the better. And those around us will notice that change, because true beauty and confidence radiate from within.

April 11

The End Of Guilt And Shame

Carrying a burden of guilt and shame can weigh heavily on the soul, acting as powerful paralyzers that hinder freedom and joy. Those oppressed by guilt and shame often experience negative self-evaluations and distress from perceived failures or transgressions. This can lead to a diminished life, revealing a sense of unworthiness and a lack of self-confidence.

And people burdened by guilt and shame may feel undeserving of a beautiful life. They might attempt to escape through destructive behaviors such as substance abuse or self-harm. The ramifications of carrying such burdens often lead to a life overshadowed by darkness.

Guilt and shame often hide in the places we don't show others—deep, self-conscious emotions that can affect every aspect of daily life. The solution is to leave these burdens at the foot of the Cross. Belief in Christ offers freedom from guilt and shame, because by His stripes we are healed. This belief is essential for lasting transformation.

If you are carrying a burden of guilt or shame today, bring it to the Lord in prayer. Christ died to offer complete freedom and forgiveness, aiming to restore your broken soul to wholeness. When you invite Jesus into your life, you are born anew, and all shame and guilt are released. Negative emotions lose their power when you call on His name.

Restoration to wholeness may happen suddenly for some, while for others, it can take time. However, as true Love fills your heart, negative emotions are expelled, and the power of the Holy Spirit replaces the influence of guilt and shame. A person freed from these burdens will laugh more, give more, dream bigger, and rarely give up. So bring your heart and burdens to Jesus today and let go of any guilt and shame. Lay these down and embrace the freedom that Christ offers.

Freedom comes with forgiveness, as Galatians 5:1 reminds us: "It is for freedom that Christ has set us free. Stand firm, then, and do not let yourselves be burdened again by a yoke of slavery."

April 12

Are You Wild At Heart?

When you are naturally wild at heart, there's a tendency to welcome risks and embrace experiences that bring valuable lessons. Much growth comes through trials, and the wild heart walks a fine line between boldness and wisdom. This balance is essential for gaining true knowledge and understanding. There's no need to play it safe when you are wild at heart.

The wild heart is brave and faithful, eager to explore the path of enlightenment by stepping out when opportunities arise. It doesn't hesitate to act, even if there's a risk of getting into trouble. While the wild heart does not seek trouble, it knows that trouble is a part of life for everyone.

The wild heart pushes through fear and, at times, rebels against the status quo and social norms. It resists expectations that stifle individuality. So, who will you trust with your wild heart? Who will stand by you through daring days and peaceful interludes? Who always has your best interest at heart? You can trust the Living God within you.

A person with a wild heart lives in a way that ensures they won't miss out on personal growth. There is a strong, unbridled spirit alive within, fueled by adventure and passion. When you know you are loved, you become bold! Naturally, you embrace your instincts and desires, living with authenticity and freedom. This approach to life is filled with excitement and spontaneity.

Your wild heart is loved and welcomed by the Lord. And being wild at heart is a good thing. John the Baptist was wild at heart. So was Peter and the other disciples. They were wildly in Love with "The Way". And although they mostly did not understand what they were doing or how things would play out, these wild at heart human beings were recorded as the example for all time.

Trust your wild heart to the Living God and know that The Lord delights in your process of exploration and learning. And when you truly have the Holy Spirit, there is nothing that will lead you away from the Truth of Jesus Christ. You are free. And if you stumble in the wilderness and make a wrong choice, you know in times that follow, there will be better outcomes.

April 13

Discipline - A Friend or Foe?

You can lead a horse to water, but will he drink? Ultimately, everyone has free will. And a person may encounter an opportunity for everything they need to succeed, but still fail to take advantage of what is presented to them. This is because discipline is required.

Discipline is a key ingredient to achieving anything great. Whether you're training for a sporting event, preparing for a test, or working to replace bad habits with good ones, we must reach a place where discipline becomes our friend. In contrast, when we lack discipline, we miss out on the goodness and excellence that life offers. No book, advice, or example can truly change our path if we do not embrace discipline.

And discipline adds to our lives and causes us to become different. Also, the root meaning of discipline is training and instruction. So when we are open to welcoming training and instruction, we are on the path to greater opportunity and further discipline.

Discipline has its rewards, but there must be a desire for transformation. Discipline instills a sense of responsibility, helping us take ownership of our actions and choices, making us more accountable. However, we must want it. If we are closed-minded or believe we know it all, we risk missing out on great achievements.

Now, discipline may ebb and flow, where we notice times, we are more disciplined than others. There may be seasons where we struggle with the process. But as we press through, we clearly notice the benefits. And hopefully, we grow to become more consistent in our ways.

Scripture tells us in Hebrews 12:11, "No discipline seems pleasant at the time, but painful. Later on, however, it produces a harvest of righteousness and peace for those who have been trained by it."

If you are a leader, the most effective way to lead is by example, and discipline is one of the best examples to set. Others may not always follow your advice, even when you offer something beneficial, but that's alright. Choose to pursue it for yourself, with God as your guide. Through this, you gain essential skills like self-control, responsibility, and confidence.

April 14

The Heights Of Possibility

To reach the heights of possibility, we must be in agreement with the Living God in our spirit. This is how we experience significant and lasting change, rewards, success, and positive outcomes. Amos 3:3 asks, 'Do two walk together unless they have agreed to do so?'

Even the slightest effort in the right direction requires agreement with the inner man or woman, because change begins and takes place in the Spirit. Change can happen overnight, or it can occur in small, gradual steps. However, for significant change to happen, there must be this inner sense of agreement. We must hold onto wisdom as we pursue our purpose.

Real change requires a continual renewing of the mind. We reap what we sow: if we sow negativity, we will see negative results. Conversely, a positive outlook filled with hope is likely to yield better outcomes. By giving 100% of our love to the path set before us, every moment is well spent. There is nothing greater than choosing love in every small interaction and decision.

Serving God is a rewarding experience that requires a commitment to Truth. And every activity, and interaction needs to be held captive to Christ, where we ask, "What would Jesus do?" Also, the best way to experience greater outcomes is to remember to ask, so that we receive, and knock, so the door will open. We must get good in our conversations with God to achieve this. This is "The Way" that brings more joy, peace, and blessings in our lives.

The goal is to end well and live with no regrets. We should seize every opportunity to make wise choices and use our time effectively. Without change and growth, we risk stagnation and future regrets. Therefore, we need to start the mindful practice of following Christ, who clearly opens the door to possibility. When Christ is at the center of your journey, there is nothing blocking you from reaching the highest potential.

It is a wonderful thing to take notice of all that has transpired and recognize the rewards of powerful change, to the Glory of God. And the beauty is revealed when you look in hindsight. Here you understand how far you have come. Loving the Lord and your life, you can commit to grow 100% every day. This is a life well lived, generally for the brave heart.

April 15

When In Doubt ~ Hold Out

Many times, when we have an idea in mind, we want to jump right into things. We may feel very sure of ourselves. Or we may have some doubts and yet still feel like jumping in. And because we are human, we want what we want. But the bible says, "thou shall not be in want". So, we need to make sure that our root motivations are toward the true desires of our heart, and not motivations toward greed, notoriety, or excess.

There are times when fear can hinder our ability to move forward with confidence and faith towards our ideas. Excessive doubt and fear can paralyze us, preventing us from pursuing new horizons and dreams. It's important to find a balance when making our choices, ensuring that fear doesn't overwhelm our aspirations.

Have you heard the expression, "When in doubt, hold out?" When we follow the lead of the Holy Spirit, we get good guidance. Often there are whispers that point us in the direction we are to go. And we can take time to consider the options. However, when we have doubts, we need to trust and wait, knowing that for the best outcome, we must have peace about our decision.

The Lord walks with you and goes before you, making the crooked places straight. While circumstances may not always unfold smoothly, waiting for clarity and holding out for peace will provide you with clear direction. Acting impulsively on desires without waiting for this guidance can lead to trouble. So if you have doubts, consider holding off for today.

And while waiting for assurance, clarification, and peace about your decision, you can make small changes to help bring new views. For instance, you can do something like rearranging or cleaning. Or perhaps attend a class or a meetup group. There is no reason to feel stagnant or stuck. Small changes can help you not lose your joy or become agitated, while you wait.

Press toward change today in small ways as you await larger decisions. Remember, for every decision, you need to have peace about your choice.

April 16

A Life Of Loving Well

No one truly knows what others are experiencing or what influences their choices. For this reason, we should refrain from disapproving of someone else's path. Instead, we should concentrate on our own purpose, vision, and intentions. And we may notice massive abilities and talents in someone and think to ourselves, it's too bad they are not doing this or that. However, people have issues and responsibilities that affect how their dreams and desires manifest.

We are here to learn lessons about Love, and true success lies in living a life of loving well. And life can change unexpectedly, so it's important to recognize that many factors influence the situations people encounter. Therefore, we need to focus on being encouragers rather than judges, disapproving of anyone's path. Further, life can be harrowing at times. And people get into trouble when they compare themselves to others. This is the place where judgment begins. And the root of a matter frequently stems from a sense of inadequacy. You may feel disadvantaged in some way, or as if you have not achieved what you believe you should have, for the time you are in. But this is not a good place to be. Instead, remember your purpose to love God, yourself and others well.

Scripture tells us to bring every thought into the captivity of Christ. And this means that we check every thought, to make sure it aligns with the Truth. We can simply ask, what would Jesus do? And the better we get at regularly taking responsibility for our thoughts and actions, the more peace we will have. The more we remain focused on the Truth, the better.

Even when thoughts of negativity or judgment creep in, we should quickly correct them by embracing the Truth that sets us free. The path may be difficult, but everything you endure is for your benefit and to help you reach the heights of Love.

Remember that true success lies in living a life of loving well. When you reach the end of your days, you will either feel content with your choices (in both thoughts and deeds) or harbor regrets about the path you took. Keeping Christ at the center offers freedom and guidance. When you misstep, He is your comforter and redeemer; when you listen and obey, He is your Waymaker. So, regardless of how difficult the path may be, do not disapprove of it.

April 17

Supernatural Grace

Fear will cause us to run from facing the error of our ways. But we can only run for so long, because the things we do in the dark, will show up in the light. And the more we choose to sing a song of repentance, the better we remain in the light to flourish.

We don't know the darkness with which people encounter daily. But one thing is for sure, what truly matters is that your soul is free. Because sin will hold you back and hold you down. And you do not need to be a slave to sin, but to righteousness.

There was a time that I was afraid of what people would think, as I sang my song of repentance. "Exodus", means "life". It rose up in my Spirit, at a time I had been redeemed from drug addiction, physical, verbal, and sexual abuse, and the curse of insecurity and loneliness. The Lord touched my heart when I was in a dark place and I received grace and forgiveness for all matters. It felt supernatural. I had fallen far, and then was changed in an instant by the Holy Spirit. This was an experience I could not hide. Love had come in. And my song of deliverance was beautiful to me.

The book of Exodus is primarily the story of the Israelites being set free from a life of slavery. And that is what God did in my life. His grace is supernatural. And you can be free too. Bring your failings and missteps to the Lord, and invite Him in through your prayer, to be set free from all past, present and future sin. Sing a song of repentance today.

Scripture says in Psalm 119:9, "How can a young man or woman cleanse his way? By taking heed according to your Word."

Sin will create a veil that can be subtle to notice, and something that will keep you from God's best for your life. So do not let sin weigh you down and burden your days. Instead, get to know the Word of God. And receive the teachings today. The Word of God reveals that Jesus Christ, and the Cross is "The Way", through repentance. And further in; Deuteronomy reminds us that when we enter the promised land, the place of our freedom, that we should not forget where we came from. And how we have been set free. This is a supernatural life changing grace, open for you to receive.

April 18

Freedom - Fight For It!

Freedom from fear is a powerful trait. And it does not come without a fight. There is a resistance that we must press through. And because people love comfort and want to be comfortable as much as possible, the desire for comfort can steal away your dreams.

The journey to freedom is not comfortable. It may appear impossible or dreadful, frightening and even against the norm. It is a trial of sorts, where we are required to face our fears and move through something that we are not accustomed to, or content with. And many people desire to take the easy route. They rarely step out and experience true freedom and change. The resistance is pressing. Add to that, delays. Many have excuses that come up, in some way or another.

Do you believe that angels are watching over you and listening all the time? Scripture says in Psalm 91:11-12, "For He shall give His angels charge over you, to keep you in all your ways."

Life is difficult and not without challenges, however, living in a state of fear is hard and has challenges. When you choose darkness over light, fear over faith, these angels move a bit further away. So we need to choose our hard, so to speak. We can either press on and do the difficult thing toward our freedom, or we can lay back and remain a prisoner, to a life with increasing limitations. And when we press through for our freedom, there is a sense of victory that brings joy, yet succumbing to fear, can bring more pain to the individual along with regrets.

What is holding you back from obeying the Lord today and following His will? You are only given a limited amount of time. And nothing is done in secret. Therefore, choose your hard today. There will be challenges. And unfortunately, most of us learn what is most profitable the hard way.

Has God asked you to do something and you have been hesitating? Don't wait any longer. You will need to fight for your freedom. But you are never fighting alone. As a child of God, there is a great crowd of witnesses and angels watching over you, to support you and go with you through the difficult things you must do. You can live in the freedom that Christ provides.

April 19

Faithfulness – Gotta Have It!

One of the best ways to gain personal freedom is to be committed to being faithful. You have the choice. Will you be faithful and tell the truth? Can you do the right thing when it feels easier to do the wrong thing? Are you a committed person?

Faithfulness to your word, actions, and interactions, is a cornerstone of trust and reliability in both personal and professional relationships. And when you consistently keep promises and follow through on your commitments, you build a reputation for dependability and integrity. This establishes a foundation of trust, allowing others to feel confident in your reliability.

Being faithful to your word and actions fosters respect. When your actions align with your promises, you demonstrate authenticity along with strong moral character. Additionally, people are more likely to seek your advice or collaboration, when they know you can be trusted to do what you say you will do. And faithfulness in your actions sets a positive example for others, encouraging them to uphold similar standards.

Faithfulness in word and deed is Godly character. And if you are not practicing faithfulness in every interaction, it may be time to repent. Bring your case to the Lord when you miss the mark, and ask for forgiveness. Ask for strength to become more faithful in things and get on track. This will produce real joy in your life, where you are walking in a good way.

And faithfulness in your everyday actions, can lead to fruitful collaborations, deeper friendships, and increased opportunities for personal development. When you consistently uphold your commitments and treat others with honesty and respect, your self confidence will be soaring. You will be at your best and feel good about your choices. This alignment with your values, will definitely lead to greater fulfillment and satisfaction in your life.

Scripture tells us in Luke 16:10, that "One who is faithful in a very little is also faithful in much, and one who is dishonest in a very little is also dishonest in much." Therefore, commit your way to the Lord and His Truth, and grow in excellence daily. Faithfulness is true success.

April 20

Gentle Yet Persistent Growth

Our actions are influenced by our thoughts. And in order to fulfill our journey, we need to implement mature efforts toward greater outcomes. And the best way to make significant progress is to step out of our comfort zone. We must press in and push through, to overcome the resistance.

And we do not need to push so hard that we suffer. Instead, we must be gentle with ourselves, in the way that we go. There is a balancing act that needs to take place. And the important thing is to enjoy every day, as we are both gentle and persistent together.

Navigating life can be a lot like picking beans. And if you have ever been a gardener, you know the lessons that come with gardening. Some beans may not be ripe yet, while others need more time to mature. Many are simply beautiful and ready to be enjoyed. And then there are those that sit hiding, overripe and overlooked; never wasted, but gone to seed.

Our lives are much like this. Each of us are at different stages. And as we traverse the path of Love and dreams, we have power and protection, when we commit to walking in Love. This is because Love is supernatural and has the ability to change situations and outcomes.

Jeremiah 17:10 says, "I the Lord search the heart and examine the mind, to reward each person according to their conduct, according to what their deeds deserve."

We will reap what we sow. And if we are passive and complacent, we will experience lack in areas. Furthermore, walking in Love means navigating life with compassion, empathy, and kindness as our guiding principles. It's about extending a hand to those in need, listening with an open heart, and understanding without judgment. Love takes effort. And when we press in, and do what is difficult, for the sake of Love, every step we take is infused with understanding.

Love has the power to create connections that bridge differences and heal wounds. It is the opposite of evil and is a journey of selflessness and generosity. Love is based on truth. And being committed to The Truth is the first step to walking in Love. You can do it!

April 21

Through Trials And Tears

Life can weigh us down with issues. And it is not uncommon to become separated from the people we love. Troubles rise up to cause what would be beautiful, to be parted. And sadly, people who are hurting, tend to hurt other people. The route can be brutal. The only way to find freedom from the pain is through forgiveness. We need to forgive the hurts that people bring into our lives, with the understanding that everyone has a cross to bear.

People in pain often lash out at those closest to them, especially family and friends. Everyone carries their own unique cross, and no one is exempt from facing the consequences of their actions. It may seem like some go through life without pain or accountability, but each person will one day face the Truth. Since everyone experiences conflict and difficulty, those who navigate it with the most freedom do so through a willingness to forgive. This freedom is often hard-won, and for most, the victory comes through trials and tears.

Scripture tells us in Colossians 3:13, "Make allowance for each other's faults, and forgive anyone who offends you. Remember, the Lord forgave you, so you must forgive others."

You can experience more potent energy, with assistance, when you say yes to the challenge of forgiveness. When helping others and doing something to make another's journey a little lighter and more hopeful, you are actually helping yourself. And as a child of God, you can rest assured that the Helper is always with you. When you go through hard things, get your mind off of your circumstances, and on to what you can do for someone else. This is the example that reveals Christ. Both in forgiveness and service.

Finally, every time you humble yourself and forgive, you gain heavenly assistance to float above your circumstances. And since Love is everlasting and goes from heart to heart, you can be committed to those around you. Your friends, lovers, relatives, leaders, and followers. The key is to passionately follow the lead of Jesus Christ.

April 22

Love Is Your Defense

In order to experience every good thing in life, we need to be clear on how we feel about ourselves and what we believe. This is an ongoing process where we put ourselves in check on a regular basis, until the right belief is permanent and predominant in our thinking.

And there comes a time for many of us, where we come to the end of ourselves and realize a need for change. And when this occurs, we must get to the truth, to understand the importance of knowing who we are in Christ. We must choose our side and whom we will serve. We do not need to worry or concern ourselves with what others will think or say. Instead, we must hold fast to what God says about us in His Word.

You are a child of God and Love is your defense. So, if you are noticing that your life is not going well, perhaps you are making poor choices. If so, there is a need for repentance. Also, people often lose their individual thinking when in groups. This can cause some to become caught up in ways that are not healthy or their own. Many people allow others to influence them, in ways that gradually move them off track and into a dark place where they are unable to hear from God.

Is it time to awaken to the Truth? Evil conditions exist, often stemming from fear and manifesting in groups of people. Rooted in pride and fear, evil intentions and actions take hold in those who are conflicted, dissatisfied, or struggling with self-worth. Those who entertain evil are often confused, caught in a cycle of unrest. The only way to break free from the influence of evil, both within and around us, is to stay vigilant in the pursuit of Truth and remain committed to it.

As John 10:10 says, "The thief comes only to steal and kill and destroy; I have come that they may have life and have it to the full."

With a focus on Love, we can learn how to discern evil and the situation of an evil condition. Let's not pretend evil doesn't exist. Instead, let's hold fast to the truth of God's Word and confront evil with every turn. Love is our only defense against evil and we need the power of the Holy Spirit working in us, to lead us every day through, to our destiny.

April 23

An Inclusive World

Our world is a beautiful tapestry of diverse cultures, teeming with life—people, trees, animals, mammals, and aquatic beings. Each has a unique place on this living planet, and everything that exists has a right to do so, according to its grand and mysterious design.

As we look out our windows, scroll through our phones, or watch our TVs, much of what we see remains a mystery. Though we often feel like we know and understand a great deal, the truth is, we do not. We are conditioned by what we see, but it is a world full of mystery, with layers of meaning beyond our immediate grasp.

Therefore, it is essential to respect the Earth and the individuality of everyone in it. Each person has their own unique place, life experience, and hope. While some may appear hopeless, that's where you can make a difference. When we put others ahead of ourselves, relationships flourish. On the other hand, selfishness and self-centeredness are often the root of breakdowns, especially in communication. Many people struggle with listening because they are focused on their own agenda rather than prioritizing the person speaking.

How can we find clarity and peace if we only consider ourselves? We must be open to taking a broader perspective to be more inclusive. Active listening is key. By truly listening without judgment and seeking to understand others' perspectives—even when they differ from our own—we cultivate empathy and openness. This broadens our understanding of the world, helping us appreciate the richness that diverse perspectives bring.

While we don't need to agree with everyone or everything, we should hold fast to the Truth of "The Way." This requires stepping out of our comfort zone and acknowledging our biases and privileges. Jesus was inclusive. In John 8:7, He said, "He who is without sin, cast the first stone." This reminds us that no one is without sin; we are connected in this beautiful tapestry of life on Earth.

By recognizing the inherent value of all things, we expand our vision to embrace inclusivity in every aspect of life—whether in the workplace, educational institutions, or our communities. We can challenge ourselves to work towards creating environments where everyone feels loved, valued, and respected.

April 24

Rebellion By The Rebellious

Rebellion makes us do dumb things. We can be rebellious in our steps because we believe our way is better than the way that God shows us. But eventually, after the rebellion, the lessons arrive. And usually with more mess to clean up, going forward.

For many people, adherence to Godly principles encourages ethical behavior, while providing purpose and meaning. However, individuals who rebel, tend to lose their moral anchor, which leads to confusion, and a lack of accountability for actions. And rebellion can steal away time. Because when we take the detour, going our own way, instead of God's way, we experience delays. We need to not waste time. We must wake and repent of thinking we know better than God.

Perhaps you are someone who has had a difficult time trusting, due to injustice. There is a need for healing. Many often feel this way. And it's vital to recognize these traits in ourselves, because with rebellion against God, there is the possibility of separation from our source of higher guidance, leading to profound dilemmas. And rebellion can foster feelings of alienation and spiritual emptiness because rebellion is the rejection of an enlightened path. And without the Holy Spirit to guide us, we likely will become impulsive and inconsistent, leading to potential chaos and discord.

And it's true that on the journey in Christ, that you can love God and still be rebellious. But it's important to recognize when you are going the wrong way. We must desire to serve the Lord above all. God is an all knowing, loving Father who has your best interest. And His presence brings wholeness and belonging in the Universe. Rejecting or denying His will is dangerous, and can lead to a cycle of searching for meaning and fulfillment through experiences that do not satisfy.

Finally, trying to find something of value outside of God's plan for your life, is chasing after the wind. And even if you fall into rebellion multiple times before you realize it, you can still change. Please don't deny the leading of the Holy Spirit, and reject connection. Pray, repent and avoid the pursuits that will not work to your benefit.

April 25

Unity In The Holy Spirit

How do we embrace both our differences and shared humanity? We do this by transcending barriers of race, ethnicity, gender, religion, and culture. Since we are all unique, we must actively listen to others' perspectives and seek to understand each other. With an open heart, we create space for genuine dialogue and respect the challenges others face.

As Scripture says in Psalm 133:1, "How good and pleasant it is when God's people live together in unity!"

To experience this "good and pleasant" state of unity, we must first align with the God of all hope and love. When united in love, our relationships grow stronger, and we are better equipped to work together toward a better world.

Ultimately, we must be in agreement with the Holy Spirit within us in order to be in harmony with our brothers and sisters. This is the key to effectively addressing complex issues. Colossians 3:14 reminds us, "And over all these virtues put on love, which binds them all together in perfect unity." Love brings the Holy Spirit, and love *is* the Holy Spirit.

Unity requires a daily mindset of humility and curiosity. By acknowledging that our diverse perspectives and experiences enrich our lives, we create opportunities for growth and learning. We must be willing to challenge our own biases and assumptions, remaining open to learning from others. When led by the Holy Spirit, we can expand our view and deepen our understanding of the human experience.

In God's Kingdom, and in the Body of Christ, we are all one—coming from various backgrounds and perspectives. Pray today to be filled with discernment and a desire for unity, so we can create a world where individuals feel valued, respected, and empowered.

April 26

Whom Will You Serve?

Every day we are given choices in small and larger ways. And each choice demonstrates the state of our heart. Who are you serving today? Hopefully you are living for God, and have a profound sense of purpose with a desire to lead by faith.

And people who live for God, find something to do for God. It's nearly impossible to be in the body of Christ, and not be inspired to dedicate time and energy to serving others and contributing positively to the community. This is because faith in the Lord is the guiding force that shapes our values, actions, and relationships.

In Ephesians 6:12, scripture tells us, "For we wrestle not against flesh and blood, but against principalities, powers, and the rulers of darkness in this world, and against spiritual wickedness in high places." So we need to be sure that we know who we are serving. It's necessary to understand what is really taking place.

In Christ, we overcome the world. No more questions as to where we will go. We are a part of the body of Christ and our spirit exists in Jesus, everlasting. And it is our actions that display the condition of our heart. It is by every interaction with the one person standing next to us, that we truly see how we are choosing.

Are you clear on who you are serving today? One of the most common ways to demonstrate your faith is through actions and acts of service. And those who walk with the Lord are often compelled to share their faith through evangelism or discipleship. This can involve teaching or mentoring others in their spiritual journey, while inspiring others to find meaning and purpose.

Finally, love is demonstrated by being neighborly and offering hospitality. By helping those in our circles who are in need, we embody the teachings of Jesus and bring hope and comfort to a hurting world. It all begins within us. What is happening inside us becomes noticeably evident in our daily actions and interactions. Who are you serving today?

April 27

Embrace The Extraordinary

Embracing the extraordinary requires stepping out beyond the mundane and opening up to new experiences and possibilities. It requires a willingness to challenge your preconceived notions of what is possible. Is it time to see the world with fresh eyes? By cultivating an adventurous spirit and a mindset of curiosity, you will find deeper meaning and fulfillment.

One way to embrace the extraordinary is by seeking out new opportunities. This may involve trying new hobbies, traveling to new places, or exploring different cultures. When was the last time you stepped out of your comfort zone? When you expand your perspective and look for inspiration in the unfamiliar, you find unexpected wonders.

And cultivating a sense of wonder is wise to do at any age. When we take the time to appreciate the beauty and intricacies of the world around us, we are greatly encouraged. Whether it's a stunning sunset, a beautiful work of art, or a thought-provoking book, finding moments that evoke a sense of awe and gratitude, enable a perspective shift that can transform ordinary moments into extraordinary experiences.

Live a life filled with wonder, adventure, and inspiration to embrace the extraordinary today. Remain open to the unknown. There needs to be a willingness to accept change as an opportunity for growth. And by approaching change with an open heart, you will find new paths you may have not yet considered. Also, being adaptable, allows you to navigate challenges with resilience, to discover extraordinary outcomes.

Finally, embracing the extraordinary requires nurturing your creativity and imagination. When you allow yourself to dream big and pursue your passions with enthusiasm, you open yourself to thinking outside the box. Surrounding yourself with inspirational people and experiences that challenge and expand your thinking, can also be transformative. Don't forget to practice gratitude. By staying present and appreciative in each moment, you'll uncover beauty and wonder in the ordinary. This heightened awareness will lead to a deeper sense of purpose and fulfillment.

April 28

Living Beyond Limits

Will you push beyond your limits today by stepping out of your comfort zone and expanding your horizons? Personal growth and fulfillment come from challenging self-imposed constraints and societal expectations. Living beyond your limits invites you to embrace the unknown and grow in the process. When aligned with God, in Love, through the Holy Spirit, you receive the wisdom to recognize limiting beliefs or negative thought patterns that may be holding you back. And it's essential to know the Word of God, which helps counter any wrong thinking.

We are never alone in our walk or in our conversations with God. So do not be shy about expressing your desires, or asking for wisdom. You can develop improved self-awareness to better explore and realize your potential, when you simply pray for understanding and wisdom in any area. Communication is key. And the Lord offers a 24/7 hotline.

When you take risks and try new things, setbacks are inevitable. However, by embracing failure as a learning opportunity, you step beyond limits. Instead of letting failure deter you, adopt the mindset that failure can expedite your growth. Painful as it may be, it's essential to understand what went wrong and identify areas for improvement.

Setting ambitious yet achievable goals is a crucial step in living beyond limits. When you establish clear and challenging goals, you create a roadmap for personal and professional growth. Breaking down these goals into smaller, manageable steps not only keeps you motivated but also builds confidence as you witness your progress. Be sure to celebrate each milestone along the way.

You were born into this world for such a time as this, and God has a good plan for you. Don't let the opinions or expectations of others distract you from what the Lord is calling you to do today. By embracing growth and discovery, you unlock your full potential and find yourself living a life that is truly extraordinary.

Surround yourself with supportive, like-minded individuals who encourage you to push beyond your limits. Engage with people who inspire you and share your values. Their encouragement and insights will help you stay focused on your path. Life is full of unexpected challenges, and navigating them with grace and flexibility is key. Remember to rest as well, maintaining your mental and emotional well-being.

April 29

Life In Full Bloom

To live a life in full bloom, you need to know how to nurture your spirit. This is an essential aspect to leading a balanced and fulfilling life. And it can come in many forms, however, it involves spending time with the Lord. Communing with God will strengthen your resolve, and foster a sense of peace, especially as you go through difficult things.

And the Holy Spirit is water and fertilizer to your soul. The time you spend in prayer and meditation will till the soil of your heart, so that you are not bound by fear or restraints. This nurturing creates emotional resilience and a sense of well-being. You can live life in full bloom. For many, this is a very natural way of being. But for anyone who has lived oppressed in any way, getting to this place takes a bit of effort in letting go.

To live a life in full bloom means to reach for greater heights. It is the recognition that you are free from any chains imposed on you in the past. You understand the seasons of your life, and the goal is to move through them gently, knowing that you don't have to diminish or rush the process of growth in any way.

When you live life in full bloom, you come to understand the height, depth, width, and length of God's love for you in Christ Jesus. With this knowledge comes freedom, clarity, and insight, allowing you to connect more deeply and discover what truly brings you joy and fulfillment.

To live a life in full bloom, you recognize the importance of cultivating gratitude and maintaining a positive outlook. Salvation alone provides a profound reason to rejoice and be thankful. However, as human beings, there may be times when we become closed-minded. Therefore, practicing gratitude helps shift our focus from what we lack to what we have.

When you live in full bloom, you actively seek out and pursue activities that bring you joy and purpose. Whether it's spending time in nature, engaging in creative pursuits, or contributing to your community, finding ways to express your heart while doing what you love will lead to a profound sense of fulfillment. And as you incorporate these practices into your daily life, you'll notice an inner joy that fuels you, making you unstoppable.

April 30

Above And Beyond

Trials and troubles approach us daily, and to move beyond them, we need to connect with our higher power. Finding the God of all hope and love helps us align with His way. Therefore, we must adopt effective strategies for personal growth, knowing that the Lord orders our steps. Being aligned with God, allows us to embrace our purpose with authenticity and His presence.

One key strategy for transcending the ordinary is to fully embrace each moment. By being present and aware of your thoughts, feelings, and surroundings, you can appreciate the beauty in everyday experiences and find more joy in the simple things. Setting clear intentions and goals will also support your decision-making and actions.

To go above and beyond, align your daily actions with your values and purpose. Reflect on what truly matters to you and what you hope to achieve today. Prioritizing integrity allows you to grow beyond limits to find fulfillment and meaning in all you do. Cultivating empathy, compassion, and understanding fosters deep, supportive relationships. While building meaningful connections with others enables you to grow and experience the transformative power of kindness and service.

Embracing change means accepting an ongoing journey of evolution. So, stay open to new experiences and perspectives. And by viewing the challenges you face as opportunities for growth, you will gain new wisdom and understanding. Always remember to pray before you step out. Because when you seek the Lord first, you receive protection and direction.

Love is a dynamic, active force that requires effort. Prayer helps to clear the way for more love to flow into your daily actions. Stay open to God's guidance, as this openness deepens your connection with yourself, others, and the world. Through a spirit-filled presence, purposeful action, meaningful relationships, and a willingness to grow, you have what it takes to go above and beyond and cultivate an extraordinary life.

MAY

May 1

The Only Way Out Is Through

There is no escaping the challenges we face. However, there is a way to go through in victory. Light casts out darkness. And while darkness is a powerful force, it is not more powerful than light. When dark times come, we must hold fast to the light, focusing on what fills our hearts and minds.

Life often involves a lot of waiting, and the better we become at waiting, the more peace we will have as we navigate difficult challenges. Each of us will face physical and emotional pain, but the Word of God is the Sword of the Spirit, which causes lies to fall and Truth to prevail. Without the Word of God, our troubles can feel overwhelming and insurmountable.

Scripture refers to the Lord as the Comforter. And being rooted in the Word of God, we have the light. Having the Truth in your soul requires repentance. This is because it clears the conscience and prevents darkness from taking over. It takes humility to do this, but through humility, we build the strength to endure. Humility fills us with light, not pride.

One day, we will leave this Earth, and God's Love will surround us. We will be pain-free, and there will be no more confusion. But today, we must believe wholeheartedly in our deliverance. Sadly, many people die by suicide, giving up without finding comfort in the Lord or His Word. It's heartbreaking, and survivors often feel deeply hurt and confused by their loved ones' actions.

The Holy Spirit strengthens and comforts us daily. And Jesus is the Comforter and Savior. Without focusing on God's Word and His promises, we can be deceived. Mental illness is prevalent in society, so it's important not to ignore these challenges. What matters most is a commitment to follow the Light of God's Word and never let go. The only way out is through.

God will carry you through when you believe and trust Him. So, get into the Word and let your faith grow strong and be filled with light always. It's crucial to finish well. Isaiah 59:1 says, "Behold, the Lord's hand is not too short that it cannot save; neither His ear too heavy that it cannot hear."

May 2

Purpose Reason And Happenstance

Do things happen for a reason? Are you one to view life through the lens of an optimist or a pessimist? Are you hopeful versus hopeless? Is everything meaningful or meaningless? There are always two ways of seeing. And we can set our sights on a view that sees everything as happenstance, or on things as having purpose. One thing is certain: there is a great order and intelligence to all things, a wisdom that surpasses our human understanding.

We are multidimensional beings, constantly multitasking and balancing multiple roles. Most of us engage in different activities we enjoy each day, always changing, learning, and evolving. As we grow, our beauty unfolds like a flower in bloom. Is this an optimistic view? Much depends on the human heart.

We are created higher than the animals and have this awesome ability to reason and to visualize things, and see them take place. Also, we have a powerful life force energy to create good in the world or to destroy life.

Therefore, we have the choice and hopefully we are choosing to grow and become more beautiful. All outcomes begin within each of us.

Some forget, due to time and space, that they have this life force energy. Daily repetition, along with responsibilities, can steal away. But this spiritual intelligence exists within you and is passed through generations by the Holy Spirit. So, today consider your purpose, consider reason and happenstance; and make sure that the hat you wear truly fits. If you are walking blindly down a path that is not stimulating, then it's time to visualize a better way and step into your evolution.

Scripture says in Zechariah 4:6, "Not by power, nor by might, but by my Spirit, says the Lord".

It is through the Holy Spirit that we become and evolve. As we honor the Living God within and around us, we become co-creators aligned with Love's intention. With eyes of faith, we have the power to change everything. Open wide to beauty. You can discover a deeper purpose when you seek the wisdom of the ages that comes from knowing The Lord.

May 3

If Everyone Was A Giver

What if everyone was a giver and lived a "pay it forward" lifestyle? In other words, instead of going to a location with funds to spend on self, those funds would go to another person's needs and hospitality. Then someone would do the same for you? This is a dream and an ideal where everyone is a giver. And it would require trust.

We need to cultivate generosity. And fear of lack, especially in tumultuous times can be crippling. Any fear of lack can steal your personal joy. This fear of lack, (subliminally believing that supply or money is not enough, or that it will run out) causes people to be uptight and stingy. It can also cause people to participate in illegal activities. Additionally, the fear itself will often bring about that which is feared. In other words, poverty.

In Luke 6:38 Scripture says, "Give, and it will be given to you. A good measure, pressed down, shaken together, and running over, will be poured into your lap. For with the measure you use, it will be measured to you."

How we live our life with money, possessions and our time, makes a significant difference in the well being of not only ourselves, but the people within our circles. Our thoughts and actions have great power. And it's apparent that we are in a time where individuals are experiencing rising costs and supply chain interruptions. For this reason, we need to become very good at thinking of our neighbors, to meet their needs, while we trust God to meet our own needs.

Having a spirit of generosity is highly beneficial, yet abundance takes time to manifest. It's important to impart wisdom, as issues surrounding money and resources are often complex. People have varying responsibilities and limits based on their circumstances. However, with the Lord's guidance, we can pray, seek, and cultivate a spirit of generosity that promotes the well-being of everyone in our circle.

There is provision for all people on the planet. This should be our focus. We do not need to live in fear of lack. Instead, we can expect blessings and abundance by trusting the Lord, as we give and share. And God is the great giver, who demonstrated His Love for us, in Christ. Now it's a matter of us getting the supply where it's needed. When we are depending on our own ways, and living conservative and greedy lives, we miss out on abundant blessings and promises from our Lord.

May 4

Moment To Moment

Trusting God is the best way forward in all things. And the Lord's will is always in the moment. For this reason, we must stay flexible. Additionally, by letting go and living in the moment, we receive the highest guidance. Therefore, we need to keep things in perspective and remember that we are here for a higher purpose. And our steps are ordered by the Lord.

Rarely do we receive answers about the path we should take until the very last moment. Often, we are faced with multiple choices, unsure of which direction to follow. With many obstacles, we may set out believing we've made the right decision, only to discover shortly after that we'd prefer a different direction. As we review our options and weigh the pros and cons, it's essential to wait peacefully in faith. This can be difficult, as waiting without clear answers is always a challenge.

Humans often feel uneasy with the unknown. We only see in part and struggle to grasp the bigger picture. However,

God's ways are higher than ours. When we're in decision-making mode, we tend to think more than we trust. Many answers arrive at the last minute. While some may say this keeps life exciting, it can be a real challenge because most of us prefer certainty.

Isaiah 55:8-9 says, "For my thoughts are not your thoughts, neither are your ways my ways, declares the Lord. As the heavens are higher than the earth, so are my ways higher than your ways and my thoughts higher than your thoughts."

God's will often comes down to the last minute. So don't be afraid to wait. And be careful not to rush in. This is where people often make poor choices and receive negative results. Problems compound when we rush and do things under pressure. It is in these situations that we are more likely to make choices that are not well thought out. We might overlook important factors, or fail to consider all the options, which can lead to long-lasting consequences.

In every choice, large and small, the Creator holds the great intelligence for your good outcome. You can rest assured that you are making the best choice, when you pay attention to the still small voice within, that often arrives at the last minute, when you need it most. This is the Holy Spirit!

May 5

Walk As Children Of Light

What makes a person decide what they will tolerate or become, has much to do with experience and conditioning. Many live mediocre lives due to beliefs. But we are called to walk as children of Light. And what this means is to hold the Truth of Christ as our righteousness. When we do this, we experience faith that can overcome all wrong thinking.

You can learn to believe and adjust your sails to all that God has for you, in glory. And what most people believe about themselves is deeply rooted in their subconscious and is either truth or lies. For this reason, discernment is necessary. When we come to salvation and receive the Truth into our heart, there is no longer any power in lies. And Christ becomes our righteousness and the cornerstone, which permits us to walk as children of Light.

Believing in the Truth of Jesus Christ, requires faith. And in John 8:32, Jesus said: "You shall know the Truth and the Truth shall set you free." So, overcoming a life of limitations, shattered dreams, damaged relationships, and scarcity, can only be accomplished with a fervent grasp on Christ, and what His righteousness provides for each of us, individually.

And when we keep our focus on right believing, over time we develop an overcoming mindset, rooted in Truth and grounded in Love. God always lets us choose. He never forces His light upon us. He does however, reveal Himself to us, in glimpses of His glory, at times through signs and wonders, wake up calls, everyday miracles and provisions. These help us to take notice of this greater intelligence, working in us and on the Earth.

The Lord requires us to choose. In Deuteronomy 30:19 scripture says, "I set before you life and death. Choose life." So, I beseech you, to not get lost in the world. Choose life. Choose Jesus Christ and invite Him into your heart today. And walk as a child of God, in the Light.

May 6

Is My Hand So Short?

When we look around at the people we do life with, including acquaintances, it's difficult not to care. And although we are not meant to connect with everyone on a deeper level, we often feel concerned over the lives of those around us. And being empathetic can be impactful for us, as we go through daily challenges. For some, it can get pretty dark.

When you are empathetic, you feel for others greatly. And there are all sorts of troubles that good people face and go through. Plenty of hearts are bleeding. And while caring for others is a high calling, we need not become codependent. Instead, we must pray and seek God's will, while speaking the Truth in Love, knowing that our steps are ordered by the Lord.

Do you agree that there is a battle for your soul? And that all the trouble and deep waters that you wade in, stem from the pull of good and evil in this earthly existence? Everyone is going through matters and for this reason, we should not discard those suffering in darkness. We can pray.

Scripture says in Isaiah 59:1, "Surely the arm of the Lord is not too short to save, nor His ear too dull to hear."

A person with the Truth inside, won't tell lies at every turn. And because the lie causes so much confusion, it can be very difficult to come out of. Additionally, it may be that if a person lives in lies, there may be less of a war waging in their soul. They may be lost to darkness, not to be made as one with the Light. But if an individual has heart, and some level of compassion, goodness, and Truth, it is not uncommon to witness a real battle taking place in their soul.

Be patient with people today on their journey toward redemption. Live by example and trust your loved ones to the Lord. We can pray for our brothers and sisters. This is one of the best things we can do. And always stay committed to The Truth. Truth holds the power to overcome evil. And we overcome evil with good. So as we do good, we trust God working, to bring about the changes needed, for Love to live and souls to be saved.

May 7

Never Lose The Wonder

Have you experienced a breathtaking scene or a beautiful view? Perhaps you felt a moment of happiness and connection with someone you love? Never lose the wonder, because you have the power within, through the Holy Spirit, to change your view and awaken to new life.

We are very small in a great big world. And wonder begins with appreciation and imagination. And even without eyes, we can see within our minds eye, the beauty, and the wonder of this great life we are blessed to experience. So if your thoughts become trivial, and unappreciative of the grandeur of things, it is time to change your focus and thinking.

With every breath, there is a gift to receive. And if you are feeling caught up in the difficulties of life, with the pain that you feel in and around you, along with the sufferings of others, you might forget the splendor of your journey. However, if you can recall the beauty in something great, something you have experienced at some time, you can change your course to experience brand new wonder in being alive.

In Scripture, Psalms 65:8-13 says, "The whole earth is filled with awe at your wonders; where morning dawns, where evening fades, you call forth songs of joy".

Please do not let the news of the day and personal troubles steal the joy that lives in your heart. Never lose the wonder. And if your happiness has been buried or hidden, you can unearth it, to find new life. Let your love and enthusiasm spread. The world needs you now.

You can be the change and commit to being different. Only remember that enthusiasm is your superpower, to overcome the evil that exists and the darkness that comes to steal, kill and destroy. And choose to be a person who uses their imagination for beauty to be realized every day.

May 8

In The Refiners Fire

Our God is a refining fire. And the person we are today is only a version of who we are to become. Additionally, when we come to salvation in Christ, and recognize ourselves as children of God, this is only the beginning of our path to Christlikeness.

We have one soul and can expect to be refined as we walk with the Lord. It is through waiting that we discover our transformation. Difficult experiences crucify the flesh and help us develop godly character, greatness, and beauty. Our true colors are revealed through these experiences. And because God is great, it is impossible to remain unchanged. We either become more beautiful and loving within or we reveal our flaws as circumstances arise and the heart is exposed.

For some, it takes a while to recognize that life is more than just survival. Many go to work each day and provide for their families and participate in worldly activities, without ever stopping to ask, "What does it all mean?" But there is purpose in every life. And being aware of the attitude of our hearts, is valuable for leading a fulfilling and abundant life.

In Malachi 3:2, scripture says, "But who can endure the day of His coming, and who can stand when He appears? For He is like a refiner's fire and like fullers' soap".

Please don't resist change, but instead welcome it. Say this: "Create in me a clean heart, O God and renew a right spirit within me". [Psalm 51:10] Time passes quickly and you don't want to wake up one day to notice people being changed and refined all around you, while you have remained the same. Furthermore, spiritual maturity requires acceptance.

In the refiner's fire, you will face difficult and challenging experiences that test your character and values. This is the time when you are forced to confront your weaknesses and make changes to become a better person. If something is being revealed to you today, something that can be improved, do not hesitate to receive the challenge as a gift.

May 9

The Gift Of Wisdom

It is not easy for some people to see God at work in the world. Especially with all the darkness that comes to kill, steal and destroy. But for a wise person, the wonders of nature, historical events, and the ups and downs of life, take on deeper meaning.

A wise person will understand matters of judgment and Truth. And the wise person has the ability to comprehend the image of God more fully, seeing the Creator as a loving Father. Also, the wise person treats people with dignity, and is able to take note of God in everything. Even that which they do not understand. This creates a position to receive further wisdom.

Someone with a gift of wisdom, will seek the Lord first, in order to stay composed and find solutions, rather than being overwhelmed and giving up. And in the face of adversity, a wise person will have the courage to make right choices, even if it means going against the status quo. And a person with the gift of wisdom, will approach life with a calm and thoughtful demeanor, always seeking to learn and grow from experiences.

When you have received the gift of wisdom, you will be inclined to listen carefully to others and consider their perspectives. Ultimately, you are always striving to understand rather than to judge. And wisdom will cause you to treat others with kindness and respect, understanding that there is value and dignity in every person. Therefore, consider your way today.

A wise person lives a life guided by the Truth of God, which produces compassion, integrity, humility, and ultimately, Love. They understand that there is always room for improvement and learning. Such a person takes time to reflect on their decisions and actions, considering their impact on those around them. They choose to walk upright and experience the goodness that wisdom brings. Do you consider yourself a wise person? To seek wisdom, is wisdom in itself. And having wisdom is empowering. So today, pray and ask the Lord to impart wisdom to you. He will answer your prayer and not withhold anything good from you.

May 10

Love Is Understanding

Understanding is a great gift that is rooted in Love. And when we have understanding, we comprehend how we need to live as followers of Christ. A person with understanding is not confused by all of the conflicting messages in our culture.

And understanding is a fundamental human need that produces compassion. Also, to truly understand, is to feel a deep sense of connection and comprehension. It's a feeling of clarity and insight that brings calm and confidence. When we have understanding, it's as if a light bulb turns on, where everything makes sense.

Scripture tells us in Proverbs 4:7, "Wisdom is the principal thing; therefore get wisdom: and with all thy getting, get understanding".

Therefore, to have understanding, you need a level of wisdom, in order to obtain higher guidance, for each daily decision. Wisdom involves the ability to see beyond immediate appearances and grasp the broader context, which helps in truly empathizing with others. It guides us in interpreting and appreciating different perspectives, leading to more profound and compassionate understanding. And so wisdom enriches our capacity to understand and love more deeply.

When we do not understand a matter, it can be frustrating. However, when we listen and attempt to truly empathize with another person, we are better able to navigate complex situations, solve problems, and make informed decisions. Understanding another's plight, forges deeper connections, and leads to a more fulfilling life. And mutual understanding strengthens relationships and builds a foundation of genuine care.

Understanding can be humbling. It is the place where we recognize the small part we play in the scheme of things. And as we grasp situations and people, our direction opens. It's here we are reminded of how much we don't know, and how much more there is to learn. It is through understanding, that we appreciate and receive an incredibly rewarding feeling.

May 11

Be Strong And Of Good Courage

Being a courageous person may be inbred for some, but courage needs to be developed in most of us. And having courage allows the required firmness of mind, for both doing good and enduring evil. Also, having courage to confront challenges, builds strength. So be strong and of good courage.

There is always a choice that we have to make. We can choose to face our fear, or procrastinate and perhaps run away. However, courage is the ability to do things that we often would rather escape. And many of our courageous actions are faith based, because we cannot see results we strive for, until we meet our goal.

So to have courage, is to have faith that we can do something. Especially difficult things. And, having faith means that we believe in something greater than ourselves. When we place our faith in God, we obtain supernatural courage that enables us to withstand and accomplish more. Also, the more we go through and choose courage, the stronger we become.

Scripture says in Joshua 1:9, "Have I not commanded you? Be strong and of good courage; do not be afraid, or dismayed, for the Lord your God is with you wherever you go."

This tells us that the Lord goes with us wherever we go. We are better equipped to do good in the world, when we have the courage we need, to stand up for what is right in the sight of God. Even if it means accepting rejection, verbal abuse, or physical harm and even death, as followers of Christ.

God understands your weaknesses. He understands your need for Love, strength and courage. He is not mad at you, and will not withhold His goodness from you. What the Lord requires is relationship. And when we rely on God, by coming to Him with our cares and needs, we grow in courage and trust, along with our ability to combat the forces of evil.

Do you consider yourself a courageous person? Are you a risk taker? Or do you tend to shy away from activities that challenge your resolve for getting through? Whatever the case, don't give up today. Keep pressing through and face any fears you have. Prayer is your secret weapon, so ask the Lord to bless you with His strength and courage. Then freely receive!

May 12

Where Rain Pours Flowers Grow

Water is essential for life to thrive. You may have heard the saying, "Where rain pours, flowers grow." And rain arrives through cloudy skies, accompanied by storms with thunder and lightning. These storms can be treacherous, as they renew the Earth.

Before Christ went to the Cross, He prayed and asked God to take the cup of His suffering away from Him. Sometimes we feel the same in our trials, facing things we wish we didn't have to. And as skies look dark and cloudy, there may be fear, pain and uncertainty about the outcome.

God never gives us more than we can handle. And through the trials, we emerge stronger. And just as the Earth is renewed after the storm, we are transformed. We may be tested and as we pass through, by the grace of God, we are all the better for it. This adversity is like the rain, that nourishes and helps everything to grow.

And as we evolve through our various challenges, the most difficult moments lead to positive outcomes, where we discover new beginnings and new growth that we had not imagined previously. Our trials create opportunities for change. So, when the rain pours into your life, pray, trust and cling to the Lord. And expect growth because 'where rain pours, flowers grow'.

Scripture says in James 5:16, "The effectual fervent prayer of a righteous man avails much."

This reminds us that we are to keep praying. Don't give up and always continue to trust Him with your heart. Believe in a positive outcome and stay open to new possibilities. Consider your challenges as catalysts for further growth—this is water for your soul, nourishing you for more.

In Christ, you are righteous not by your deeds, but by what Christ did for you on the Cross to reconcile you to Him. Always remember that you are the Righteousness of God in Christ Jesus. You belong to the Lord who is your Father. And He has your good outcome in mind. He will never let you go and will deliver you through every trial.

May 13

Made In His Image

The image of God is a complex and deeply personal concept that can evoke a wide range of emotions and feelings. And to comprehend the image of God, we must first recognize that it is a metaphorical representation of the divine, rather than a literal image.

In Genesis 1:27, Scripture tells us that God made man in His image. This means that we possess qualities and characteristics that reflect those of God. And some would suggest that humans have a spiritual essence or consciousness that mirrors God's being, while others focus on having the ability to reason, create, and exercise free will, like God.

The image of God, can conjure feelings of awe and wonder, as we contemplate the power and majesty of the Lord. Many people surely feel a sense of comfort and reassurance, imagining a loving and caring presence. Nevertheless, being made in His image, reminds of the importance of treating others with respect, compassion, and dignity, as all people are made in His image, and are inherently valuable and worthy of Love and care.

The image of God can also be a source of confusion and doubt. For many, it is complex, to reconcile the idea of a loving God with the pain and suffering that exists in the world. It can be difficult to understand how we can embody the image of God in our moral, spiritual, and intellectual nature, while we experience so much death and evil in and around us. However, much of our dissatisfaction with faith and believing, stems from our own lack of awareness, obedience, and rebellion. For this reason, we need to remember that God is Love.

Love is a reflection of our deepest aspirations and longings. And with Jesus as our example, we can choose to connect with God's greatness within ourselves. This is a personal relationship with the Lord. And in return, we better understand our path. Are you a loving person? Then you are an expression of the image of God, and God is in you.

May 14

A Change Is Gonna Come

Sometimes change comes, and we feel as if we're being downgraded to a less favorable situation, making it difficult to make sense of things. For instance, we might be in a comfortable place, content with our circumstances, when suddenly, change arrives beyond our control. We find ourselves in a melting pot of discomfort, facing trials in a situation that feels far less opportune. Or perhaps the change affects a friendship, leaving us feeling forgotten or left out. Somehow, we are thrust into an experience that feels like a step down from what we're used to.

Scripture says in John 21:18, "Assuredly, I say to you, when you were young, you girded yourself and walked where you wanted to go; but when you are old, you will stretch out your hands, and another will gird you and carry you where you do not want to go."

God's ways are not our ways. We are frail and have ever-changing needs as we grow. Yet, the Lord knows exactly what we need for a good outcome in every situation. Even when things don't seem to align with our expectations, we must trust Him and hold onto peace. For many, this is not an easy or pleasing reality. There are times when changes come that we don't choose—unpleasant and discomforting. But through it all, the Lord walks with us. The true test of faith is revealed in our attitude as we pass through these difficult trials.

We may have tears, but do we have peace? We must remain steadfast through difficult times, especially when we feel crushed and out of control. True peace doesn't mean the absence of pain but the presence of trust in God's plan, even in the midst of our struggles.

Have you been downgraded lately? Do you feel like your best days are behind you? When you miss out on personal comfort, while continuing to shine your light, you are situated to receive God's best. And as long as you are alive and breathing, you can choose to be a loving person. This is how to make the best of the journey. Love is also the way to fill up your spirit with strength as you pass through the fire of change. Say this: "The joy of the Lord is my strength".

May 15

God Will Meet You

We gain clarity and guidance when we invite the Lord into our circumstances. And by remaining open and receptive to receiving, we can tap into higher awareness that helps us to see more possibilities and options. Ideas that we might otherwise miss.

It's important to not go in the wrong direction, in the first place. But often we do. And sometimes, matters can't be taken back. So it is refreshing that God meets us precisely where we're at. Little by little, we see resolution to a situation that seems impossible. His mercy endures forever, and His Love is towards you.

When the Lord enters a soul, transformation can happen in an instant. However, after salvation, individuals often need time and experience to evolve and grow in faith. This is because we have strong self-will and can often be our own worst enemy. If we're honest, we recognize that we don't always walk in Love as we should. It's a learning process, one where we are corrected when we stray. Over time, with each correction, we begin to notice that we are making progress and moving forward in our faith.

The gift of salvation marks the beginning of our identity in Christ, ensuring that we move forward in the direction of Love. In knowing pure Love, we become aware of our imperfections. As new believers, we come as we are—with our sinful nature—yet reconciled in Christ. We are given a fresh start and a clean slate. However, more is needed, for within, we require transformation. So, we step forward, trusting God to change us as we strive to live by His example.

The Lord is in the restoration business. And as we see the consequences of our choices, we become deeply aware of the mercy and forgiveness we have received. Now, we must learn to trust, for God meets us exactly where we are—in our brokenness and humility. His Love is immense, and daily He shows us that He can be trusted to work things out for our good.

Are you struggling with addiction, feeling broken, bruised, or confined? You are accepted and loved just as you are, despite all your mistakes and wanderings. The One who began a good work in you will see it through to completion (Philippians 1:6). Invite the Lord into your heart today with a simple prayer, and watch your life transform into something truly beautiful.

May 16

The Working Of The Lord

Maybe you're feeling disappointed today because things didn't go as you envisioned. A dream didn't come true, or a relationship you longed for failed. It can be challenging to understand why these things happen, especially when something you had faith in falls apart. We might struggle to piece things together, but we must place our faith not in circumstances or ideas, but in God alone.

The Lord makes your path straight and orders your steps. There may be times when your faith wanes—when you feel close to God and strong in your belief, only to suddenly experience doubt and lose interest in seeking Him. When this occurs, it's important to explore what's deeper, as His purpose is for Love to grow within you.

A good way to return to a place of unwavering faith is to whisper a simple prayer, such as 'I love you, Lord' or 'Thank you, Lord.' Offering a prayer of affection and gratitude as you continue moving forward can be powerful. With each new day, you may begin to see the

Lord's work more clearly in your life. Walking by faith through the unknown leads to exponential growth.

The path to our dreams is often unpredictable, and we may find ourselves surprised by the circumstances. Yet, God shows up when we invite Him to walk alongside us. His work in our lives is beyond our comprehension. Therefore, we must continually refresh our focus, inviting Him in and trusting His will. This is how we will see the working of the Lord in our lives.

In Luke 12:48, Scripture tells us, "For to whom much is given, of him will much be required." So, do not hesitate to have faith through the difficult times and believe for greater things. By trusting the Lord and placing your faith in Christ, you gain freedom, understanding, vision, and purpose.

Finally, Love is a mystery and God is mysterious. So look and take notice in your daily steps, to clearly see the working of the Lord in your life. Deuteronomy 31:6 says, "Be strong and courageous. Do not be afraid or terrified because of them, for the Lord your God goes with you; He will never leave you nor forsake you."

May 17

God Will Supply

Many people live in fear. And plenty wonder how matters of life and death will work out in the end. But with faith comes help. And an underlying fear can actually bring about negative results. In contrast, when there is faith in believing, especially in the Word of God, a soul is more capable and better able to counter sabotaging fears along with deception.

Knowing the Word of God, provides Truth in the soul, that strengthens us, through the trials. And believing that God is our supply, helps us as we trust for our provisions. We do not need to spin our wheels or worry. As we trust, we notice that we get what we need. And by grace, we have victory.

Scripture says in Philippians 4:19, "But my God shall supply all your needs according to His riches in glory in Christ Jesus."

This tells us that there is no need to stress, or try to fix things, or over contemplate to figure things out. Because God will supply all of our needs, when we believe. And having our needs met requires patience and faithful reliance. We cannot see what is ahead. However, God knows.

In Matthew 6:26, Jesus said, "Look at the birds of the air, they neither sow nor reap, nor gather into barns, and yet your heavenly Father feeds them."

God will provide for you, as long as you are willing to listen and obey. If the Lord offers you plenty of opportunity to take a job or employment position, and you do not walk through those doors, you will find a real struggle exists. So you must be willing to do the Lord's will in the moment, in order to fully receive the blessing of provision. Love is an action word.

And the more obedient you are, the more God is active in your life. He comes through, when you trust that circumstances will work out, in your favor and for your best interest. The more you can let go of self will, the better your needs are met. So trust, pray, communicate and listen. He will supply all your needs according to His riches and glory in Christ Jesus.

May 18

Change Takes Time

Change may come instantly for some, but for most people, it's neither straightforward nor immediate. Some days can seem to last forever, while others pass quickly. Everyone's pace is unique, and each day brings its own rhythm. Thus, evolution ebbs and flows, especially when facing numerous issues that need resolution.

Many people resist change due to fear of the unknown, fear of failure, or fear of losing their identity. When trust is lacking or when someone is unwilling to let go, change can take longer. Progress may come in baby steps. Additionally, individuals who grow up in supportive and nurturing environments may find it easier to adapt to change compared to those who experience hostile, abusive, or neglectful environments.

For those who do not feel God's Love, favor, guidance, or blessing, change can be a struggle, and emotional healing may take longer. This is because the soul needs to learn to trust, and without trust, it can be difficult to receive God's best. However, as we build trust, we begin to see more of the blessings and miracle-working power that God brings. We gain greater clarity when we walk in a position of trust, believing in a good outcome.

Sometimes we find ourselves uncertain about what to believe. We look at the world's strangeness and observe how others navigate their paths, often choosing by example. However, when we reach a moment where the future is shaped by the past and we stand at a crossroads, we come to fully understand our need for dependence on God.

Nothing in this life is assured or promised except the Truth of God's Word. Scripture tells us repeatedly, 'I will never leave you nor forsake you.' While we may not always have earthly support or a team cheering us on, we can trust that God will always be there to help us.

May 19

Pray Your Way To Success

Prayer is a powerful and comforting tool that everyone can use. It can be practiced in secret or openly, but one thing is certain: prayer helps us focus our thoughts and release them.

Do you believe you can pray your way to success? Most of us have doubts and fears, and unknown questions and answers that we consistently wonder about. And prayer not only deepens our relationship with God, but also provides comfort and relief from negative thoughts that twirl within the mind. Prayer has a way of clearing things up, to get to the core of matters and make progress.

And our prayers are conversations with God. When we pray, we are reminded of our purpose and what we want to achieve in this life. This focus helps us to stay motivated and driven towards our goals, even in the face of challenges and obstacles. And prayer does not have to be long and drawn out. A simple prayer can help to refocus and clear the way in our thinking.

When we pray, we are essentially turning our attention towards something greater than self, which helps to put worries and concerns into perspective. And God requires fellowship. So this is a joyful exchange. It is also a time for releasing pain. Whatever the case may be, sharing our heart, while casting our cares, and listening for answers and guidance, as well as giving praise and thanksgiving, can lead to success, and also be pleasing and fun. Prayer can put the spring back in your step!

When we pray, we can expect comfort and direction. And as we release our issues to the Lord, we create space for a centered state of mind. Additionally, we grow in intimacy by remaining open and receptive to the Holy Spirit's guidance. This is how we tap into a higher level of awareness, to see things that we otherwise might miss. Doing this, we edge closer to success in our endeavors.

Praying your way to success involves aligning your goals and desires through heartfelt communication with God. By seeking guidance and support, you invite clarity and strength into your endeavors. Prayer helps you focus on your objectives, overcome obstacles, and stay grounded in faith, turning challenges into opportunities for growth. And as you trust in God's plan and seek His wisdom, you pave a path to success that is not only fulfilling but also deeply rooted in purpose.

May 20

Surrendering For The Win

When we surrender our will to God, we are in agreement with the Lord. Here we relinquish control to His sovereignty and trust Him with our lives. This includes our dreams, hopes, and fears. And surrendering for the win, is a continual process of letting go of our will and desires, while submitting to God's plan and purpose for our lives. He guides our journey.

Humans can be very strong willed. We have our minds made up about things, and often there is no changing a perspective. However, the more we flow with the changes, the more we experience a manifestation of purpose, to gain experience. When we resist, we can delay progress and set ourselves back. We might even miss out on a blessing!

So, surrender for the win today, and do not focus on your limitations. Instead, receive strength from the Holy Spirit with a greater appreciation of God's grace. You can learn to walk by faith, so that you are better able to relax and discover your true purpose and calling. Even when it is uncertain or difficult, you must trust and rely on the Lord completely.

In 1 Corinthians 9:24, Scripture says, "Do you not know that in a race all the runners run, but only one gets the prize? Run in such a way as to get the prize."

The prize is yours when you surrender for the win. This is the continual process of trust in God's plan. And by surrendering our lives to Him, we are better able to make a meaningful impact in the world. A good daily mindset is to pray the Lord's prayer. "Not my will, but your will be done". This is how to develop trust in letting go, while cultivating humility.

Surrendering our will to God, for the win, helps us to find peace, as we release our worries, fears, and anxieties, to grow in calmness. And when we trust that God has our best interest, we experience a sense of freedom from the burdens of life. Additionally, our faith is deepened as we hold the intention to live a life of strength and purpose.

May 21

Grow In Grace

The Bible is filled with stories of God's grace and how it has transformed the lives of people throughout history. And this grace is a free gift that is often unexpected and a surprise. Grace is a demonstration of God's character, and a reflection of His perfect nature, which is a transformative force that can change people and the world for the better.

And God extends His grace to us, despite our flaws and shortcomings. Not because we deserve it, but because of His infinite Love, favor and mercy toward humanity. This grace is extraordinary and can feel like a miracle of sorts. Also like a new day dawning. Grace can feel like a turn of events where everything changes and a revelation occurs.

And grace is a lifelong process that involves developing a deeper understanding of God's Love. We must allow Love to inspire our thoughts, attitudes, and actions every day. Additionally, grace is an act of kindness that when freely given, inspires us to extend grace toward other people.

And with prayer, we get help in extending grace to others when it is difficult. We must demonstrate the same kind of Love and mercy that God has shown us.

Grace can be frightening, because of the way it unfolds. It manifests and does not appear linear. It comes in like a flood, in our favor, and working for our good. And there may be situations where it is difficult to forgive ourselves or someone, who has hurt us deeply. But grace helps us along, as God reveals areas in our lives where we need to grow.

Ultimately, growing in grace requires us to surrender. We must allow the Lord's love and mercy to transform us from the inside. And by committing ourselves to this process, we seek guidance, to experience its fullness and to live a life that reflects God's love in the world. This love is a free gift, made possible through faith in Jesus Christ. It is a rescue from hopelessness, and the unknown.

God's love is a priceless gift of salvation and forgiveness. Have you welcomed Christ into your heart? In every moment, there is grace. Reflect on how God's grace has impacted your life. When have you been able to extend grace to family, friends, colleagues, or even strangers? By persevering daily, you position yourself to fully experience the profound benefits of God's love and grace.

May 22

Do Everything In Love

Love has the power to ignite spirits, bind us together, and transform our lives. And in 1 Corinthians 16:14, Scripture tells us, "do everything in Love". This means we should approach life with a mindset rooted in compassion, empathy, and kindness. Love should be the driving force behind our actions, decisions, and interactions with other people.

When we operate from a place of Love, we transcend self-interest to embrace deeper understanding. And each of us will encounter multiple opportunities every day, to apply the principle of doing everything in Love. We are called to approach others with open hearts and minds. Seeking to understand rather than to judge. And to empathize rather than criticize.

Have you ever said something you wished you could take back? We all have. And watching our words is a very important component to our happiness, because our trouble often stems from things that we say. This is why we need to approach Love as learners. We are always learning to apply the principles of Love. And looking through the lens of Love, we see the inherent worth and value of every person. Are you doing everything in Love today? Is this your mode of operation?

Doing everything in Love means embracing forgiveness and reconciliation. And conflicts and misunderstandings are all a part of the human experience. We understand this. However, Love encourages us to approach these challenges, with a willingness to heal and restore. Love empowers us to let go of resentment, and to live with humility and grace.

Love has the power to bridge divides and to dismantle barriers and bring people together across differences. It unites us in our shared humanity. Also, Love in action compels us to help those in need. Jesus Christ was Love personified. So as we do everything in Love, we can simply ask ourselves in any given moment, "What would Jesus do?" This helps our direction.

Finally, Love brings encouragement and validates the experiences of others. Love knows no boundaries of race, religion, or nationality. Love recognizes that each person has a unique story, with unique struggles and dreams. Love will extend compassion and kindness while creating the spaces for healing and growth to occur.

May 23

Inspire And Illuminate

In a world often shrouded in darkness, letting your light shine before others is significant. We are the pathway to illuminate. And we hold the potential to radiate goodness and inspire others around us. Our light represents the qualities that make us unique and the virtues that guide us, which must include love, kindness, empathy, compassion and forgiveness.

What does it mean to let your light shine? It goes beyond merely existing or going through daily life. It's about living with intention and purpose, aligning your actions with your deepest values. By letting your light shine, you not only showcase the good within you but also glorify God and contribute to a brighter, more compassionate world.

And we gain insight into where our light can shine brightest, when we look deep within. It may be through acts of service, creative expression, leadership, or simply being a source of encouragement. However, letting your light shine is not about seeking recognition or accolades.

It is not driven by ego or a desire for personal gain. Instead, it is an expression of genuine care and love for others. It is selflessness, without expectation of reward.

Good deeds, both big and small, have the power to uplift and inspire others. It can be as simple as offering a smile to a stranger, lending a hand to someone in need, or actively listening to a friend who is going through a difficult time. But every act of kindness, no matter how small or large, has the potential to create ripples of positivity in the world.

Are you letting your light shine today? You hold the power to ignite the light within others. And your actions speak louder than words. So remember that you can bring hope, joy, and healing all around you as your light is a beacon of inspiration and an agent of change. Today, be a catalyst for transformation, encouraging others to tap into their own goodness.

Letting your light shine before others requires courage, vulnerability, and a willingness to step out of your comfort zone. It entails facing challenges and overcoming obstacles. And the rewards are immeasurable as you follow the pathway that inspires and illuminates.

May 24

Seeds We Sow

Life is a journey of choices and consequences. And every action we take, sets in motion a chain of events that lead to outcomes. This reflects the idea of cause and effect, demonstrating that deeds and intentions shape the future that awaits us.

And just as a farmer carefully selects and plants the right seeds, nurturing them with care, we too are responsible for the thoughts, words, and actions that we put into the world. Are the seeds you are sowing today good seeds? What harvest will you reap tomorrow?

Consciously or not, you are sowing seeds that will inevitably sprout and yield results. And some seeds take more time to grow and bear fruit. So plenty of patience and perseverance is required. Also, factors beyond our control can influence the results we obtain. The timing and manner in which we reap, may not always be immediately apparent. However when we sow positivity, kindness, and compassion, we can expect to reap the rewards of happiness, fulfillment, and meaningful relationships. Conversely, if we sow negativity, selfishness, and dishonesty, we will likely experience the consequences of discord, and a loss of trust.

Scripture says in Galatians 6:7, "Do not be deceived: God cannot be mocked. A man reaps what he sows."

This principle applies not only to individuals but also to society as a whole. The actions we take collectively, as communities and nations, have lasting consequences. If we sow seeds of cooperation, understanding, and social justice, we can expect to reap a harmonious and progressive society. Conversely, if we sow seeds of division, injustice, and indifference, we will face inequality and unrest.

Therefore, we need to thoughtfully consider the implications of our choices, before we act. By consciously striving to make a positive impact, we increase the likelihood of positive outcomes. Here we are active participants in shaping our destiny and the world around us.

Have you thought about what you are sowing today? You can lead an intentional life, when you navigate with wisdom, to create a positive ripple effect. Today, cultivate virtues such as integrity, empathy, and resilience, knowing that these qualities will ultimately contribute to your growth and well being, along with the well-being of all those around you.

May 25

Incremental Progress

Our world celebrates instant gratification and overnight successes. And because of this, the concept of starting small may seem counterintuitive. But this is where we are to begin when we step out to do something great. Especially when serving the Lord in any capacity.

We are bombarded with stories of rapid growth and monumental achievements, leading us to believe that significant progress is achieved through grand gestures and dramatic leaps. However, there is immense value in starting small and embracing the journey of incremental growth. By taking small steps consistently, we lay the foundation for lasting success.

And one of the key advantages of starting small is the ability to build momentum. Whether a personal goal or a professional project, the sheer magnitude of a dream or task can be overwhelming. In fact, for most, it is easy to get paralyzed by the enormity of the challenge and succumb to inaction. This is why trusting God step by step, is necessary. He leads us with manageable tasks, in the moment, to gain a sense of progress and triumph.

And as we consistently work toward achievable goals, we transform our lives in profound ways, while breaking down challenges. Whether it's learning a new skill, adopting a healthier lifestyle, or nurturing meaningful connections, starting small, helps to set a path for continuous improvement and fulfillment. Achievable tasks can develop discipline, focus, and perseverance. And these qualities become the building blocks of success, enabling us to stay committed and motivated even with obstacles and setbacks.

Building the character needed to stand in the glory of greatness takes time. God will guide you daily with courage and humility to face each task. There's no need to rush or get ahead of yourself—simply trust the Lord with every step. Don't wait to pursue your dreams. Set a goal and go after what you envision. By making incremental progress, you can achieve big dreams through small steps, no matter your age or the challenges you face.

May 26

The Great Commission

When something works, you just want to share it. It feels good to point someone in a positive direction, knowing that they will receive freedom to flourish and grow. For this reason, we must share our testimonies and stories of salvation. This is "The Great Commission". It is a mandate to go forth into the world, with the message of hope, salvation, and love through the redemptive work of Jesus Christ.

In Matthew 28:19-20, Jesus says, "Go and make disciples of all men."

The Great Commission encapsulates the spreading of the gospel, not merely through words, but also through actions. We set the example in living out Christ's teachings everyday. And the Great Commission calls us to love one another and to serve others selflessly. Our witness reveals the power of faith, while introducing and bringing others into a personal relationship with God.

Have you shared your testimony recently? Are you open to helping someone along their journey? In our interconnected world, The Great Commission is no longer limited by geography or time. Thanks to technology, it's easier than ever to reach audiences across physical barriers through media and social platforms. Your personal message can inspire and nurture faith, connecting with communities around the globe.

Fulfilling The Great Commission extends beyond sharing words; it requires living out the teachings of Jesus Christ in a way that reflects His love and character. It means embracing humility, kindness, forgiveness, and empathy in our interactions with other people every day. It also means being a source of hope, comfort, and encouragement to those in need.

We are here to share the hope that comes from knowing God's grace. And by heeding this call, as believers, we participate and continue to shape history, bringing healing, redemption, and a glimpse of God's kingdom to a world in need. We can strive for justice, and advocate for the marginalized, while promoting peace and reconciliation. This is a sacred mission that embraces the responsibility of sharing the life-changing message of Jesus Christ.

May 27

More Strength Daily

Life is a complex journey filled with trials and tribulations. From personal setbacks to professional obstacles, challenges are an integral part of our journey. And each of us would welcome more strength. Would we not? When we are strong, we can take on the world!

Relying on the Lord for strength, we know that a great intelligence is at work in co-creating our direction and outcomes. And when our faith is in God, we are equipped with the flexibility and adaptability necessary to embrace growth, increasing our chances for success. Tapping into the source, who is God, we are supported by greatness. We do not rely solely on ourselves. Daily, we receive the strength to tackle challenges with clarity, focus, and determination.

And it is good to know that we do not have to go through life's challenges alone. When we welcome Christ as Lord, the Holy Spirit comes to live inside us. And the Holy Spirit is known as "the helper" to transform our challenges into stepping stones. Through prayer, we become energized to embrace challenges we face with a positive mindset, trusting even in adversity.

It's through facing situations that we build resilience and keep the wind in our sails. As time passes and we continually rely on God to guide us on our journey, we adapt, learn, and grow through challenges. Walking with the Spirit to receive daily strength helps alleviate the uncertainty that often accompanies trials.

Through prayer and faith, as we pursue our aspirations and grow with God, we are empowered to confront our emotions head-on. We rely fully on the Lord to transcend and push beyond the boundaries of our comfort zones. By His strength, we gain the resilience to persevere and the courage to face the unknown.

Strength has a ripple effect that extends beyond our lives. And as we display more strength in the face of challenges, we become a source of inspiration for those around us. Our resilience, determination, and unwavering spirit serve as a beacon of hope, inspiring others to face their own challenges with renewed strength each day. As you walk this path, remember to pray daily for more strength to keep going. You are capable of more than you realize!

May 28

Harmony And Tranquility

Becoming a peacemaker is an important mission that we can choose, to contribute to a more harmonious society. And in Matthew 5:9, Jesus said, "Blessed are the peacemakers, for they shall be called children of God." These words emphasize the importance of fostering peace and harmony in a world often marred by conflict and discord.

And to understand the essence of being a peacemaker, we must recognize that peace extends beyond the absence of physical conflict. It encompasses human relationships, unity, and reconciliation where understanding, compassion, and forgiveness can flourish. And being a peacemaker reflects the nature of God. So, as we become peacemakers, we demonstrate kinship with the Lord, and the joy that comes from fulfilling this calling. Further, in order to radiate peace outwardly, we must first cultivate peace within ourselves.

Through connection and guidance from God, we gain a sense of contentment, and a willingness to embrace forgiveness. And peacemakers are not passive bystanders. Peacemakers seek to heal broken relationships, mediate conflicts, and foster understanding with efforts driven by empathy, humility, and a genuine desire for unity. Our peaceful actions today create blessings that serve as catalysts, making us agents for reconciliation.

A core principle of peacemaking, is to embrace the diversity that characterizes our world. Do you allow differences to fuel division and animosity in your life, or do you seek common ground, celebrating the unique contributions of each individual? With Love in the lead, we can choose to walk with understanding using dialogue, respect, and acceptance. This approach is the bridge between cultures, religions, and ethnicities.

When you embrace the role of a peacemaker, you embody attributes of God, igniting a ripple effect of positive change. Do you strive for peace, even when it seems difficult? Even the smallest acts of kindness can spark a transformative movement, touching countless lives and leaving a legacy of peace for generations to come. We are the instruments through which God's blessings flow. Today, take Jesus' teachings to heart and commit yourself to being a peacemaker. Embrace the calling to build a wonderful world filled with Love, understanding, and lasting peace.

May 29

As Children Of God

Grasping the idea of being a child of God, brings comfort, value and a sense of belonging to many, and signifies a personal and intimate relationship with the Creator of the Universe. As we surrender our lives to the guidance and direction of the Holy Spirit, we are strengthened to further embrace our identity as children of God.

Through the Holy Spirit's gentle whispers, promptings, and convictions, we have wisdom, discernment, and clarity. This leading, aligns our hearts and actions with God's will, enabling us to honor Him and reflect His character. Do you consider yourself a child of God?

In Romans 8:14, the apostle Paul, in his letter to the Romans, writes; "For those who are led by the Spirit of God are the children of God".

When we awaken to the idea of being a child of God, we acknowledge our true identity in Christ. And this powerful Scripture affirms our identity as believers while highlighting the redemptive and transformative role of the Holy Spirit in our lives. Our journey further evolves, as we inherit His grace and eternal promises. By the Holy Spirit, we are empowered to shed our old nature, with its selfish desires and sinful inclinations and embrace a new life characterized by love, joy, peace, patience, kindness, goodness, faithfulness, gentleness, and self-control.

As children of God, it is evident that the Spirit works in our hearts, renewing our minds and conforming us to the likeness of Christ. We are no longer bound by past mistakes or the burdens of guilt and shame. Instead, we are liberated from chains, and empowered to walk in freedom. The Holy Spirit continually intercedes on our behalf, bringing our prayers before the throne of grace. This intimate connection fills our hearts with peace, joy, and a sense of belonging. Here we comprehend that we are eternally cherished by an unfailing love.

We are called to reflect God's character and share His Love with the world. Through the Holy Spirit, we experience transformation, freedom, and deeper communion. Equipped with love, compassion, and truth, we are empowered to impact and serve others globally. We are never left to navigate life's challenges and decisions alone. And our lives are a testament to divine connection.

May 30

Wisdom's Instruction

Wisdom is something we should regularly pray for. It keeps us from trouble, and moving into what we dream. To heed wisdom's instruction, we must cultivate a humble heart and a teachable spirit. And wisdom requires the courage to let go of our limited perspectives.

Scripture says in Proverbs 29:18, "Where there is no revelation, the people cast off restraint; but blessed are those who heed wisdom's instruction."

This verse highlights the significance of divine revelation and the transformative power of wisdom's guidance in our lives. When we embrace God's vision and wisdom, we find purpose, direction, and the strength to walk in alignment with His will.

Wisdom reshapes our character to reflect the virtues of love, kindness, patience, and justice. And wisdom enables us to make decisions that honor God to benefit those around us. In contrast, when wisdom is absent, we are prone to selfish desires. An unwise person will often prioritize immediate gratification over long-term fulfillment. And a lack of wisdom can lead to an erosion of values and a disregard for others.

Wisdom's instruction equips us to discern between right and wrong, making us better prepared to face adversity and build meaningful relationships. Have you prayed for wisdom lately? You can gain insight that will guide your life. The Truth provides a compass, offering direction, and a foundation to build a better future when you prioritize wisdom and ask for it in prayer.

It takes courage to request great things. And to expect great things. So today and every day, embrace wisdom's instruction and allow it to shape every aspect of your life. As you receive wisdom, you gain understanding of truth, along with guidance, which grants the strength and clarity to persevere through difficult situations.

May 31

God's Limitless Power

Walking with the Lord is an exciting adventure. And when we align ourselves with God's purposes, we witness the awe-inspiring manifestation of His limitless power in our lives. His ability to accomplish the extraordinary, surpasses our expectations and imaginations.

In scripture, Ephesians 3:20 says, "Now to Him who is able to do immeasurably more than all we can ask or imagine, according to His power that is at work within us."

So God can do more than what we imagine on our own, especially when we pray and believe. And believing in the amazing power of God enables us to live lives of impact and abundance. And our finite minds often struggle to comprehend the vastness of God's capabilities. But He is not constrained by human limitations or restricted by our doubts or uncertainties. Instead, God's power extends far beyond what we can conceive or articulate.

The Lord delights in going above and beyond our expectations in ways that astound. So we need to trust more. He is not limited to answering our prayers within the boundaries of our understanding. And by trusting in His goodness and sovereignty, we open our hearts and minds to a higher plan, where we clearly notice and see daily provisions and breakthroughs.

Do you remember a time when you witnessed the awe inspiring power of God? The Lord invites you to dream big and approach Him with confidence. Furthermore, to fully experience this immeasurable power, you must have faith and surrender to His will. We are called to embrace boldness and remember that our Heavenly Father is not confined by human limitations. So as we fully grasp the magnitude of His willingness to work in and through us, we are emboldened to step out, further in faith, to serve and answer the call with fervor.

Experiencing God's limitless power is exciting, fulfilling and often mind blowing. So stay open to a view that is more than what you can imagine for yourself, by honoring the Lord today in all you do. Remember He is in control and has the highest good for you.

JUNE

June 1

Room For All

Having a Christlike mindset means that we are to live our lives judgment free, knowing that Jesus is the door for each one of us. We also understand that love is the only thing that can heal and counter human evil. Especially the trouble we struggle with from time to time.

Are you afraid to reach out? Do you have trouble accepting yourself or other people? It's very important to know that love makes room for all individuals. Furthermore, there is a battle for your soul. And the only way to win the battle, is to step out against the lies of the enemy, with a commitment to The Truth. This requires discernment.

And a person may go through great tragedy, in many ways, suffering great losses and incomparable struggles. And plenty hold secrets inside, while protecting and preventing outsiders from entering in. But the Lord never intended His children to live this way.

Scripture says in John 8:32, "You shall know the Truth and the Truth shall set you free."

We must commit our way to the Truth with complete integrity. To receive love, we must not fear sharing it. By letting go of judgment—toward others and ourselves—we open the door to more love and diversity in our lives. Whether inside or outside the church, in a nightclub, coffee shop, grocery store, or community space, when we open our hearts with a desire for inclusion, God meets our needs in even greater ways.

The 'Sword of the Spirit'—the Word—empowers us by distinguishing truth from lies and provides guidance for our souls. You have the choice to embrace this expansive love and live fully alive. However, it's crucial to actively overcome the falsehoods that may derail your positive outcome. A strong prayer life is essential to this journey.

Each of us can choose to embrace love today by seeking ways to help others and placing their needs above our own. Have you noticed that some people fear those who love and believe in the Word of God? This often stems from human judgment. However, when you walk with a focus on love and goodness, there is nothing to fear.

June 2

More Divine Appointments

There is nothing like holding Scripture in your heart to recall when your soul needs refreshing. Scripture offers a wellspring of comfort and guidance, grounding you during uncertain times and renewing your spirit with strength and hope. It prepares you for whatever comes your way. Understanding the height, depth, width, and length of God's Love in Christ Jesus reveals the secret to abundant living. This is the fullness that comes from divine appointments.

Are you ready for more divine appointments? When we honor God, He honors us. Even when it feels like no one is listening. So rest assured that God hears your prayers. Divine appointments are moments and encounters that seem orchestrated by God, bringing meaning and purpose to our lives. These events provide opportunities for growth, guidance, and blessing, whether through meeting new people or gaining valuable insight and revelation. They represent God's hand in guiding and shaping your life through encounters that turn out to be significant.

As you seek to find your people, the hope is that friendships will flourish and love will abound. These people may not be blood relatives but are likely like-minded souls. As life unfolds, people change—some move on, and some pass away. You might feel out of place or wonder where everything went. In moments that feel desolate or disheartening, turn to the Lord and deepen your relationship with Him. You are not alone; God understands what you're going through and has destined you for more divine appointments.

God is at work beyond our understanding, and His desire is for you to fully trust Him. With that trust, you can navigate difficult times with victory. Humility is essential on this journey. Though the path may seem daunting, it need not be feared. God knows your needs even before you ask, and every prayer you offer is a divine appointment leading to more opportunities for you to serve.

Question: Would you give your attention to someone who does not honor you with theirs? Likely not. Similarly, we need to spend time with the Lord, casting our cares and expressing everything we are feeling and going through. This practice fosters a deep relationship where we can freely receive from Him. God's Love embraces each of us with complete understanding. As we serve others, we discover that we reap what we sow and are strengthened by God's presence within us. Learn to pray about your concerns and trust in the Way that Christ clearly demonstrates.

June 3

Wonder About Love

There are certainly plenty of things to wonder about on Earth. And our existence holds mystery with answers we seek to find. Illusions are everywhere. And although it appears things are moving along in directions, it can also be as if nothing is happening. However, Love is not an illusion. And the Lord orders everything with perfect intelligence and brilliance.

And because we are an advanced society, we strive to harness resources. Including from other planets. This is truly remarkable. It's as if we can touch the sky. But all of the resources and knowledge in the world are still unable to penetrate the deeper mysteries of Love. So, it's important to not become too mighty in our thinking, having a sense of false security.

Love is both our greatest mystery and the ultimate reveal. It invites us to reflect deeply on its meaning. Many do not fully understand what it means to walk in Love. Love is tangible; it requires action and practice. It produces results, brings about change, and heightens awareness.

When we ponder Love and strive to live fully within it, we become more vibrant, healthier, and more satisfied with the time we are given.

You may have much to remember and much to forget, but with every interaction, are you placing Love at the center? Let's hope so, for a life with fewer regrets. It's never pleasant to wonder if you could have done more. Instead, focus on Love and how you can grow in it. It is a true blessing to understand Love in all its wonder.

Everyone has moments they wish they could forget—times when their best wasn't given, and mistakes were made. It's during moments of pressure that we truly see what a person is made of: is it Love or fear? As believers in Christ, we are given a clean slate, and moving forward is essential. It's never too late to begin wondering about Love. You can choose to live and walk in it. Love is amazing, and it's our most important resource.

June 4

Mercy Is The Principle Thing

Our reputation with people is never going to be perfect. But it can be good. And when we walk with a contrite heart that values integrity, we build trust with others. People may see our shortcomings, just as we can see theirs, however, mercy is the principle thing.

And sometimes our mistakes bring about changes we wish we did not have to go through. So we must remember that all things work together for good, for those who love God and are called according to His purposes. Additionally, God chastises those He loves. So we are not surprised when we are rebuked for failings and poor choices. It's all for our benefit.

And when we invite Christ into our hearts, we receive mercy and freedom from the oppression of sin. Our past, present and future sins are all forgiven. We are learning to walk with Jesus and stand in the light that shines bright. There is no hiding. And as we comprehend the "The Way", we can choose to respect matters and make things right with those involved and especially where needed.

When we bring our confession to the Lord, we receive mercy. We do not dwell on our faults, but are learning from the lessons as God reveals them to us for our benefit. Also, we do not continue to feel bad or downtrodden about ourselves because we missed the mark. We receive God's forgiveness. And just as we receive, we must remember to forgive quickly. To provide mercy speedily, offering the same courtesy to people, because mercy is the principle thing.

No one is perfect, but we are being perfected. So let us receive the Lord's mercy and continue to walk in a way that is pleasing to Him, one day at a time. Mercy is the principle thing.

Scripture says in Micah 6:8, "What does the Lord require of you? To do justice, to Love mercy and to walk humbly with your God."

June 5

In The Light God Keeps Us

When we walk in the light, there is no hiding. And when we walk in the light, all is open and revealed. In contrast, to hide something means to put it under some cover, or out of sight and away, so it cannot be seen. Therefore we cannot expect to succeed as we move toward the light, when we are hiding something to protect ourselves or our reputation.

Our actions, motivations, and successes, along with our shortcomings are all revealed in the light. And in the light, God keeps us. Everything is open before the Lord. So, we must accept the fact that the way to have joy and victory is by keeping a clear conscience. Everything must be out and into the open. This complete clarity comes from repentance.

Furthermore, to reach maturity, we must hold fast to The Truth. And when we slip up with things like lying, prideful actions or wrong motives, we can expect that these will rise to the surface, where we experience a level of discomfort and a need for change. We may not have been taught properly. Perhaps we had very few good examples. But in the light God keeps us.

When we first come to Christ, we are washed clean to begin like newborn babies with plenty of growing to do. We are born again, and as born-again believers, we are being perfected. As we mature, the road becomes narrow. And often we do not know what the hidden issues are, although we must acknowledge wrongdoing and have a desire to choose what is right going forward.

And in the light we have peace. Our souls receive rest and we are stronger. In the light, we have confidence and better health. All of this comes as we choose not to live in and fulfill the flesh. In the light, our thinking has clarity and direction. We have fewer doubts. This refining makes us beautiful within. And far better able to stand in the face and day of adversity.

June 6

A Love Story Redemption Brings

Love is an action word. And Love is about change. And although your life story and past may appear unattractive and even hopeless, God is in the business of making your life beautiful. He is not finished creating a true love story that only redemption brings.

And you may feel relatively content, or perhaps sense that something is missing. Either way, life is in constant motion. So we need to ask ourselves, 'What direction am I going?' Am I progressing and experiencing more of God's love in my life? Do I have the peace I'm meant to embrace? Or is something still missing?

As believers in Christ, we have been redeemed by the blood of the Lamb. And when we accept the gift of Grace in Jesus Christ, our redemption is the action of being saved from sin, error, and evil. We go from glory to glory, and we're not the same people that we once were. This is because the Lord is re-writing our story. This is the redemption story of our lives.

And sin is a progress blocker. What we believe about ourselves, affects our outcomes. People can strive and read all the self-help books in the world, but until a person comes to the end of self, and the ways that do not encourage love, progress is muted. So we need to bring our broken places to the foot of the cross and be honest with the Lord.

Remember that when you were redeemed, you returned to the One who loves you most. And being transformed by trusting the Lord, you are not the same person you once were. Now you are glued at the hip with this great love that comes from receiving what Christ did for you, to set you free. This is a true love story that only redemption brings.

In Christ, your redemption unfolds without the shadow of your past mistakes. It is through complete forgiveness with deep understanding that the Lord brings you through. And your story is a testament to the resilience of the human spirit and the transformative power of God's love, that proves that through redemption, true love can flourish.

June 7

The Beauty Of Redemption

We are a beautiful work in progress that glows with more light every day. And the Lord knows what you need, exactly when you need it. His timing is perfect. And akin to a puzzle, where all the pieces are placed in order, at the right time, God knows how to change you, deep within your soul, to create a beautiful image, where all the parts fit together perfectly.

Redemption means receiving. No more pushing away the things you are afraid of. And redemption comes with protection. When you are redeemed, you know within, that you belong to the Living God. And you have a covering that comes with belonging. You are not afraid of what's to come.

Scripture tells us in Ecclesiastes 3:11, "God makes everything beautiful in its time".

We must trust the Lord as we walk through the redemption story of our lives. When faced with rugged mountains we don't know how to climb or bring low, we need help. We also have crooked places that need to be made straight. 'I will do it,' says the Lord. Though you will never be perfect, you are being perfected. You can recognize the redemption in your life by the words you speak. When your words are respectful, you reflect the great gift of life as a child of God. For example, when you pray, 'Nothing more and nothing less than Your words on my lips,' you demonstrate a heart that is truly redeemed. Your words ring of Love inside, revealing your heart, soul and spirit.

And when you have understanding, about where you have been and where you are going, you are being redeemed. This is when you recognize that in the world you will have trouble, yet you choose to cheer up and go through with a positive mental attitude. And when you declare, 'The Lord is my light and salvation, whom shall I fear?' you are living out your redemption story.

Being redeemed, you are guided with each new day, to live courageously, comprehending Christ, who paid the price to reconcile you to God. And being redeemed brings a sense of excitement. There is a confidence which provides further protection. You are awake and alive to love and are vibrating at a very high level. As your energy rises, you simply trust and observe the Lord at work. God is at the helm, where anything great can happen. This is a love story only redemption brings.

June 8

Crossroads, Changes And Shifts

There are times when things do not go the way we hope, or the way we plan. And when these situations occur, we feel severely let down. But we can still thrive, and not get off course, even when things do not go the way that we think or expect that they should.

Maybe you've hoped for something for a very long time and believed you'd see your plan or vision come to fruition, only to have your hopes dashed. A door closes and things don't appear to be working in your favor, or according to your ideas. It's a real let down when this happens. But we must continue to hope and trust the Lord, who knows just what we need at every stage of life.

Please don't lose heart or get angry with God when challenging moments arise. Continue to make plans, but hold them loosely, remembering that God knows what is for your highest good. This might be a time to rest and regroup. Avoid acting irrationally. Instead, be gentle with yourself—take time to pray, rest, and eat healthily as you wait for guidance. Use this period for restoration so that you are prepared for the next steps.

In Psalm 37:23, Scripture says, "The steps of a good man/woman are ordered by the Lord." It continues, "And He delights in his way." When we put God first, we can trust in the divine order of all things, knowing that God has our best interests at heart and is guiding our steps.

Now you may be at a crossroad and need to prepare for changes and shifts. Please continue to have expectations for success. Sometimes, we get a big wakeup call. And big wake up calls, help us to not resist the Lord's leading and will for our lives any longer.

Finally, there are times when we need to change something. Trials and difficulty will come. But we overcome by embracing these changes and losing our self-will. We must be able to listen and obey the Lord's leading. And surely we know and expect that trouble will come. And we are made all the better for it, especially when we let go and let God!

June 9

Who Can Tame The Tongue?

There are times that we all say things that we should not. And we may try to watch our words, but it is by grace that we move, live and have our being. So each one of us, at one time or another, will say more than what is needed.

You can be relatively mature with spiritual practice, but still fail over words spoken. And there may be times that we are brainwashed into believing that we are helping another person by being forthright, only to discover that we have said too much. Pridefully we think we know better. However, some words are better off left unsaid. And once words are released into the Universe, they stand forever. Good or bad, you cannot take them back.

Scripture says in James 3:7, "All kinds of animals, birds, reptiles and sea creatures are being tamed and have been tamed by mankind, but no human can tame the tongue. It is a restless evil, full of deadly poison."

Challenges with words, occur until we get them right. And it's true that people who are hurting, tend to hurt other people. So if negative words are being spoken towards you, they are probably coming from a hurting soul. This is key in not taking offense.

Some words can be harsh. They can sting and do great damage. For this reason it is good to consider and be aware of motives and root causes. The less trouble we need to clean up, due to our words, the better. And thankfully, God's mercies are new every morning.

Every day, we must put Truth front and center. We are on a living planet, serving a living God with a purpose to grow in Christlikeness. Ask God to change you and recognize that what comes out of your mouth is important. Also, it is best to settle a matter. When we acknowledge our failings and move forward, we grow in self control and especially Love.

June 10

Wishes And Dreams

Do you ever find yourself wishing? Saying "I wish", when referring to hopes and dreams? "I wish this could be, or I wish that would happen"? Wishes don't make dreams come true. And while wishing may provide comfort or motivation, wishes rarely lead to tangible results.

There are two primary things that will deliver a winning edge. The first is integrity and the second, perseverance. And to truly turn your desires into reality and achieve your goals, it is essential to engage in deliberate planning, consistent effort and proactive behavior. By setting clear objectives, and creating actionable steps, your aspirations will become attainable.

In Matthew 5:37, Scripture says, "But let your 'Yes' be 'Yes,' and your 'No,' be 'No'. " For whatever is more than these is from the evil one".

Having your yes mean yes, and your no mean no, is very important. And making wise choices and sticking with them, takes character. It's important not to give up early, but instead to trust the Lord and yourself through difficult times. At the core of all things, you need to keep it real.

Do you struggle with sticking to decisions or listening to your heart and following through? When you cultivate perseverance and integrity, good results follow your efforts. Dreams are not achieved by wishing but by developing Godly character. It's crucial to be honest, reliable, and to stand up for what is right, especially when failure or missteps occur. Emotional strength means having the courage to confront issues rather than avoiding them. The goal is to leave no situation unresolved. This is how we truly love people and support them through challenges.

It takes courage to do the right thing. So stay humble and persevere. Let Love grow within you. And taking the easy way is not where you find the rewards. Rewards come with maturity and perseverance. This approach not only increases the likelihood of success, but fosters resilience, and a sense of accomplishment.

June 11

Your Worth And Value

Many struggle with self-worth. But every person has value, and we are all equal in God's eyes. People need to be treated equally in human kindness. No one person is more valuable or worthy of kindness than another. And when our value is in being a child of God, we get the small things right.

Scripture says in Galatians 3:28, "There is neither Jew nor Gentile, neither slave nor free, nor is there male or female, for you are all one in Christ Jesus".

You have great worth and value as you grow and discover your place in this world. And hopefully, you come to learn that your value is not in what people think of you, or in how they act toward you, or even in how they treat you. Your worth and value is not in the money you make, or the position you hold. Instead your worth and value is in God alone. And equality is your birthright.

Life brings complications to all. Women are sometimes raised to believe that they are less valuable than their male counterparts. And in many job positions, women are not paid equally. Countless females are dismissed and not respected or heard, where men are revered. And in some cultures, women are severely oppressed from birth.

In contrast, men struggle, due to societal pressures and traditional expectations that emphasize strength, success, and stoicism. Many are conditioned to equate their worth and value with their ability to provide and protect, which can lead to significant internal conflict when they face setbacks. And the pressure to excel along with the fear of being perceived as weak, can exacerbate feelings of inadequacy.

We often place our trust in those who lead the way. But are we being led astray? When someone doesn't respect or honor you as an equal, it cuts deep, much like the pain of racism, where people elevate themselves above others. Yet, God's love is ever-present for the underdog, and when your worth and value are anchored in Christ alone, nothing can stop God's blessing in your life.

Remember to renew your mind daily. No one is above or beneath another. And if you find yourself thinking otherwise, it is a sign of pride. Seek alignment with God and walk in a way that pleases Him. Your worth and value must be found in Him alone.

June 12

Love Yourself Well

Your ability to love yourself well, is a direct reflection on how well you connect with God's unconditional love. And when you love yourself well, you will love other people well. So what does it mean to love yourself well? It is not a puffed-up state of being. It is a humble heart that receives mercy, grace and forgiveness.

Loving yourself well comes from experience. And when you commit to Walking in Love, the more you do it, the more you see love develop in your life. Also, love is patient and kind. It does not envy or boast. It is not proud or easily angered. Love keeps no record of wrongs. It is not judgmental. It does not delight in evil, but rejoices in Truth. (1 Corinthians 13)

To love yourself well, you need to release any past missteps, through repentance. Where there is shame, humiliation, or guilt, it is necessary to let it go, leaving matters at the foot of the Cross, to be remembered no more. Now you have a clean slate, so you can commit to purposefully "Walking in Love".

Also, when Walking in Love has not been modeled for you, it takes practice through trial and error. The more you do it, the more open and evolved you become. Also, one of the hardest things to overcome is insecurities. Insecurity can creep up and enter into your interactions with other people. And even though you may have become good at Walking in Love, occasionally you may feel insecure. Because insecurity is a human condition.

And we are diminished when insecurity causes us to feel as if we don't measure up. So to better understand our feelings and thoughts, discernment is needed. Using discernment, you can gain clarity to know which thoughts to let go of, and which ones to acknowledge. And deceit, in our thoughts, can be disheartening. We may consider that we are not attractive enough, or that we don't make enough money, or maybe that there's someone more talented than we are, coming along. The better we become at knowing and believing what God says about us, in His Word, the better we are at correcting our thinking.

This life is passing away, and our time on Earth is very temporary. So, remember who you are and keep your security in God first. Remember that you are the righteousness of God in Christ Jesus. And learn to receive from the Lord. The rest will follow. Love is a seed to grow, planted in God's soil, to produce a bountiful harvest, available to share with others.

June 13

Amazing Love - Amazing Freedom

Everyone, at one time or another, has wondered what might be coming around the bend. And we can either have an expectation for trouble, or an expectation for good. And while countless individuals go through the day without much contemplation, many live with an underlying fear, or even dread that something negative or bad will happen.

Having the strength and freedom to trust God, is an amazing place to be. And Jesus said in John 16:33, "I have told you these things, so that in Me you may have peace. In this world you will have trouble. Cheer up! I have overcome the world."

This tells us that trouble will come. However, trusting and placing our lives in God's hands brings contentment, peace and even cheerfulness. And the more we know God, the easier it becomes to trust Him and rely on His guidance, in all areas of our lives.

Trusting God is not a sign of weakness; rather, it is a demonstration of strength and wisdom. And as we release control and surrender our plans, dreams, and desires to His will, the burden of trying to orchestrate every aspect of our lives is removed. We embrace freedom and cheer from God's divine orchestration. There is wonder in His ways.

To draw near, we must cultivate a personal relationship, spending time in prayer and seeking His presence. Scripture is powerful too, because throughout the Bible, we find countless promises of provision, protection, guidance, and Love. And the more familiar we are with these promises, the more strength we have, to approach life with confidence, knowing that God will light our way.

Trusting God has transformative effects. And there is no need to dread or fear. Through consistent communication, you can develop a better understanding of His character. This is how to grasp His amazing love. And His faithfulness uncovers amazing freedom. Freedom from codependency, failure, fear, dread and death, to live with a boldness that carries us to the next level.

June 14

Bold Faith To Touch The World

Chasing dreams requires risk. And boldness with imagination are both necessary ingredients for dreams to come true. So, as you pursue opportunities and face challenges, please do not allow fear or doubt to hinder you. You need to have a bold faith to touch the world.

In Matthew 9:21, a woman who had been ill for some time, noticed Christ walking by. She said to herself, "If I can just touch His garment, I shall be made whole." She was desperate and also bold and full of faith. She needed to be made whole. So she touched His garment and was immediately healed. Her great faith was born out of desperation.

Faith requires us to release our fear of failure or rejection, and to focus on God's promises, goodness and guidance. This is how to experience growth in ways that we never thought possible. And when we trust God and act boldly, doors open. Also, by nurturing our imagination, we gain strength to see beyond our present circumstances, to comprehend the Lord working all things together for our good. He is creating new beginnings in our lives.

The Lord is with you every step of the way. So when things do not go the way that you think they should, do not lose hope. For it is in these moments of uncertainty and adversity, that we are tested the most. By trusting God, your perspective is transformed, to align with His purpose and will.

In Christ, you are empowered to face challenges with resilience. And perceiving the entirety of our lives in a single glance, we know that God's plan is higher than ours. So to greatly receive, we must step out of our comfort zone and embrace the unknown and move forward. Are you ready for a miracle? Overcome doubt with imagination and boldness today. Reach out and touch the world!

If you feel distant from God today, invite Him into your heart now. He hears your prayers, so pray with bold faith. Ask the Lord to forgive your sins and make you whole. Then, ask Him to guide you on the path you should take. He delights in giving you the desires of your heart.

June 15

Do You Know What Time It Is?

Wasting time often leads to regret, so it's important to consider how you spend your days. Many people don't pay close attention to time, wandering through life as if they have all the time in the world. It's like thinking it's three o'clock, when in reality, it's already nine.

Just as the Lord knows every hair on your head, Scripture also tells us that our days are numbered. Time is a mysterious force governing our existence, flowing in a constant rhythm, shaping our experiences, and offering opportunities for transformation. Though we perceive time as linear—past, present, and future—God transcends these limitations and exists beyond the confines of time. Do you know what time it is?

We often strive to control every aspect of our lives. We long for things to happen on our terms and according to our timelines. However, there is a higher power at work, which orchestrates the events of our lives with divine precision. And from this vantage point, every moment, every delay, and every leap forward serves a purpose. So we must be willing to surrender our desires and expectations, and trust God and His perfect timing. This means acknowledging that our limited perspective does not comprehend the intricacies and complexities of the Universe.

And God uses all things together for good, to serve a far greater and more expansive plan than our own ideas, and understanding. Letting go can be difficult to comprehend. The idea that we are not in control. However, when we recognize that God's wisdom surpasses our own, and His timing is perfect, we have an anchor that provides solace and reassurance, during moments of uncertainty.

Have you ever felt as if God's timing doesn't align with yours? You may desire something and not get it. However, God knows what you need, exactly when you need it. And you are not wasting a moment, when you wait. The important thing to remember is to keep walking in faith and love, so you can fully reap the benefits of living your dreams. By trusting in God's plan and staying true to His guidance, you'll experience the fullness of a life well-lived.

June 16

Gifts Without Repentance

When we are born into this world, there is a purpose and place for our talents and gifts. Romans 11:29 tells us that the gifts of the Lord are irrevocable, meaning our talents, abilities, blessings, and calling—our vocation, purpose, and mission—are without repentance. God does not change His mind. Your gifts are not subject to withdrawal based on your actions or behavior.

Many people don't recognize their gifts until they come into fellowship with the Lord. They may follow a certain path in life, only to later discover a different calling. God stands with us as we uncover what truly fulfills us. The gifts woven into our personality remain with us as we grow and evolve, through both adversity and blessing.

Are you serving your fellow man with purpose and understanding? Are you passionate about your life? Does your purpose include a resolution for faith, healing, prophecy, proclamation, teaching, administration, reconciliation, compassion, and self-sacrificing service or charity to help and encourage others along?

We may see ways that we could have made more progress, in different areas of our life. However, the beauty of salvation is that the gifts we are given, continue to work for our benefit, even through our mistakes and missteps. Our gifts remain with us, even in our failings. So do not lose heart, in pursuit of your talents and gifts.

Perceiving, serving, teaching, encouraging, giving, ruling, and mercy are the gifts found in Romans 12. These attributes provide a foundation for work in the world that is unique to each of us. And when we understand what our specific gifts are, we know what direction to take. Also, we may have more than one gift.

Gifts that you receive are not meant to be hidden away. They are meant to be shared with the world. And your gifts hold the power to ignite hope, bring healing, and create profound shifts in the lives of others, while at the same time, providing you with a sense of joy, contentment and reward.

June 17

Never Lose Hope

It may look like the end is near, or that a dream you have, may not come true, but as long as you are alive, God is working to bring your heart's desires to fruition. It is important to remember who holds the plan for your life. And to never lose hope.

And when hope runs thin, look for the moments when God's direction and blessing were evident. It may be the job offer that arrived when you needed it. Or the encounter that led to a lifelong friendship. These instances remind, there is a higher intelligence at work, orchestrating the events of our lives with precision and care.

Hope is more than a mere wish or desire. Hope is an emotional anchor that keeps us grounded amidst life's storms. And hope breathes life into our dreams and infuses our hearts with resilience, strength, and optimism. It is the inner knowing that, no matter the challenge, there is always a possibility for things to improve. And hope provides the courage to persevere when the world seems bleak and dark. Hope is the strength that helps us walk through. Also, hope possesses an incredible healing power. It mends broken pieces in our hearts and revitalizes our spirit. Hope reminds us that even in the midst of sorrow, wounds can transform into wisdom.

In moments of pain, grief, or loss, hope serves as a soothing balm, offering comfort and solace. And with our hope in Christ, we have immeasurable strength to endure whatever comes our way. No day is promised. Yet, with hope, we rise and march forward. We do not know when our time will come to rise up into heavenly places. However, as we hope in Jesus, by faith, we naturally carry a radiant glow that illuminates our path.

Never lose hope. Even in the darkest moments, when the path ahead seems uncertain, hope keeps us steady. It reminds us that no situation is beyond God's reach and that every challenge holds the potential for growth and transformation. By trusting in His timing and staying faithful, we open the door to new possibilities and brighter tomorrows.

June 18

Redemption Is The Word

Jesus came for the lost and broken. He is a spiritual physician who arrives when we need Him most. And many who believe they have it all together, are mostly blind to their need for redemption. However, when all seems lost, Christ makes sense.

When we come to the end of self, we comprehend redemption. And those at their wits end, facing big trials, follow the great teacher, who gave His life as a ransom for many. This all encompassing, demonstrative love, lifts the weight of our burdens, as we leave them at the cross. And redemption is a process that can take time. So we commit to carrying our cross, just as Jesus carried His.

The moment we come to Christ and receive the Truth, our transformation begins, lifting us above the past. We overcome by the blood of the Lamb and the word of our testimony (Revelation 12:11). Now, as God's children, we see with new eyes, attuned to His image. It is here that we discover great joy and freedom for our soul.

How do we carry our cross? We continually confront our truth with The Truth. We face our weaknesses and shortcomings, sharing our story with humility. We understand that redemption is a daily deliverance from sin and shame, a process that rewrites our narrative while embracing our imperfections.

Knowing we are redeemed by the blood of Christ, is cause for celebration! And with this gift, we are changed in our soul. As we navigate the intricate path of redemption, to lead a more authentic and fulfilling life, we begin to experience profound personal growth. Each step forward opens the door to new possibilities and opportunities.

Our redemption fosters deep gratitude. Those who have been redeemed from much have much to be thankful for. This newfound freedom and life inspire significant thankfulness. When you encounter someone excited about what God has done, it's clear they have overcome significant challenges. And a thankful heart is a testament to a heart that has been truly redeemed.

June 19

The Blessing Of Salvation

When we come to salvation, there is relief for our soul. And most of us feel a sense of reassurance, knowing that we no longer have to do life alone. And even with loved ones around, we can feel lonely. So when God enters into our living experience, there is comfort.

Salvation brings with it a sense of understanding, where everything about ourselves has resolution. We can relax and walk in a way that is significant for all the right reasons. The wrong things about ourselves, the doubts and fears about the future, all disappear as we place our trust in the Lord and His will for our lives. God is Love and we feel loved by the blessing of salvation.

And we no longer need to run the show. When the blessing of salvation comes to us, Love is the moral code that we live by. And mostly with an overwhelming sense of joy and gratitude. It fills our heart with an inexplicable happiness, knowing that we are loved, accepted, and forgiven. This joy transcends our circumstances and provides an unwavering source of strength and contentment.

And while many struggle to give and receive love daily, when salvation comes, the doors swing wide open for new love to form and multiply. The blessing of salvation offers liberation, from guilt and shame. It has the power to save, transform, and guide us individually, toward a more meaningful and righteous existence.

And the blessing of salvation requires repentance. With repentance comes a transformed heart, turning away from sin and toward the fullness of God's grace. Now with salvation, we embrace a deeper spiritual journey. Have you received the blessing of salvation? Are you living with a newness in every step, and hope at any stage? Do you understand what it feels like to be saved?

When we walk in the blessing of salvation, we rejoice in leading a life characterized by love, compassion, integrity, and service to others. And when we embrace the principles associated with salvation, we notice apparent positive changes that impact our lives for the better.

The blessing of salvation is assurance of God's Love that provides comfort, along with a desire to live life with purpose, intention and confidence. Because we are saved, our faith, commitment, and relationship is secure. We can do more, as we hold a sense of peace that dispels all doubts within.

June 20

Step Out To Find Out

Step out to find out that God will meet you and bring a new start to your dreams. Leave your comfort zone, to discover the hidden treasures in the beyond. And when you step out into new experiences, knowledge and opportunities, miracles happen, empowering you to grow, learn, and succeed in ways you never thought possible.

Change can be intimidating. But you do not have to go it alone. When you walk with the living God, your prayer is an enormous helper. This communication aids in letting go of fear, embrace the unknown to explore and understand the world around you.

And when stepping out, you will likely discover failure is a stepping stone towards success. When you try something new, you are bound to face obstacles. However, with guidance from the Holy Spirit, these can be minimized. It's important to listen to the direction that God provides. Where there are setbacks, you will need to adapt to new strategies. The goal is to keep moving forward with resilience and determination.

And stepping out to find out, requires pushing boundaries and challenging limits. It is through bold actions that we discover our true potential. With every achievement, a testament to our courage, perseverance, and unwavering determination, in unleashing creativity, innovation, and passion.

Finally, stepping out is not a one-time event. It is a lifelong journey. So don't forget to celebrate your successes, no matter how small they seem. And remember to embrace accomplishments with gratitude and humility. Ask God to open new doors for you today and take the next step to embark on a journey that will transform your life with possibilities. Embrace the unknown and let the adventure unfold. Step out to find out.

June 21

Are You A Truth Seeker?

Are you a seeker of The Truth? Countless people are vying for attention. And in this vast landscape of information all around us, it can be a challenge to discern fact from fiction, truth from lies. However, when we walk with the living God, and rely on the Holy Spirit for direction, we have the tools to navigate with confidence and accuracy.

We must have our wits about us at all times. Especially as we develop the ability to discern the lie from the truth. The goal is to become skilled in navigating life's complexities. And because every choice impacts our journey, it's important to keep things in perspective, and not think that we are more than we truly are, which appeals to the ego, versus the spirit of truth. Humility is required.

The lie is tricky. It sneaks in when you are not paying attention. And many are deceived and do not know it. However, when we hold and honor God's Word, we have a message that reveals the whole story. This is the reality of The Truth, passed down through the ages. It has always been with us. We are now only experiencing it, in a new way, and in an advanced time.

Our time on Earth is limited. And as seekers, we can grasp that we must be patient in tribulation. We know that matters we face and go through may be very painful and difficult, however, we stand on God's Word as we seek to understand. And with understanding, there is protection and guidance, along with the recognition of evil. Our eyes are open to see both sides of matters.

Thankfully, we have an example. Because God loved us, He sent His Son, Jesus, as a ransom for our souls. This brings glorious freedom and relief from darkness and deception. When we put Jesus first and ask ourselves, 'What would Jesus do?', we are on the right path to discovering the Truth. The Holy Spirit will provide the answers you seek—ask, and you shall receive.

June 22

Loneliness And Poverty

When you are fighting and battling with an injury, everything is more difficult. You're not going to be so strong, as you navigate, protecting that injury. And when you have a poverty mindset, or if you are consumed with loneliness, you will likely make poor choices and have difficulty flourishing. So loneliness and poverty go together, in making poor choices.

When you are broken, your choices often reflect that brokenness, making them more difficult. In contrast, when you are whole, you are battle-ready, moving forward with strength. This makes the journey exciting, effective, and rewarding. And in that, there is beauty.

We must let go of what hinders us. Perhaps you live with a feeling of lack or the belief that you do not measure up or have what you think you should. This type of thinking causes negative results. So if you want to break the chains of negativity, you must let go of loneliness and poverty.

In God's Love, there is strength and beauty. And it's the simplest things that we try to get back to, when we notice that much is lost and broken. Like basic kindness, necessities and the understanding and feeling that we are loved. Without these, we struggle further.

With God in the center, we are rich and never alone. We live and do by the grace of God. And life flows in perfect timing and wonder. Our journey may not be elaborate. It might be simple. However it can be pleasing and effective. And because we have understanding, our journey is bountiful.

You can let go of loneliness and poverty, knowing that you have free will and the power of choice.
Pray and invite the Lord in today. And receive His love. Commit your way to The Truth. You must learn and know who you are in Christ. Reading the Word will help you with this. Also, let go of any root of rejection. Have you been rejected? If so, this may be one reason you struggle with loneliness and poverty. Begin a new way today. You will reap the rewards of following the pathway out of the muck and mire, while having fun at the same time. The choice is yours.

June 23

Faithful And True

What does it mean to be faithful and true? It means that we are loyal, trustworthy, and committed to relationships, promises, and principles. It means that we have hope and courage. When we are faithful and true, we also possess a gentle and honest reply. And being faithful and true, we do not give up easily, instead, we have what it takes to persevere through trials with understanding.

Being genuine and honest means being sincere in our words, actions, and deeds. It requires that we neither deceive nor mislead others. We are authentic, not pretending to be something we are not. Our dreams are rooted in truth, and as we truthfully discern our own motives, we move forward in a way that creates love, light, and lasting beauty. While we may test the waters, with practical experience, we grow into a higher design.

People go through difficult experiences, some so traumatic they feel unreal and nearly impossible to overcome. However, by staying true, we can approach these matters with wisdom. If we question acts of violence, disrespect, or dishonesty but fail to take action, we delay the promise of meaningful change.

No one can serve two masters, so we must choose wisely and be prepared to do what is right. If we fail to stand up and make the right choice, we neglect our own soul and forfeit a great blessing. Hopefully, when we stray, we recognize it and find our way back before it's too late.

When we act in favor of the good, we will find it. By choosing to be 'faithful and true,' we walk with integrity and loyalty. It's about being someone others can rely on and trust, and it involves a strong moral and ethical commitment in how we conduct ourselves. In living this way, we reflect the very character of God, bringing light and hope to those around us.

June 24

Your Lasting Treasure

It's natural to reflect on the impact you've had on others and the legacy you will leave behind. And the way that you will be remembered, hinges on the impressions you've made in your life. Your actions, words and the way you treat people, really matter. All of these are a reflection of your character and your values. What will be said about you when you are gone?

Scripture says in Jeremiah 29:11, "I know the thoughts and plans I have for you, says the Lord. Plans to prosper you and not to harm you. Plans to give you hope and a future."

Walking with the Lord blesses not only our present and future but also eternity. Your impact shapes what people will remember about you. Those who know you intimately may reflect on your kindness, compassion, and how you made them feel. They may recall your generosity and support during difficult times. Colleagues might remember your work ethic, contributions to projects and causes, leadership skills, problem-solving abilities, and the way you inspired through your actions and dedication—or simply the warmth and positivity you brought to their lives. For this reason, always walk with love at the center.

Ultimately, what people say and think is a reflection of the heart. Whether you are an employer, employee, homemaker, activist, volunteer, mentor, or advocate, your efforts to improve the lives of others leave a lasting impression. The legacy you build through love and service becomes your lasting treasure, one that continues to inspire long after you're gone.

What will remain when you are gone? Are you trusting the Lord to light your way and direct your path? If not, now is the time to change. Thankfully, God is in the restoration business. So if you've been walking in a way that's less than stellar, now is the time to make things right. Invite the Lord into your heart with a simple prayer and nurture your relationship with the living God. It's the relationships we nurture and the contributions we make that reveal our lasting treasure.

June 25

The Age Of Sorrows

Are we in an age of sorrows? Sorrow is different from pain. Pain refers to physical or emotional discomfort, distress, or suffering caused by injury, illness, or loss. And sorrow is an emotional response to loss, disappointment, or grief. It involves deep sadness, regret, or melancholy often triggered by death, separation, failure, or unfulfilled expectations.

An 'Age of Sorrows' is marked by major challenges, including moral decay and existential crises. It is a time of trials such as wars, natural disasters, societal upheavals, and spiritual crises. In such an age, ethical values decline, and people grapple with questions about existence and meaning.

Our issues begin within humanity's soul, everyday. And if we don't face our own personal matters, we contribute negatively to the whole and we suffer. We will always have pain and sorrow. And history is often punctuated by cycles of prosperity and adversity, where periods of growth and enlightenment are followed by periods of struggle and introspection. We understand this.

Scripture says in Romans 8:22, "For we know that the whole creation has been groaning together in the pains of childbirth until now".

This shows us that our groaning has been since the beginning of time, however we must look within ourselves, to understand the complexities of our collective journey in our present time. When we experience periods of decline, we can find meaning in the face of our challenges, as we discover where and when we have gone wrong. We must turn and change direction. We need a contrite heart, a heart of repentance and awareness to confront mistakes.

Is it too late to change? Are we capable of changing? Turning the tide, begins with each one of us individually. It starts in our hearts, and is moved forward by standing up for transformation. Are we committed to the betterment of society? Love is the answer and we must consider future generations and what we are leaving for our children. This is what it means to be aware, awake and repentant. And repentance is required for resilience and hope, amidst any adversity.

June 26

Pray For Others Today

In a world characterized by individualism and self-interest, the act of praying for others is a powerful gesture of empathy and goodwill. And prayer is a form of positive energy. So when we direct our daily prayers to God, towards another, there are benefits that ripple beyond self.

Studies have shown that prayer and positive thoughts contribute to reduced stress, improved coping mechanisms, and better health outcomes. And when we pray for another's well-being, we reinforce the bond of our shared humanity. This alone brings spiritual and emotional healing.

And when you don't know what to pray for, this is the time to bless someone near to you. Praying for another, nurtures empathy and the ability to understand feelings. When we take a moment to lift someone in prayer, we acknowledge their struggles, joys, and aspirations. This deepens our connections while cultivating compassion.

In person prayer is powerful. Whether in relationships, or larger societal contexts. And when we pray for loved ones, friends, and even strangers facing adversity, we express our solidarity as well as our support in tangible ways. This fosters trust and intimacy, creating a foundation of mutual care and understanding. So it is good to come together and pray.

Scripture tells us in Matthew 18:19-20, "Again I say to you that if two of you agree on earth concerning anything that they ask, it will be done for them by My Father in heaven. For where two or three are gathered together in My name, I am there in the midst of them."

Prayer provides reassurance and allows us to tap into the energy of goodwill and positivity. By looking beyond our own concerns and acknowledging the blessings and struggles of those around us, we enrich our spiritual lives. And a prayer of gratitude for the people and blessings in our lives is especially powerful, as it strengthens the soul. It requires humility and is an act of love that honors and recognizes the source of all blessing. So, remember to pray for others today.

June 27

Make An Eternal Difference

In our fast-paced world, immediate gratification takes precedence. And often we do not consider making an eternal difference until it's too late. The idea goes beyond a lifetime, and involves the long-term effects of our actions on individuals.

And no one can see the future, but Lord willing, we can attempt to look into it. As we live in the moment, outcomes are not always apparent. For instance, breaking the chains of child abuse, or addiction, resets the trajectory of lives, for generations to come. And in the midst of these types of situations, there's simply evidence of something new. Further, inventors might invent something that changes the future. The task is done in faith, as the outcome is unknown.

Do you want to make an eternal difference for good? Then stay motivated in the direction of love. Whether promoting education, advocating for social justice, or fostering compassion, clarity of purpose and purity toward love, will anchor your efforts. And your birth in time, is not by accident. Everything you do, potentially has a lasting impact. So it's up to you, how big that impact will be.

Are your endeavors working toward a better world? You are here to share your knowledge and skills generously. And whether mentoring, teaching, or leading others to discover their own potential, you are born to effect and enact positive change. So live your dream and create, and cultivate meaningful relationships with family, friends, and community members.

Making an eternal difference is a deliberate and sustained effort to create a legacy of positive change. Every action, no matter how big or small, has the potential to ripple outward and make a lasting impact on future generations. And when the Lord is at the helm of your heart, you are well able to chart a course that makes an eternal difference for the good of all mankind.

Scripture says in Matthew 6:33, "But seek ye first the kingdom of God, and his righteousness; and all these things shall be added unto you."

June 28

No Respecter Of Persons

When the Lord gives gifts, He gives them for keeps. And He does not favor people in the giving. No one is above another, although our society places precedence on those who may be more qualified and educated. God is no respecter of persons. And He uses the weak and the foolish things to confound the wise. [1 Corinthians 1:27]

In Acts 10:34, Peter opened his mouth, and said, "Of a truth I perceive that God is no respecter of persons." This statement indicates that God does not show favoritism or partiality based on external factors such as wealth, social status, race, or any other human distinctions. This concept underscores the idea that all people are equal in the eyes of God.

The Lord judges individuals based on their character, actions, and faith, rather than on superficial or worldly criteria. And God's grace and justice are impartial and fair to all, regardless of one's background or circumstances. God is Love and His love abounds to all who seek His face and desire to live a life in fellowship and service. A life of integrity in Christ.

Because of this, we need not place certain people higher than others. We must acknowledge our shared humanity, knowing that every person has value and is worthy of respect. Have you preferred someone over another in your story? Perhaps someone preferred another over you in a situation. When this happens, it does not feel good.

Our relationship with God matters. And when we acknowledge The Truth and walk in a way that honors the value of all people equally, we welcome the favor of God in our lives. We are not perfect. However, we can follow the lead of Christ, to know that there is a way that is beyond our natural tendency to favor the rich, or those who may have achieved some level of notoriety.

Knowing that the Lord is no respecter of persons, brings comfort to those who might feel inadequate or unable to be used by God for great things in their lifetime. And based on this, anyone who receives Christ, to acknowledge and fellowship with the Lord, can effectively listen and honor the Holy Spirit and move in a way that honors God, for His purposes, in all things.

June 29

Freedom In Christ

Freedom is something that most everyone desires. People want to live the way they choose. To go where they want, when they want. However, when we come to Christ, chances are, we have not been free. We have lived with the chains of life, in a worldly fashion.

When we live for material things, money, or power, dissatisfaction arises. This is because the things of this world are not the things that bring freedom and peace to our souls. Neither do they bring security. And if we are honest, we can see that what does produce peace and freedom and security, are quite the opposite of what the world offers.

Life is terminal and how we live is important. When Christ comes into our hearts, our sins are no longer a burden that we carry. We are no longer weighed down. And because of this, we are ready and inclined to serve and acknowledge the Lord wholeheartedly. Our willing obedience, devotion, and alignment with God's will, is what brings personal freedom and joy.

In Romans 6:22 scripture says, "But now that you have been set free from sin and have become slaves to God, the benefit you reap leads to holiness, and the result is eternal life."

Are you free today? Free from what others think or say about you? Free to understand that your days are numbered? Are you free to make an impact for the time you are in? Your freedom is not an invitation to live autonomously or selfishly. It is a call to live a life yielded to God.

Freedom in Christ allows you to rise above your circumstances and live in peace, which stems from your trust in God. Surrendering to God's purposes brings true, complete freedom. For example, Paul was in prison yet still experienced the spiritual freedom of the Holy Spirit. And as you welcome God's authority into your life, you will increasingly reflect the character of Christ, which leads to genuine freedom.

June 30

The Light Of Hope

There is a light that shines far differently from the lights that shine when the cameras are on. This light shines brightly in the darkness—it is the light of hope. In the depths of darkness, where despair often reigns, this light has the power to pierce through even the thickest shadows, offering comfort in times of distress.

Jesus said in John 8:12, "I am the Light of the world. Whoever follows me will never walk in darkness, but will have the Light of life."

The light of life in Christ is not a passive presence; it actively drives us to seek solutions. It is the answer in darkness, a guide on a rough road, and the glimpse at the end of the tunnel. This light shines brightest through adversity, acting like a lifeline, offering us strength to keep moving forward. When the world seems bleak and challenges feel insurmountable, it's crucial to recognize the light as it reveals the way.

Jesus is the light of our salvation, and His resurrection is the cornerstone of our hope, signifying victory over death. Through faith in Christ, we experience the indwelling of the Holy Spirit, empowering us to live according to God's will and purposes. This becomes the foundation for living in love, with faith guided by the anticipation of God's promises.

Scripture says in Romans 15:13, "May the God of all hope fill you with all joy and peace as you trust in Him, so that you may overflow with hope by the power of the Holy Spirit."

Hope is a light that burns brightly within us, fostering resilience as it is uniquely shaped by our personal experiences and aspirations. It is found in the embrace of loved ones, in quiet moments of reflection, or in the pursuit of a cherished goal. A revelation of this light ignites faith, empowering us to believe in God's higher purpose.

When we have the light, we have hope—and as long as there is hope, there is the possibility of overcoming any obstacle and emerging from any darkness. The light of hope reminds us that, even in our most challenging moments, there is a reason to believe and strive for a better tomorrow.

JULY

July 1

All Is Vanity?

Life is a breath. We are here one day and gone the next. And how we spend our time, and what we do and say, is important. We build families, serve communities, build businesses and create art. However, we need to check ourselves, because without the Lord in the lead, our influence and service to humanity is all vanity. And God knows what is for our highest good. He is sovereign.

We are here to redeem the time. And most have much to accomplish. Hopefully, we contribute, participate, and offer perspective. And each utilizes free will, to make both healthy or grave choices, depending on the circumstances. And as we chart our direction, we notice the choices we make have repercussions. Here, we become keenly aware that we don't hold all the power.

So we do not need to strive for the wrong things. Fortune, fame, or glory, is not everything in this temporary life. What is good, is to look inwardly and to seek the Lord with your whole heart and learn to hear His voice. And Ecclesiastes 1:2 tells us that everything we do is "vanity".

Empty, futile, and short-lived, because everybody dies. Therefore, much of what we do on Earth is vanity.

Our vision is limited. And because we each experience legacy differently, we may falsely think or believe that we are the author, director, or finisher of our experience or existence. However, John 21:18 tells us, "Very truly I tell you, when you were younger you dressed yourself and went where you wanted; but when you are old you will stretch out your hands, and someone else will dress you and lead you where you do not want to go." This sounds unpleasant, but it is our reality.

And Scripture says in Psalm 119:37, "Turn my eyes from looking at worthless things; and give me life in your ways." Here the Psalmist offers up a heartfelt prayer, acknowledging the potential to become distracted, and to look at that which is not beneficial or prosperous.

July 2

Mix And Shine

The world needs you to be the light amidst the darkness. So, get into the mix today. Because when you get in the mix to shine, this is how you demonstrate Christ's Love, which at best, means that you are able to love the unlovely and walk humbly with the Lord.

Are you a loving person who values mercy and justice? Because Micah 6:8 says, "He has told you, O man, what is good; and what does the Lord require of you, but to do justice, to love mercy, and to walk humbly with your God?"

When we follow what the Lord requires, we become refined. And daily, we grow further refined, having more grace than yesterday, to embrace situations where we shine forth in Love. And we do not need to fear or avoid people because they are difficult. Our growth is through direct connection and conflict. And walking in Love, we have much to offer.

And people need inspiration along with a helping hand. So, we are here to lead by example. Humility is required.

We may offer encouragement; however, we do not want to cast our pearls before swine, remaining in places that are less than desirable. Also, we do not need to circle with people who are always pristine in their behavior and thinking. When we attempt to be around only those who appear to have it all together, we miss the mark.

So remember that Love is patient and kind. Especially with those who appear a bit rough around the edges. And we can be patient, because we have our own rough edges as well. However, we might get into the mix and say, "Oh no Lord, I can't do this!" But this is not true. Because we are light, we can do this. We must bring the light of Love.

Being Christian brings with it a covering. And welcoming the Holy Spirit into your heart brings superior direction, supernatural healing, wisdom, and protection. So, when you get in the mix, and take it to the streets, you are equipped to step out into the places where people have real needs. These are the gritty places. And this is how to make a difference.

July 3

For Such A Time As This

You were born for such a time as this. And all that affects you regarding your personal development is precisely right for Love to shine through you now.

Perhaps you are unhappy at your job, or you are going through a health crisis. Maybe you are required to move to a new location and you feel very alone. Certain times come and you may wonder; "Why must I go through this situation?" This is the time to seek the Lord. Because God wants to share the journey with you.

There will always be difficulties to conquer. And the best way is to face the dark places as times of testing. You are here to bring the light. So trust there is a higher purpose going through the trials that come and go. Share your concerns via prayers for guidance and strength. It's essential to learn to wait and hear the still small voice of the Lord. And while waiting, stand on the Word of God.

The steps of a good man or woman are ordered by the Lord. (Psalm 37:23) So each step we take, along with things we go through, are especially on purpose to develop, in us, Christlike character. To make us brilliant, like a shining diamond.

You were born for such a time as this. And in the grand scheme of things, connection with people is important. Every interaction is a reflection, as in a mirror. There is no need to be pushy with people in hopes of seeing them change. Instead, take the focus off others and shine the light on your own metamorphosis.

Finally, some changes take longer. So, don't give up or give in during the hard times. God's timetable is different from yours. Remain patient, and in faith. And pray for strength to go the distance, because you were born for such a time as this!

July 4

Get Your Joy Back

How can we have great blessings and somehow lose our appreciation for them? Is it boredom? Could it be that the days all seem and feel the same? Why do we switch from gratitude and Love, to indifference or disdain?

Sometimes we take for granted the many wonderful gifts and experiences available to us. Perhaps we lose sight of the good? Or maybe we become familiar, to the point of everything appearing mundane. Have you lost your appreciation?

Scripture tells us that "it is the little foxes that spoil the vine". Bit by bit, fear and doubt can creep into our thoughts and steal the joy of daily living, especially if we are not careful to pay attention. And when this occurs, it's common to become self-consumed.

When we are self consumed, the beauty around us fades. And when we lack appreciation for life's many blessings, we need to ask ourselves, what does it take to get back on track? The first step is to check our faith. It's also necessary to get to the root of a matter, because a loss of appreciation is often rooted in a deeper issue.

The path to gratitude requires us to face Truth. Is it time to get your joy back? If you feel at a loss, unappreciative and downtrodden, get back on the gratitude train. And take a look within, to see where you may have missed the mark in some area.

Finally, remember Christ is our Cornerstone. And if you have not yet, invite the Lord into your heart with a simple prayer. Simply say, "Jesus, come into my heart. I am a sinner and I believe you died to set me free". "Show me where I have missed the mark and forgive me." This is how miracles happen and new joy is revealed.

July 5

Hold The Bright Light

Holding the bright light requires embracing the depths of your being. It is a life of excellence. And in this world of dichotomies, with good and bad, the light and the dark; we need to embrace and face the darker parts of ourselves, in order to experience the bright light.

And many avoid looking in the mirror, to make an honest assessment. Some have little desire to expose and release imperfections and errors. Mainly, because facing these can be painful. For this reason, some walk on, while avoiding deep seated issues and hurts.

But we need to become accustomed to taking time with God to face the Truth. And as we transfer our concerns over, from our personal management into God's higher management, we notice an increase of happiness, clarity and health. This is an important and necessary undertaking. Especially if we want to hold onto the valuable sparkle that shines through our eyes. And although repenting doesn't seem like a happy place, it does produce happiness.

Do you need to take responsibility for your actions today? When we confess our sins to God and to one another, we are healed. In contrast, you might live the status quo, where a veil falls over our experiences and learning. Maybe there is darkness or sadness?

We need to feel our pain and let it go. And countless do not like to look at places where they could benefit from correction. Also, the arrogant tend to think they know it all. However, there is something we miss when we are like this, because there is more.

So grow in Love today, and bring your concerns to the Cross, where the Light shines forth, rightly bringing you an enjoyable reward. Commit your way to The Truth, where a brilliance bubbles over and produces Light. And when you have the Light, it is because of something that you understand to be good in your life. This is a pure heart before God.

July 6

The Gift Of Insight

There are traps that attempt to enter through the phone, computer, or the door. And if we are not awake, we can easily make costly mistakes. And most of us have encountered something dangerous at some time. Hopefully, we have protections to alert us, and defenses like doorbell cameras and home alarms, to keep us safe. But what about the warnings within, that protect us from big trouble? If we are not paying attention, we might miss great leadership. And this can be detrimental to our good outcome. If we are not listening to guidance, there may be added pain.

Insight is guidance that comes from God. It is more than intuition. Insight produces clarity. And insight is a gift of the Holy Spirit. Insight can keep you from walking into the wrong places and connecting with unsavory people. Insight is God's perfect timing in all things. It is a knowing within, that can save from a lifetime of regret.

And to receive insight, we must be right with God. Common sense is necessary, but it is not the same as insight. Insight is the still small voice that knows what is to come, which way to go, and how to get there. Insight can be like a flashing signal, or a warning light that brings you to safety. Insight is the capacity to gain an accurate and deep intuitive understanding.

We have important choices to make. And, once you receive the idea that God is all knowing, and for your benefit, (just like protective software) you will gain clarity and wisdom with guidance toward the best possible outcome. And to receive insight, we must know that we are not completely in control. We have free will, but there is a greater intelligence at work. Therefore, we must use free will, in accordance with this Great Intelligence, knowing our steps are ordered.

The gift of insight is for the brave heart. It is not for weak minded people. And if we are not able to discern the still small voice within, likely, we have not yet let go of being in charge! So today, acknowledge God's sovereign authority in your life. And finally, if you have been partaking in evil doings, you must repent and turn away. Christ came for this reason. For the salvation of your soul and for guidance into the heavenly realms. So receive Him today for guidance and insight.

July 7

Respect And Admiration

Every person's story matters, regardless of their successes or failures. And as God's children, each person is worthy of respect. To foster this, we should strive to become better listeners and recognize the good in others. Furthermore, healthy individuals admire greatness and goodness in others rather than focusing on themselves, encouraging mutual admiration.

We live in a world where there is a spirit of death. And the thief comes to kill, steal, and destroy. (John 10:10) So the spirit of death is directly opposed to the Spirit of Life. For this reason, we sometimes make grave choices. However, the more we walk in the Light, the better we are at respecting ourselves and others.

Furthermore, people are faulty and at times needy. For this reason, we must honor others and forgive quickly. And Love sees the best in other people. Love encourages admiration and respect. Therefore, when a person desires more respect, first they must respect their own soul.

Self-respect and respecting others is a choice we make in little ways every day.

Admiration is respect, multiplied. It is the ability to recognize greatness in another human being. And admiration is established by one's ability to make smart choices. We might notice a level of accomplishment or motivation. Maybe it's a sweetness that exists. But the reasons we find people admirable are unique. Including how a person carries themselves around others. But admiration should never be about one's outward appearance alone. We might admire someone who looks or carries themselves well, but it's the inner man or woman that we need to value and consider.

So, amidst all the disrespect we see around us, we must remember to find a few things to admire in others. And when it comes to putting your life into another hands via relationship, it's best to be sure there is mutual respect and admiration in all of its fullness.

July 8

You Are Meant To Shine

Our faces are meant to shine. And every day we're given a gift. However, the older we get, the more challenging it can be to rise and smile with a will to live. Depression is real and plenty struggle with it. So we need to encourage ourselves. And when we hope in the Lord, we are better able to withstand the pull of darkness. We know the Earth is not our home.

And self-centeredness is a poison that will remove the shine from your eyes. It's also a lack of trust in God that demonstrates that faith in self alone, will eventually fail. However, faith in God propels us forward in strength. Have you noticed drone images of people moving about below? Looking from above, we appear like ants. Gathering in groups and wandering about. We could be squashed in a moment! And this is very possible. So remember, we are small.

And we see people having difficulties. We also see those who go before us, leave too soon. For this reason, occasionally, we are beaten down by sorrow and feel unenthusiastic. Yes, there will be grief. Yet, when we hope in Christ, who perpetually demonstrates how to live victoriously; we understand what is to come, as we ascend onward.

When we hope in the Lord, we take our mind and focus off self. We learn that what we can do for someone else, is what causes us to thrive. And we shine because we focus on being a blessing. Further, Christ demonstrates how to love one another, as well as how to be helped ourselves. In Him we find joy and delight in the darkness.

You are meant to shine. And things of this world are passing away. So put your hope in the Lord today, and not in the things of this world. And the light of Love, hopes in you, fondly. So remember that a good state of mind to hold, is what you can do to bless someone else. Or how you can make a difference. With the correct mindset, you will be joyful.

July 9

In The Refiners Fire

Real change comes from God, within our soul. And when we are born again, we are a new creation. And though we are the same person, we are not the same. We are in the refining fire. Being refined daily, to grow and gain important understanding.

We are unusual people, who sometimes do things we never would have imagined. And when we step into something, we reap the consequences. However, when these moments come, we need not feel bad or downtrodden about ourselves, because we are in the refiners fire. Instead, we can share the situation with the Lord. Also, scripture tells us to confess our sins to one another, so that we may be healed.

And some matters rise up that appear out of character. They may be little lies, or gossiping to a neighbor. Whatever the case, when we are tired, we tend to be more vulnerable. And because we miss the mark from time to time, we should not give up on God. Or feel that we have failed and allow failure to break our connection. We can strive to do better next time, knowing that we grow from glory to glory, by the Spirit.

In the refiners fire, we are being changed. And there are times when this feels good, and other times when it does not feel so good. Therefore, when matters come that make us feel less than great about ourselves, we must immediately embrace the forgiveness that Christ offers. Our evolution is to become better going forward.

So, when you fall, do not spend time feeling bad about yourself. Instead, freely receive what Christ died to give you. Freedom. And with repentance you grow. Prayer is powerful. So pray and ask God to strengthen and teach you. Love is the most excellent way. And this life is a learning experience for Love. So never stop learning how to Love well. You can do it.

July 10

The Heart Speaks

Have you listened to your words? Or paid attention to your thoughts? Have you considered where they are from or how you are transpiring to others? Have you noticed what is created through you? Because, "out of the mouth, the heart speaks."

We are living and breathing, in the flesh and have one body and can feel our skin. Along with our inner emotions. And having an awareness of thoughts and words is important, because "in the flesh" we are complex. We have a heart that beats, and a "heart" we refer to as our spirit. And our thoughts perpetuate our movements wherever they lead. While our words impact our destiny.

When we are receptive, we grow exponentially. And when the flesh ceases to carry us, what then? Does our spirit have more to learn? Have we mastered or harnessed our experience, toward the next level of being? Perhaps enlightenment outside of the body? These are intelligent questions for the spiritually receptive person.

In the beginning was the Word. And words are influential and significant in showing us who we are. Are you condescending, demeaning or unjust with your words? Check your heart and listen to your thoughts. Do you have a mouth full of defeat? Or perhaps perversity that says, "I think nothing of profanity. Everyone does it!"

Scripture says in Matthew 12:34-40, "For out of the heart, the mouth speaks. The good person out of his good treasure, brings forth good, and the evil person out of his evil treasure, brings forth evil." So your words speak of the state of your heart.

So consider the root of your words today, and pay attention to your thoughts. Listen to what comes out of your mouth. This is where the path begins. Deep within, where thoughts enter the world through words. Words show people who you are.

July 11

Bear Each Other's Burdens

People can be quick to write other's off, at the first sign of dysfunction. However, God calls us to be long-suffering and to bear each other's burdens. And some do not know what long-suffering means. This is one reason why so many people are lonely today. They fail to take into consideration their own need for redemption and metamorphosis, and are unable to provide others the same necessity to improve.

And when people are given room to grow, there is hope for lasting friendship. We don't expect perfection, however, we can offer mercy. Additionally, it may be easier to be long-suffering with a person who is not in our close proximity, because being around someone daily, makes for an increase in challenges, including control issues.

Also, mental illness runs rampant in our society, along with bipolar disorder and narcissism. And each person's history is somewhat of a mystery. But Love is a redemption story. So it's best not to be too quick to judge, but instead, quick to forgive. By offering grace to another, the darkness is canceled out. We need patience and mercy, and to pray for those who demonstrate a need, while not allowing the darkness to invade the light of our souls.

And when people are difficult with each other, as they sometimes are, the heart that gives Love, is filled with light. So do the best you can. Also, Love is patient, and kind. It is gracious. So mercy is the principal thing. Because no one does everything right all the time. And since we have redemption, we are equipped with an abundance of grace for others.

Finally, in every instance, we have a choice. Will my actions produce Love? Or will they cause division and pain? Boundaries are important, but not walls. We can set boundaries that respect our personhood, and those around us. But if we are not careful, boundaries can become walls. So work through matters, and get to the other side of every situation. This is how to benefit and live in a redeemed state, while not being held back by unforgiveness.

July 12

His Grace Is Sufficient

We do not know the way forward. But His grace is sufficient. And you may be dreaming of doing something new. Perhaps, you're inclined to help someone or fill a need. Maybe you are eager for something more for yourself or someone you love? Desiring to grow is good. And we can have ideas of how to get there by doing this or that. But how we arrive at what we envision, is a path that only God knows.

We have choices to make and often struggle to understand why we must wait. While the hardest part as we go, is not knowing in the present moment. Perhaps you're searching for a place of comfort. Maybe a home of your own, and every day is a waiting game. Or maybe you are not sure about which direction to go? God, who is this Great Intelligence, Loves and understands and His grace is sufficient. He will reveal The Way to you when you wait on Him.

Scripture says in Psalm 127, "Unless the Lord builds the house, the workers labor in vain."

Without the Lord to satisfy us, we often strive and stress to reach our goals. If we do not rest in God, we often miss the mark, causing more problems that can set us back. Our self-will comes into play, and our motivations might not be aligned. We may face resistance and try to make things happen on our own. While taking action can be beneficial, we do not always know what is for the highest good. There may be random matters and connections that need to be in place. Therefore, we must trust the One who knows.

Finally, the time will come, when you will see the changes you desire, transpire. And the vision may evolve as you move forward. So it's smart to hold on loosely to your ideas. Further, not knowing everything is ok. So treasure and enjoy the journey, and trust God for your good outcome, knowing that His grace is sufficient.

July 13

Through Faith And Patience

Miracles can happen in an instant. However, most come through faith and patience. And it's true that without faith it is impossible to please God. This is why scripture teaches that "faith without works is dead". (James 2:14)

Faith requires stepping out and being proactive. And we must seek the Lord, to know the best way to proceed. Sometimes we experience a miraculous development, but more often, there are indications of a miracle taking place over time. So, within the moment, we don't see the miracle. However, being proactive and patient, we see in fruition, a miracle developed in good faith.

Have you heard the saying "insanity is doing the same thing, over and over, expecting different results? Well, if we desire a miracle in our life, whether it be for health, love, prosperity, or experiences, we need to step out of our comfort zone and do something different. Prayer is the answer and the first step.

The Holy Spirit is listening. And perhaps your miracle was a healing in some area of your life. Maybe there is something that you have hoped for, for a very long time, and it's now coming to pass. Whether these marvels are instantaneous or gradual, miracles graciously abound, where we can see clearly, the hand of God at work.

Finally, miracles work for our benefit, arriving in a way where we recognize that the miracle is not of our own doing. And even though you may have been waiting for some time, please do not give up, because most miracles take time. And the timing belongs to the Lord. He brings these surprising and welcoming events to us in divine and supernatural ways, through faith and patience.

July 14

God's Perfect Timing

Delays and circumstances arise that can affect our plans. We have destinations, deliveries, people to influence, help to administer, and much hope for development. And it can be difficult to wait, while you may wonder why some changes take so long to transpire.

However, when we comprehend that our timing is not God's timing, we can let go and trust. There is no reason to become upset or full of doubt, knowing there is a higher purpose at work, for our good outcome. The Lord's timing is perfect. And as we wait through circumstances, we can be proactive, to especially not waste time.

God loves His children and as a child of God, He wants the best for you. He knows what you need even before you ask. And when you are good at listening to the Holy Spirit for direction, you will make better choices and have added clarity that brings blessings and positive results. Also, trusting the Lord when things don't go your way, is a sign of maturity.

We learn from experience that actions we take in our own strength can potentially bring negative results. And God given ideas may require delays. For instance, we might plan on selling our home or moving in the fall, but issues come up that push things back a bit for whatever reason. Or we could have our heart set on a spring wedding, and then as the season changes, the destination may have to be relocated due to weather. There are many factors that go into our outcomes, which often involve other people.

So do not become distressed when things don't happen on your timetable. You can wait and rely on God's will and perfect timing for what is to come. Because the Lord has your best interest and knows the beginning from the end. He will bring it to pass according to His perfect will for your life. Have you noticed in your life when God's timing was perfect?

July 15

Give Them What They Want?

Are you a soul on the path to enlightenment? Do you have hope for understanding? Do you sometimes wonder and ask "why?" Our actions tell us about ourselves. So if you are curious, it's likely you are seeking the motivations behind your maneuvers.

Sometimes we go along for as long as we can, before we are fed up. And that's the time when many of us give in and "give them what they want". And while every person has limits and boundaries, we learn a lot about ourselves when we stretch. We might find ourselves on the edge, holding a devil may care attitude.

There may be a need to find something out. And you may wonder, why did I fall so quickly into temptation? To find what is real? Every action has an outcome. And for countless people and especially women, it can be a challenge to say the hard things. Some feel it is easier to remain quiet and move along. And women who speak boldly are sometimes referred to negatively in society.

They are described using the "B" word. And that's not a respectful playing field, where men are revered for speaking up and women are demeaned.

Strangely, when we "give them what they want", we see that the Lord does the rest. Should we ask why? Why not! We are here to learn how to become better people. And the primary way we learn is through experience. So the thing to remember is to not be too hard on ourselves when we mess up. We can look for answers, but to grow in the inner man/woman is a greater outcome.

All of this evolution belongs to God, who is working in us. And when we fall into temptation, we must remember that matters of concern are lessons to be learned. They teach us how to be brave and better, and eventually, we grow strong to resist and stand. This takes practice and resilience. And through experience, we follow our heart with integrity. Only remember that Christ is "The Way". And in Christ, we have humility, repentance and Truth.

July 16

In The House Of The Lord

Those who are planted in the house of the Lord shall bear fruit in old age. They shall be fresh and flourishing to declare that the Lord is upright. There is no unrighteousness in Him. (Psalm 92:13)

There is significance to having a satisfied soul and a peaceful spirit. This is a person who goes through their days, without strife or fear. They do not look outward for things to complete them, but instead, to Christ who lives in them, reconciling all things toward wholeness. And aging is not for sissies. The fact that one is old is a blessing, because many die young, before old age. And with age, likely comes wisdom.

To be planted in the house of the Lord, means to have roots that go deep in God. And there is a clarity and awareness when souls are planted in the house of the Lord. Also, to be fresh and flourishing in old age, is a gift. It comes from a purposeful sense of living, along with a complete trust in God to direct the path. Additionally, those who are planted in the house of the Lord, have a sense of service, where every day there's something valuable to give.

God desires to be known and will achieve His purposes in the world. And having the mind and body as one with the Lord, is a profound relationship. Not a surface experience. While being planted means that there is growth in visible places outwardly. And while resisting the Lord, does not assure one will die early, those who have God's Love in their heart, often shine brighter, as the Lord is the fertilizer that drip feeds the soul through trials.

Further, those who are planted in the house of the Lord will have a testimony. Their story is likely remarkable. And they tend to live longer to tell others about it. So don't waste another day. Get planted in the house of the Lord and invite the Holy Spirit to live in your heart today. Consider your story, and what God has done in your life. Especially to set you free.

July 17

Are You Mad At God Today?

Have you ever been angry at God? Perhaps your prayers were not answered the way you had hoped. Or maybe you suffered a severe loss and wondered, "How can a good God allow this to happen?" Many people, from time to time, have an underlying disillusionment. They feel let down by God and simply detached from having a personal relationship.

Some feel that they cannot trust God. Especially when they've been hurt or let down severely. And it can be a challenge to make sense of things that happen that are out of our control. However, how we respond, sets us on a path of healing or destruction. And trust can grow, when we make the first step in the direction of Love and especially forgiveness.

And while most people believe that trust is earned, God shows up when we take the first step, usually through dark days and trials. We may need to look in new ways, with eyes of faith. Usually we are at our wits end. And counseling can be a big help. Especially when we need to make sense of things that are near impossible to figure out. But the real healing comes when we seek God and recognize that we are not the Great Intelligence of the world.

And when we learn to trust God even in the midst of terrible trials, we are on a path to heightened recovery, guidance and keen awareness. Here we notice His presence and purpose in our lives. Likely, we have fought through the darkness and not succumbed to the evil we may have experienced. We have found the light.

Scripture says in Daniel 12:3, "Those who are wise will shine like the brightness of the heavens, and those who lead many to righteousness, like the stars for ever and ever."

The time you spend on Earth is temporary. What is important is the condition of your heart. So forgive today and learn to walk with the awareness of God's Love for you. And begin to lead a fulfilling life that goes beyond your wildest imagination.

July 18

Are You Using Your Gifts?

You may feel unenthusiastic about using your gifts. And it's not always easy to put yourself out there and do the hard things. There are great challenges. However, the reward shines through when you do. And your gifts and talents are unique to you.

When you are keen to live victoriously, you will give your time and energy to the manifestation of these. And many are not clear about their gifts and are not sure how to impart them to the world. They get up and go through the daily motions without a sense of purpose. And this comes with an underlying dissatisfaction.

Have you asked yourself, what are my gifts? What do I love doing? And would it please God to do this thing? These questions can help determine your happiness. And when you use your talents and gifts for good, happiness is greatly produced. In contrast, when you are not using your gifts and talents on purpose, there may be regrets. And sometimes we do not know what our gifts are, until we are fully mature. That's ok. It can take longer to get to know what truly fulfills you. The important thing is to find out, because your time is limited.

Now you may have a gift for encouraging others. Or perhaps teaching is your passion. Maybe you enjoy helping people by managing finances. Or you have a store that supplies products for daily life. Whatever the case may be, when you are committed to your calling, good things will come your way. It is essential to not waste time, or become distracted.

It's never too late to make a difference, so be brave, because the answers will come when you listen. A good place to start is with prayer. When you seek God first, good things happen. Also, reflect on what made you happy as a child and consider those interests in your current situation. It may not mean doing that exact 'thing,' but finding a niche in that area is possible.

July 19

Is Your Conscience Seared?

Can you discern right from wrong? Truth from deceit? Are you able to hear from God? If not, your conscience may be seared. And when the conscience is seared, there is a numbing in the soul, due to times the conscience has been ignored.

Having a seared conscience can be permanent. And those with a permanently seared conscience, no longer have a choice. They are too far gone. For example, someone with a permanently seared conscience could be a drunkard. Someone whose soul appears to be missing. Perhaps there was so much continued alcohol abuse, that over time, they are not the same person they once were.

A seared conscience stems from disappointments. It can be a feeling of giving up or even burnout. It is a wretched state of being that can cause anguish when not corrected. And a person with a seared conscience lacks hope. Also, the wounded heart can have a seared conscience.

Having an open mind and heart is essential to healing the burn of a seared conscience. And the first step is to listen intently and arrive at a place of humility, versus ego. A person with a seared conscience must believe that they don't know it all. And they must be open to the idea that they can be healed. And while countless individuals do not acknowledge their pain, when a person is willing to receive forgiveness, they can begin to heal. And Jesus is the answer where healing initiates with a simple prayer saying, "yes" to the Lord.

There may be many times a person has been wounded. And the repercussions of the wounds often are to hurt self or others. However, with Jesus as the Cornerstone, the person that chooses life, can be saved. This is a choice that has to be made by the individual. And reconciliation can rescue a soul, from the point of no return.

We have one life to live. So, listen to your conscience and tune into your past, present and future. It's not too late to recognize something you have been afraid to look at. You will grow when you get to know the Love of God in Christ Jesus. And having a sensitive spirit is good. Yes, it is possible to heal from a seared conscience. Turn now before it's too late.

July 20

Do You Love God?

It's one thing to believe in God, but do you love God? If you are going to meet Him one day, it might be a good idea to get to know Him, and even fall in Love. And when you love God you know it. You are witness to the many times God has shown through situations, to see that they are not coincidences, but rather synchronistic events that happen on purpose.

And certainly, God loves His children. Also, when you love God, you will enjoy fellowship with Him. It is through this give and take of Love, that the Lord becomes a soft shoulder to cry on, and a cherished friend to share the joys of life with. There is comfort as you rest assured, knowing you are never alone and that He is with you, rooting for you and holding you up, guiding your steps.

Unfortunately, some people are angry with God. Perhaps things did not go as they had hoped. Some were abused or abandoned as children, while others lost a loved one and never understood why they were taken so soon. Many question why God would allow something tragic or terrible to happen. Some choose to abandon their relationship with God, while others deny His existence entirely. Often, this stems from unforgiveness, which leads to building emotional walls.

God is relational and God is Love. It's as simple as this. And you are made in His image. And the more you acknowledge God, the more He acknowledges you. And as you trust Him and cast your cares on Him, via daily prayer, you will see His Love shine forth in your life. And when difficult matters arise, you know God is with you to provide courage.

Scripture says in Mark 12:30, "'You shall love the Lord your God with all your heart, and with all your soul, and with all your mind, and with all your strength." This is the first commandment, so it's important for your personal well-being.

The world is a dangerous place, and we encounter various forms of evil firsthand or through the news. Furthermore, each of us will face trials such as financial challenges, health issues, or difficulties in relationships and home life. However, when we love God with all our heart, mind, and soul as the first commandment suggests, we can expect the best possible outcome from a loving Father who always has our best interests at heart.

July 21

Be Your Authentic Self

In a world driven by consumerism and the constant pursuit of material possessions, it is easy to fall into the trap of mirroring other people and coveting what they have. And coveting is a desire to possess something that belongs to someone else, whether it be their possessions, achievements, relationships, or qualities.

Coveting may seem harmless at first, but it can have detrimental effects on your overall contentment. And most people are easily influenced. At least until they learn not to be. You've heard the saying "Monkey see, monkey do?" It is not uncommon to fall into this trap. Plenty believe they are authentic, when in fact they are copycatting their neighbor or some person of influence.

Sadly, when we compare ourselves to others, it can result in a never-ending cycle of unhappiness. This is because there will always be someone who appears to have more, or better things than we do. And comparing, and coveting, leads many to anxiety, depression, and a lack of self-worth. This is because their value is measured based on external ideas rather than internal qualities.

When a person loses sight of who they truly are, they become needy for external validation. And if we compromise our values, we lose our authenticity. Also, when we follow the crowd, or the influencer of the day, instead of listening to the Holy Spirit and who God made us to be, we set ourselves up for disappointment, where we often lose sight of our own goals and aspirations.

You are a unique creation. And your mind and blueprint are all your own. And you can repent today and turn from the sin of covetousness. Your energy and resources are better spent pursuing your passions and working towards your personal growth and fulfillment, rather than trying to replicate someone else's life. And true contentment comes from embracing your unique qualities while staying true to yourself, rather than trying to mold into someone else's image.

July 22

Take A Faith Vacation

Our world moves at an alarmingly fast pace. And often we find ourselves caught up in a never ending cycle of work, responsibilities, and obligations. Additionally, we receive stimuli from every angle, while the pressure to be productive and achieve success can be overwhelming. And in our relentless pursuit of dreams, visions and ideas, it's easy to overlook our well-being, which requires rest and recovery. So we need to take time out, for rest and recovery.

Now this can be a time out from responsibilities, however true recovery is time spent with God in meditation, with faith building activities, such as prayer, contemplation, and dream building. And contrary to popular belief, taking time out to rest, is not a sign of weakness, but an essential ingredient for personal growth, enhanced productivity, and overall well-being. So, to achieve optimal performance and a balanced lifestyle, take your hands off the wheel and let go.

Time spent in contemplation and solitude can help rekindle your passion and enthusiasm. And as we allow ourselves to unwind, we create a buffer that shields us from the negative effects of prolonged stress and overworking. Furthermore, by quieting our minds, we are open to hearing and direction. In contrast, if we are going all the time, busy with tasks and responsibilities, we may not be hearing and listening for new ideas that build our faith and expand our thinking.

So consider a faith vacation today, by spending time with the Lord. This is where you plan to fellowship and enjoy your time away from the routine of everyday life. Here, new dreams and beginnings are birthed. And more than just a getaway, or a day off, a time of fellowship with God, is restorative in ways that a standard vacation break is not.

Finally, great leaders understand the importance of time spent with God. They seek clarity that comes from knowing the way forward amidst the noise. This takes practice in solitude. And not only does time with the Holy Spirit produce clarity, but it heals the body and improves reasoning.

July 23

Focus On Possibilities

Where is your focus today? To find contentment in all circumstances, we need to focus on things that are true, noble, right, pure, lovely, and admirable. By doing this, we are better equipped to succeed and at the same time, keep our minds off negative influences and distractions.

There is no stopping the goodness of God and when you believe. And when we are rooted in Truth, while certain of God's purposes for our lives, there is no reason to not believe in great things. The sky's the limit, as we move from Glory to Glory, doing the small things daily.

Doing the small things daily is the key to not giving up. And sometimes, we need to expand our thinking and step out of the box, to explore new possibilities. When we do, we often discover new opportunities. The only requirement is the courage to follow our heart and do something different.

Having your heart in the right place is valuable. And when possibilities have to do with edifying others, being a blessing, and serving God in some way, along with the goal of making the world a better place, you are on the right track. However, it takes focus to persevere, because most endeavors take time to evolve and manifest into a successful reach. Also, they require a financial investment, and this can require multitasking and outside support.

But God never gives us more than we can handle. And if our mind is focused on the possibilities and our heart is in the right place, we are on track to accomplish our goals. The supply comes, and we get what we need to fulfill God's purposes. Our direction is made clear through daily prayer and fellowship with God. And with God in prayer, He answers your needs according to His will.

Are you using your gifts and talents for good? There is a world of possibility at your doorstep. So seek the Lord and consider the many ways you can do what you Love, so that you are leading a fulfilling life that is rewarding. Do not resist the Lord and spend your days as a slave to doing what you hate. God would not want that for you. God is Love and if you cannot find Love in your situation, it's time to step out in faith and do something different. Focus on the possibilities.

July 24

Rise Above Negativity

No one can serve two masters. It's crucial to recognize where your loyalty lies and understand your beliefs about yourself. We must seek fulfillment through righteous living. And when we are clear on this path, we gain the strength to rise above negativity.

Ephesians 6:10-12 says, "Finally, be strong in the Lord and in the strength of His might. Put on the full armor of God, so that you will be able to stand firm against the schemes of the devil."

Negativity can enter our lives from any angle. So we must be built up and wearing the full armor of God, because the devil is contriving and tricky. Imparting schemes that sneak into our psyche, in ways that we would not expect. It can start with a small notion, or a negative perception.

And a negative mind reveals itself through our words and actions. When we are negative, we are not believing what the Lord reveals in the Word about us. And it's normal to experience negativity from time to time, however, we need to correct our thinking immediately, when we notice this, by imparting the Truth of God's Word, to call out deception, which can turn into depression.

We can rise above negativity, to purposefully change. It is a choice, and it takes work. And the full armor of God, includes the belt of Truth, the breastplate of righteousness, the shoes of peace, the shield of faith, the helmet of salvation, and the sword of the Spirit. This is the covering we need everyday, to be battle ready. And cultivating these characteristics may take some time.

Begin now, because the battle is in the mind. Everyday, we must take into captivity to Christ, every thought and impression to ask, "What would Jesus do?" and "What would Jesus say?" The better we are at this, the more power we have to rise above negativity. Further, the more we impart scripture and what God says about us, over the lies of the devil, the better we are at walking in the Spirit.

Are you believing the promises of God today?

July 25

Contentment In Christ

In the hustle and bustle of modern life, we often find ourselves yearning for something more profound. Something that transcends our materialistic pursuits to bring lasting contentment and peace. And our relationship to the Lord is the answer to this and a guiding light where we can find solace, purpose, and inner harmony. It is in Him that we have true contentment.

When we place our trust in God, we learn the art of surrendering to the present moment. Regularly, we lay everything at the cross of Christ, letting go of past regrets and future anxieties, with the understanding that everything happens for a reason. This cultivates a sense of calm that allows us to weather life's storms, with grace and resilience.

One important key to contentment is a heart of gratitude. So, count your blessings and find joy in the simple things. And if you are searching for something to be grateful for, look and appreciate the beauty of nature, the warmth of friendships, and the unconditional love from family. With an attitude of gratitude, we shift our focus from what we lack, to what we have.

Furthermore, as we walk with Christ, we comprehend empathy, compassion, and unity. And when we magnify His Love, we are more conscious of the interconnectedness of all living beings. This awareness motivates us to spread kindness and Love. And we know that our purpose is to alleviate suffering any way that the Lord leads, especially to make the world a more peaceful place.

In order to walk in contentment and peace, we need to embrace repentance. And when we bring our flaws to God in prayer and lay them at the foot of the Cross, we receive forgiveness. Further, we are released from the burden of resentment and guilt. This paves the way for emotional healing and personal growth that allows us to emerge stronger and more resilient.

Life unfolds in the present moment. And to have contentment and peace while being fully present, we need to bring every thought into captivity to Christ. When we do this, we savor life's experiences while embracing its imperfections. Finally, we can let go of the constant need to control, and have contentment in the ebb and flow, trusting that God's divine plan is ideal.

July 26

Direction Straight Ahead

Knowing the way to go is essential when choosing important paths. And the way we know our choice and direction is ideal, is by peace. In other words, we need to have peace about our decisions. So pray, because God will direct your path when you ask and let peace be your guide.

And on this journey of pursuing your dreams, there is an undeniable force that will propel you forward. It is the power of vision. So fix your gaze straight ahead, unyielding in your determination. Strive to manifest your deepest aspirations. Your dreams are not distant fantasies, but instead, real and tangible possibilities, that empower you to overcome obstacles with unwavering resolve.

And when you encounter roadblocks, disappointments, or heartbreaks, your forward gaze acts as a compass, redirecting you toward your dreams. And like a guiding light, illuminating the darkest night, when you set your eyes firmly holding a clear vision, you discover a beacon of inspiration.

Now, throughout your day, learn to deny distractions. Because a steadfast vision nurtures resilience. And no journey to success is without setbacks. Therefore, if detours or distractions attempt to steer you off course, turn to the Lord, who is your trusted companion. In Him, you will obtain the strength to rise after every fall. Trust God's purposes for your life. And remember that success is not always a smooth ride, but an endeavor worth fighting for.

In 1 Corinthians 9:24, Scripture says, "Do you not know that in a race all the runners run, but only one receives the prize? Run in such a way that you may obtain it."

When your dream is a God given dream, you will get there. So, set your direction straight ahead. And today, remain determined and undeterred. Keep your gaze fixed on the prize. And remember that each obstacle is an opportunity to strengthen your commitment to the dream you hold dear. It is this unyielding determination that sets the stage for transformation and ultimate success.

July 27

Astounded By Grace

Grace, in its essence, is a quality that emanates from the depths of empathy and understanding. It is a gift that we don't deserve. And astounding grace, is God's unmerited favor, forgiveness, and compassion, in a world often marred by turmoil, conflict, and uncertainty.

Astounding grace enters our lives to offer kindness and forgiveness, even in the face of wrongdoings and transgressions. It is the Lord's extending hand of mercy. And grace challenges our primal instincts for retribution, while inviting us to see our potential for change. In grace we grasp that all things work together for good, and for our growth, rather than a reason for exclusion.

Astounding grace has come to us through Jesus Christ, offering us the free gift of salvation. God's timing is perfect. Romans 5:20 says, 'Where sin abounds, grace abounds much more.' Thus, there is a thread of charity woven throughout our lives. Through astounding grace, we recognize our shared humanity, and grace manifests even in our darkest moments and difficulties.

When the issues of life come along, astounding grace guides us to take the high road. Grace carries us to the next level. So we do not become downtrodden, because the grace we are offered is a new beginning. And as we navigate life's complexities, we remember that grace is a gift that we can offer to others as well, in order to uplift, inspire, and bring about positive change.

God's astounding grace brings the answers that we seek. It shows up when we least expect it and especially when we need it the most. Can you recall a time when grace entered your life, and brought hope and relief to your situation? Astounding grace is the relief that comes after the confusion. And the degree in which it shows up, is precisely the degree of faith that we have.

So give thanks today for God's astounding grace. It is the gift of redemption that flows freely, according to the Lord's perfect will and timing. This grace is a miracle. And it is astounding.

July 28

Can You Take Correction?

Many people have trouble with correction. They think of it as a negative, and take it personally, as if there is something wrong with them. However, in Truth, correction is good for us and has everything to do with our actions and thinking. Not who God made us to be. Therefore, we must remember that correction is a tool for growth, rather than a measure of our worth.

Correction helps us to become better individuals and is necessary for personal refinement. And scripture tells us, "do not let yourselves be easily offended". So when we are being corrected, we must understand that a person who is able to receive correction, is someone bound for glory.

What someone suggests, may help us to become better. And the choice is ours as to whether we will consider what is being said, and implement it? Or discard it. We can ask ourselves, "is there a motive to demolish our ideas and purposes?" Hopefully, we have enough discernment to understand what is being said. Is it coming from a good place? A person wanting to help us to become better? Or is it suggested in foolery? The choice is ours, what we take to heart.

And when we welcome correction, we welcome an idea for growth, along with excellence. And because we are able to discern the motive behind correction, we are ready for next level living. Each of us is a work in progress. So having humility and a heart that desires to grow, means that correction is a welcome friend that keeps us on the path to enlightenment and improvement.

The ability to receive correction is valuable, because corrections contribute to our personal development. And correction challenges us to step out of our comfort zones. This is how we refine our skills. And if we value others' insights and are willing to make adjustments based on their feedback, we are strengthened in our connections, while mutual respect increases.

Finally, receiving correction can be challenging, because ego, fear of failure, and the desire to maintain a positive self-image can all influence our response. And it's natural to feel defensive when efforts are criticized, or when we're made aware of mistakes. However, understanding that correction is not an attack, but rather a means to enhance our abilities, is crucial and impactful.

July 29

Do You Love People?

Love is the foundation of human connection that transcends boundaries, cultures, and backgrounds. And when you Love God, you will Love people. In fact, the more you Love God and have the Love of God within you, the better you will be at loving people. Even those who hurt you, or those who have nothing of value to offer you.

And science supports the idea that loving and being loved has tangible effects on our mental and emotional well-being. Studies show that every act of Love triggers the release of oxytocin, also known as the "love hormone". This adds to trust and connection, fostering a sense of safety and mutual support. Every loving act, whether physical touch, words of affirmation, or supportive actions, can reduce stress, anxiety, and depression.

With Love as our guide, we nurture empathy, understanding, and healthy relationships. And while most people center on family and friends and their inner circle, when we focus on the one person in front of us, whoever they may be, in every instance, we create a chain reaction that has the power to change the world. It is not always easy. Especially with difficult people.

Our journey in Love, always is a two-way street. And as we invest our time and understanding in accepting others, we grow to Love ourselves more profoundly. Whether it be partners, friends, family members, or colleagues, Love requires action and it is a choice. Also, to Love the unlovely, requires help from the Holy Spirit, where we develop greater patience, compassion, and tolerance.

So remain close to the Lord in your communication and understanding today. By doing this, you are less likely to become selfish, and more capable of cultivating a nurturing environment that encourages growth and emotional well-being. It is only by the great Love of God, that we receive grace, where daily we demonstrate affection, kindness, and respect for others, at all times.

July 30

Enjoy Your Life!

Do you have trouble enjoying your life? Perhaps your days are simply too much toil under the sun? Maybe you feel undeserving of the experiences that life has to offer? Whatever the issue, burdens will steal your joy of living, especially if you are not careful and paying attention. And many are heavily burdened with sin, while others are laden with trauma that may have occurred in their past. This pain is like a sun block, that keeps the light from entering in.

In John 10:10, Jesus said, "The thief comes only to steal, kill and destroy; but I came that you may have life, and have it more abundantly."

An unforgiving spirit undermines our confidence and wellness. Regret often arises from missed opportunities and unfulfilled desires. If someone has hurt you or you are hurting, it is essential to take your concerns to God, releasing the weight of your burdens and sins. Wasted time is common among those who do not confront their personal dissatisfaction and pain. When there is resistance to facing the truth, it can lead to even more regrets over time.

Only the Truth will set you free. And what a wonderful promise we have from the Lord who sets everything right. While we are reminded that there is a power that works to our destruction. And as we bring our matters to the Cross, they are washed away. So do not let painful issues hold you prisoner. Please don't wait. Further, it is sinful to have wasted time and even wasted years.

When we confront dissatisfaction through prayer and fellowship with the Lord, we are better able to trust and enjoy our days. Time is a gift and we are only promised the moment. So, if you are not enjoying your days, you need to ask yourself why? It's very important not to continue in a state of dullness or dissatisfaction. You must confront the darkness that is shielding you from the light.

Isn't it time to enjoy your life? The impact of a life well lived, extends far beyond your own experience. Your attitude and actions influence those around you. So enjoy your life. Jesus came to set you free. Invite Him into your pain today, and receive the forgiveness that only He can provide. You can embrace enjoyment, as you confidently move forward, without the weight of "what ifs."

July 31

Love And Understanding

We all need affection, connection, understanding and Love. And without these, something is missing. It is the recipe for contentment. And Scripture tells us in Matthew 7:7-8, "Ask and it will be given to you; seek and you will find; knock and the door will be opened to you. For everyone who asks receives; he who seeks finds; and to him who knocks, the door will be opened."

We are social creatures, created to naturally receive. And when we are out of balance, it is detrimental to our happiness. If something is lacking, we feel it. And our days are imperfect, however, one of the most poignant reasons to face our fears and embrace healing, is the fact that time moves swiftly. Our moments today, become memories tomorrow.

And things get broken for various reasons. For instance, maybe you were a child of divorce, or you did not have two healthy parents. Perhaps, it could be that the parents who raised you, had a cool or cold disposition, and rarely gave you hugs, or told you that they loved you. Or possibly, you felt as if no one was listening. A person who has never been touched, may struggle with accepting affection. These examples result in more brokenness, when not resolved.

So, to have a great life, not lacking in any way, Christ is the answer. Following Him, helps to face whatever it is that you may need. And hopefully, as you grow, you forge strong bonds and relationships that are built on shared experiences and emotions. If you are lacking, you must get to the bottom of matters and work through things, to get the proper ingredients into the mix.

Life is a precious gift and a journey filled with a myriad of experiences, emotions, and opportunities. And having the courage toward healing, helps extract the richness of every second. You can have it all. There may be pain to confront, but you can have affection, connection, understanding and Love, regardless of the challenges you face.

So, bring your situation to the Lord, He hears you. God will lead you. He will bring the ideal people into your life, at the precise time. And when you are ready to face issues, the Lord will give you everything you need to flourish and enjoy your life. You must be willing to face Truth and heal.

AUGUST

August 1

God Is Our Healer

God is great. And when we believe in His greatness, we clearly can see that He does and will do great things. He is our healer. And when we place our faith and trust in Him, we connect on a deeper level, where He heals us and brings wholeness to our broken lives.

Every person needs healing in one way or another. And healing can happen in an instant or it can take time. You may notice progress in small steps or large transformations. However, being in the land of the living, we are, and will be a work in progress. Additionally, moving mountains is a big job! So our healing requires our willingness and participation with God daily.

We are being made whole. And as we call on the Lord to breathe into us by the Holy Spirit, we receive greatly. It is the fervent prayer that avails much. So, pray with focus, and receive all that God has for you. Keep in mind that, sometimes, in some cases, healing is the transition to our heavenly home. And when this is His way, our hearts are made right for the journey.

Now while you have your mind set on healing, it is good to keep your focus on the Fruit of the Spirit. Because your interactions and circumstances reflect your state of mind and being. And as you focus on the fruit, you notice where you are growing and where you may need more practice. And the Fruit of the Spirit is, Love, Joy, Peace, Patience, Kindness, Gentleness and Self Control.

Christ is referred to as "The Great Physician" so call on the Lord today, because there is power in the name of Jesus. You are healed by faith, so listen to your heart and the Holy Spirit within you. Do not leave room for doubt, because when you do, healing will not be fully activated. Instead, be brave, and if you have sin that is holding you back, repent and clear it up. Sometimes we are healed in an instant, but it is also comforting to know that the Lord's timing is perfect.

August 2

Purpose And Reinvention

Purpose is a powerful driver. It is the meaning behind what we do and how we do it. And when we do things on purpose, we proceed for a greater reason than ourselves. Because of this, we follow through with a level of excellence that delivers beyond average results.

Now because the dream and journey takes time and never usually comes overnight, there are moments toward the goal, where we need to reinvent ourselves. And reinventing can feel like the death of one dream, and the beginning of another. But reinvention is healthy, and mostly an addition to any God given dream and purpose, already activated, through faith and hard work.

And purpose and reinvention, may be the secret to a long life and lasting joy. While there may be better ways to go forward on your journey now. One way to tell, if the time is right, is when the old ways are not working or manifesting results any longer. Is it time to take a step toward reinvention?

Sometimes we may feel as if we are losing our purpose, because we cannot see ahead when a change is coming. We might feel disillusioned, or a bit lost. However, as we contemplate a new goal, our purpose evolves too. Here we are, ready to serve the Lord and our fellow man, as we step into new endeavors to continue manifesting. We can embrace change as a welcome friend.

There is no need to despair, grow bored, or feel useless with the time you are given. We live in a changing world. So, it is essential to remain flexible to grow. And even though at times it may be painful, at any age, you can find purpose in serving humanity. So, if you are undecided on your current purpose and what it is that you can do, (perhaps you have physical restraints) there is always a way to serve. Ask the Lord to show you purpose today, and reinvent your dream.

August 3

Pray For Courage Everyday

We can never have too much courage. And there is always something challenging coming down the pipeline that we must face head on. Having strength to do the hard things is something we ought to pray for, because we need courage, to stand amidst whatever comes our way. Also, we need courage to do the right thing in the face of temptation. Or to embark on a new endeavor, or perhaps we need courage to face a physical issue, to make amends somehow.

Regardless of what the issue, courage requires strength. And courage empowers us to face our deepest anxieties and challenges head-on. Remember to pray for strength too, because confronting hard things requires a great amount of strength, which produces courage. And God is with you, to assist you, when you simply ask for courage and strength in prayer.

It's good to make peace with your need for courage, versus running from things. This is the way to experience a brilliant life. And you can't have brilliance without plenty of courage. Furthermore, it seems the older we get, the more courage we need to go through difficult matters. And if we procrastinate, perhaps believing that what we face will be easier later, we undermine our growth.

So remember today that you do not have to go through issues alone, or face giants without God's help. Be brave and pray first. Also, remember to stay positive. There may be what looks like a mountain ahead. And it's true, we can only do so much, in our own strength. But with God, we can do so much more. In Him, we can do whatever it takes to face life's mountains.

And in your moments of daily prayerful reflection, you are strengthened, with courage and determination when you pray. So, tackle the mountain, one step at a time. Here you peel off the layers of fear, by being courageous over the little things first. This is a good way to proceed. And you don't need to be a SuperHero. You only need to begin and remember that God is with you.

August 4

Cherish Your Existence

If you are in the land of the living, there is a reason for it. Your soul and the spirit within you, share your outward life experiences. Your body carries you during your time here, which is valuable and limited. And every thought you think, along with every word you speak, relates to creation. The creation of who you are, and what you are here to do. Also, how you are to grow.

Each day is a gift, and whether you are young or old, rich or poor, broken or whole, you have value and there is a significant conversation to embrace with the Almighty. You can do much, when you simply believe and appreciate each day. And our world offers an abundance of beauty. So cherish and enjoy this beauty, and the wonderful gift of life by saying, "I am a friend of God!"

The pursuit of your passions, dreams, and values, gives life its unique significance. And embracing life's marvels, allows you to cultivate gratitude, empathy, and compassion. Even amidst the challenges, every moment you live is an opportunity to create memories, forge connections, and leave a positive impact in the world. So embrace your life and approach each day with wonder.

There are things we are here to learn. And because you never know when your time on Earth will expire, it's important to connect with God. A good place to start is with gratitude and appreciation. When we focus on the things we can do to make our world a better place, we are honoring the Lord and living our best life. So, always remember to be thankful and stay true to the Lord.

Eventually, you will return to dust and your time on Earth will discontinue. And if you choose to disregard the gifts you are given, you are not going to experience your best life. Also, when time is wasted, there may be regrets later. So use your time wisely. And cherish your existence. Honor God in all you do, and experience a heightened sense of belonging that adds dimension to your life.

August 5

Practicing Non Judgment

Practicing non judgment is for all of us. And no one is without faults, so it is best for us not to judge one another, for what our eyes think that they see. Only God knows the heart. And Jesus said, "He who is without sin, cast the first stone". So let us not judge, but let us love one another.

Love is the only thing that can heal the human heart. And when we judge others, we tend to push people away. However, what is really needed is for individuals to come together. Additionally we find that by judging others, we ourselves will be judged. It's a losing situation.

In Matthew 7:4-6 Christ said, "How can you say to your brother, 'Let me take the speck out of your eye,' when all the time there is a plank in your own eye? You hypocrite, first take the plank out of your own eye, and then you will see clearly to remove the speck from your brother's eye."

It's true this world is composed of every kind of person. And creation is a beautiful tapestry of lives, all colorful and unique. And by your own example, you can be more honest and loving, just as Christ was. You only need to remember that God alone is the judge and your path is unique.

Everyday, we can enjoy each other. Therefore, keep your focus on how you can demonstrate grace. This is the way to have clarity and be better at practicing non judgment. We do this by individually embracing repentance. When we repent regularly of our own sins and faults, to receive grace, we are better able to extend grace to others. Further, when we are forgiven, we are better at forgiving others. We clearly understand the measure of grace, which is lavishly provided.

Most people believe that when this life ends, we'll stand before the Lord and have a review of our journey. Therefore, let us nurture one another into God's Love and Kingdom. We may experience right and wrong, successes and failures and more. However, there is no need to fear judgment, when the soul and conscience is clear. And because the Holy Spirit lives inside you, you can pray for Truth, to receive daily mercy, forgiveness and guidance that leads you further, into Love.

August 6

Persevere Toward Greatness

The dreams and efforts you are involved with daily, are yours for a reason. And it's true that every great accomplishment begins with small steps daily. So, don't give up. Keep going forward and rest if you need to. But persevere. Because perseverance leads to completion.

Perseverance is the key to dreams coming true. You may not have seen the results you hoped for in your 20's, 30's, 40's or even fifties, but don't give up. And if your dream is a God given dream, it is better to go to your grave giving it all you have, then to throw it away, believing it will never come to pass. Holding your hope and persevering through times of rejection or loss is very necessary.

And perseverance builds character. At times, we are producing and believing, and we cannot see the reason why we need to keep going. Perhaps we think that our efforts are futile because we did not see the results that we expected. But when we look in hindsight, we can see that faithful efforts are a character-building endeavor. Additionally, we learn not to have too many expectations.

But instead, we can remain open to whatever God is doing and what is meant for our good.

When we persevere through tough times, we gain and obtain an inner delight. We are happier and more satisfied, by pressing through and not giving up. Also, we may notice added peace of mind, because we have put forth effort toward our good outcome. Additionally, our conscience is clear, because we have upheld our belief. And in retrospect, we witness the world more eloquently.

So today, choose to meditate and pray for the best way forward, in manifesting God's greatness. Please don't give up on your dreams, or your sense of purpose. Adversity teaches us to adapt and overcome obstacles, and to emerge stronger. And your ability to learn and evolve, is a testament to your faith. So persevere and face what comes your way with courage and determination.

August 7

Wisdom Through Experience

There are times we may find it difficult to understand why we are in a particular situation, or going through something terribly strange, stressful, oppressive, or unfair. We can't see the wind through the trees. And sometimes we struggle with understanding a situation, long after it occurs.

These struggles are experiences that become our teacher. And wisdom is primarily a learned quality. Our trials encompass a vast array of experience, including physical and emotional challenges, intellectual pursuits, and moral dilemmas. There may be many things you wish were different. Things you wish did not have to happen. But those instances and situations have made you who you are today. They produce wisdom from experience, and a deeper faith within.

Now, you may think that you are in control, but you are not. You are simply passing through this earthly place. And there is a greater intelligence at work for your purpose. Further, the trials and tribulations you face, are an integral part in the process of molding and refining you. They challenge your preconceived notions and beliefs, leading toward personal growth and maturity.

And embracing uncertainty, requires humility and an openness to alternative viewpoints. You may read self help books and listen to others stories, as they describe their experiences. However, people only tend to learn bits from others. It's our own life experiences that teach us, and work together for our growth and good, as God's children.

Jesus is the Great Teacher, and the one who shows us the more excellent way. And as we take time to pray and seek God's face, we receive the answers we need to walk in wisdom. Additionally, as we embrace lessons learned from our life's challenges, we are grounded in empathy, along with profound understanding of the world, and our place in it. And this enlightenment enables us to make informed decisions, utilizing insight that contributes to the growth of our own souls.

August 8

The Still Small Voice

You think you hear the still small voice; you try your best to follow, but sometimes you miss it. Then there are those whispers we hear, that tell lies, intending to derail us and bring us down.

As believers in Christ, we do our best to be receptive as we are guided by the still small voice of the Holy Spirit within. This voice is a great treasure that we learn to tap into, through prayer and contemplation. It offers protection, guidance, direction, and wisdom. And as we follow the whispers of Truth and Love, we discover we attain better results, in our daily lives.

And paying attention to God's voice, offers insight. However, most of us, from time to time, struggle. Especially with negativity. We may become confused as to what the Holy Spirit is saying. So, it's important to become keen at identifying the whispers that are good, versus the ones that are not. We must learn to practice discernment. We do not want to quickly accept all whispers.

In Scripture, Deuteronomy 30:19 says, "I set before you life and death. Choose life."

So as we seek the still small voice of Truth, we must listen for peace. Because when God leads us along The Way, we will have peace about our decisions. And when we miss it, we experience negative results and end up with a lesson to learn. So, it is to our benefit, to hone the skill of listening to the still small voice of the Holy Spirit within. We do not need to concern ourselves with what others think, believe, or choose. Instead, we must follow God's guidance, individually.

God's guidance is valuable to your journey. More than intuition, discerning the still small voice of the Lord brings deliverance. Here we follow peace, to receive protection and direction. Additionally, the more time we spend in fellowship, the better we are at discerning His voice. Finally, clarity comes when we know and understand what the Lord says about us in His Word. Therefore, when you need more discernment, you can find the Truth in the Word of God.

August 9

Signs And Wonders

Hopefully, there comes a time, when your eyes are opened and a miracle ensues. You see with a bigger view and notice the grandeur of this world, along with the wonder, and your purposes in it.

For years, I was unable to recognize the signs and wonders in my life. My sight was dull. I did not know I was a musician or a writer. I was floating through time. Bouncing from here to there, not paying attention to much more than my carnal desires, and my need for survival. I was unaware of my purpose for being. But after meandering for some time, I found myself injured, to the point where I had to be still. And at this time, I sensed God was attempting to get my attention.

All of us from time to time, experience insights that point us in the direction that we should go. And when we are open minded and alert, we notice the signs. We may be amazed at what we are seeing and learning. However, often we don't see the signs. But they are there. And as they guide us, we experience wonders. Are there signs and wonders that you are not seeing today?

When your eyes are wide open, you experience wonders. And when you find the Truth, miracles abound. Friends, open your eyes to the signs. Believe today and see the wonders. Time moves quickly and missing what God has for you, can mean missing your destiny. Please do not say no, or ignore the good things that can come your way, when you choose to say "yes" to the Lord.

You can avoid much trouble by paying attention to what the Creator lays out, for you individually. Today, invite God to open your eyes with a simple prayer. Say, "Lord open my eyes and show me your will, for my life. Lead me in The Way that I should go. Amen."

August 10

Submitting To Authority

Serving your fellow man and having a successful level of personal strength, requires submitting to authority when needed. The teacher must first be taught. And the leader must first be led. And if we are not teachable, while unable to be led, how can we expect to be leaders and teachers?

Being a courageous person requires boldness. It involves leadership, because courageous people frequently do not follow the crowd, instead, they set out on a path less traveled. And coming under authority for a strong minded individual, is not an easy thing. The flesh wants to rise up and fight. However, the authority of God is in place for a reason. And the key to any success and being a great leader, requires our ability to submit to the authority in our lives at the proper times. And if we are not accustomed to this, we may choose rebellion and experience negative results.

It is the courageous person who blazes a trail. And each of us will be challenged by authority at some time. And this is a testing time. The authority may be our boss, the police, or perhaps a parent. However, the testing often comes, when we are prideful. And submitting to authority can be painful. This is because it hurts our flesh. Our pride is very powerful.

There is a time to stand up to authority, but not until we are first able to come under authority. Remember, that this is a test. And we will either pass or fail. All rebellion will catch up with us. However, once we pass the test, we are on our way to great relationships, and other successful life skills. So, please do what it takes, for the call of God in your life. Do it for the sake of Love.

Testing times will come and they are not easy, but you can do it. So pay attention to your feelings in every instance and say, "I can do what it takes". When we get this right, we are ready for the next step up the ladder, where the rewards are great. Especially the reward of Godly character.

August 11

Keep Moving Forward

The clock and calendar are ever marking, as we move through time and space. And all of the Earth with everything in it, is evolving. We're constantly changing, though at times it appears, we remain the same and are standing or sitting still. And because of this, it's important to not get stuck in old ways, with thoughts of despair, and/or grief over past experiences.

There is a resistance that wants to hold you back. And emotional hurts that stem from things such as broken relationships, loss of loved ones, and rejections, can be difficult to overcome. Also, there could be a spirit of depression or fear that might ensue. Nonetheless, you must press through and keep moving forward, with the intention of letting go of things that are behind you.

War, tragedies, and events that appear to come from nowhere are a shock to our system. Often, we feel a sense of disbelief. Further, many people suffer PTSD and require long term therapy due to reoccuring trauma. Yet still, we must commit to keep moving forward, as best we can.

When I was younger, I lost my brother. And at the time, I could not understand how life could keep going. I lived in depression and fear for ten years, due to a multitude of heartbreaking events. I was stuck in the past. And this did nothing to help my situation. It only delayed my healing.

What I learned is that we must feel our pain, as we simultaneously cast our care upon the Lord. Also, we need to demolish arguments and every pretense that sets itself up, against the knowledge of God. We must cast down lies. And as we move forward, we take captive every thought to Christ consciousness. By doing this, step by step, and little by little, we grow past what holds us captive.

So, keep moving forward today. And if you feel stuck, begin with a prayer. Ask the Lord to help you and lead you in the way that you should go. Don't be afraid to feel your pain. The Lord is for you, as your best friend. He will help you overcome every obstacle, as you rely on Him.

August 12

Your Grand Adventure

This is your grand adventure. And we come into this life, our little bodies, in need of care. And we learn to be self-sufficient as best we can. We go through good things and bad, to then finally leave our bodies behind when our time is up. But what does it all mean?

Each of us has a unique path. And our society and culture favors the idea that to be happy, you must be in a relationship. But the Truth is, we need to be in relationship with God. And the key to happiness is wholeness, whether with a partner or not. And going places alone is courageous because, in many group settings, churches, events, etc., people gravitate toward favoring couples. However, people come and go, live and die. And there are no guarantees.

The distinctive life is one that does not follow the crowd. It's the idea that there is wholeness for each, independently. And what completes us, is the Lord, who dwells within us. Not another person. And while another person may add to delight, Christ needs to be the center.

Furthermore, when you are at peace with God, and joined with the Father as His child, your best friend goes with you, everywhere you go. Therefore, there is no reason to fear being alone.

We are a codependent society, even though interdependence is key to the distinctive life. And statistics show that over half of all marriages end in divorce. Additionally, people are remarrying multiple times, and sometimes to unhealthy partners, due to their fear of being alone. However, both being married and single are equally good, even though we are conditioned to believe that being single is somehow, in some ways, a negative.

In the time of Christ, leaders of the day presumed that those most acceptable to God were Jewish male, free citizens and married people. Gentiles and Samaritans were despised. Women and slaves had little value and single people had no place in society. Then Jesus entered the culture and turned those ideas on their head. He inaugurated a new society where one's status was not dependent on distinctions like Jew or Greek, slave or free, male or female, single or married. Now all could find fulfillment and their identity in Christ.

August 13

Awaken Love

Economic struggles, isolation, and loss of livelihood due to health concerns and other issues, can be devastating. However, by stepping out and spending quality time with people around you, such as neighbors and friends, (new and old) you can make a huge difference in the world toward your own happiness, while encouraging others along their way.

And when you reach out to people with kindness, you will find the light. You will notice the light shine, through the eyes of those you touch with your selfless deeds. You can go with boldness and a cheerful disposition. And because the need is great, don't wait for someone to come to you, but be the first to reach out. Have you stepped out lately?

Be the first person on the move, by making a visit face to face. Do not think a text message is enough or even a phone call. Although, it is better than nothing, when you make contact in person, it is encouraging for all. Further, a simple smile, a furrowed brow, or a warm hug, communicates emotions that words alone cannot capture.

These interactions allow for the subtleties of human expression to shine through, enhancing your connections.

Face-to-face interactions are instrumental in building trust and rapport. When you meet someone in person, it fosters a sense of authenticity and genuineness that text messages simply cannot replicate. And your ability to look someone in the eye, shake their hand, or give a warm hug and share a physical space, creates a strong foundation for trust to grow.

So, whether it's a spontaneous road trip with friends, a family gathering, or a heartfelt talk, when you share moments, in person, you awaken Love and enrich the lives of others. For these reasons, remember to visit people. And as you do, notice the light that shines in your eyes and theirs.

August 14

The Brutal Darkness

It's God's plan for you to live a triumphant life. A life not pressed down by oppression or depression, but a life filled with hope, trust and understanding. And in this world of light and dark, Love and hate, good and evil, it's crucial to recognize the battle that exists.

Everyone has their own set of circumstances that influence their thinking and present reality. And in my life, at one time, I experienced a spirit of depression. And most of us know someone who suffers from depression (it may be you). The struggle is real, and just as the Spirit of the Lord brings light and hope, the brutal darkness can steal, kill, and destroy.

When depression sets in, or a negative state of mind, it is necessary to get into God's Word and listen inwardly to discern the Truth. The bible says that we war not with flesh and blood, but principalities and powers and wicked things in high places. So by seeing things as they truly are, we are better able to bring every thought into the captivity of Christ consciousness. When we do this, over time, the darkness dissipates. This is The Way to have victory over the darkness.

Even though the battle is the Lords, we need to do our part to fight the brutal darkness. First, we must start with the Truth. You need to know who you are in Christ. Second, cultivate a spirit of gratitude. Consider what you can be grateful for. And third; practice having a strong prayer life. It's hard to imagine someone praying for deliverance for a season, and not getting it.

Our Father is a good, good father. He is Love, and His desire is to bless you. Primarily, God desires a relationship with you. And your prayer life is important. So spend time with the Lord today and cultivate a connection with the Holy Spirit. This is a form of worship. Further, when you do not give God the time of day, it's easy to understand how the brutal darkness can slip in.

We all experience moments, where we feel as though we are being forsaken, or thrown under the bus. But God will never leave you or forsake you. You will get through this situation, to the other side, by pressing into prayer and the Word of God. And with time and practice, you will move farther away from negative thoughts and the brutal darkness, to find healing and light in the Truth.

August 15

Love Compels Us

God is Love. And when Love motivates us, we are compelled to do things that we would not normally do. Love is also considered the most profound of human emotions. And Love requires action and is also a choice. It is an energy that takes on many forms as it grows and encompasses romantic, familial, friendship, and agape Love for all humanity.

And having Love within, we are better able to Love our fellow man. Love inspires us to make sacrifices, take risks, and invest our time and effort. Love propels us to forgive. It is merciful and long suffering. And one of the most striking ways that Love compels us, is through the act of sacrifice. When we Love, we are willing to offer ourselves for the sake of others. It may be a friend providing support in a time of need, or a parent who springs into action for their children. Whatever the case may be, the profound impact of Love on human behavior is undeniable.

In John 15:13, Jesus said, "Greater Love has no one than this, that one would lay down their life for his friends." And that is exactly what Jesus did. He died for us, so we could walk free from sin.

Love elevates our devotion and produces courage in the face of fear. And when we hold Love in the center, we have an increased capacity to help people. In fact, people who are typically reserved or anxious, become fearless in the pursuit of protecting or nurturing those they Love. And whether standing up against injustice, or facing personal challenges, Love acts as a catalyst to overcome obstacles that would otherwise seem insurmountable.

Do you consider yourself a loving person? Love brings a sense of fulfillment like nothing else can. It has the power to heal and strengthen your soul. And Love is so powerful that it can break down social norms and conventions. It leads people to challenge traditional expectations, to follow their heart, despite external pressure. Love compels us. And God is Love.

Do you need more Love today? Do you desire to be a better partner or friend? Remember that Love manifests in the form of selflessness. It inspires us to engage in acts of kindness and generosity. So whether helping a stranger in need, or volunteering for a cause, or offering emotional support, you can live beyond the ordinary. Go to God with a simple prayer and ask for more Love. Seek to become a more loving person and watch your Love grow.

August 16

Use Your Voice

Every person has an experience and a story to share. Our stories teach us and often help others along their way, revealing that people can be a force for good in the world. However, some stories can also be used to destroy and cause pain. The question is, will you use your voice to bridge divides, or will you use it to cause divisions?

How will you use your voice today? There are times, we choose to use our voice for good, when kind words are hard to come by. Additionally, many people desire to be accepted by others, but worry about unconventional ideas that might not be unaccepted. Will you compromise your values for the sake of approval? Perhaps for likes or popularity? Or will you stand for what you believe?

Often women straddle the fence of oppression and independence, in the home and in the workplace. Currently, in the United States and other countries, women have gained more equality and respect, along with freedoms. They follow a path of their own choosing and not one that culture insists on choosing for them. However, many do not. And freedom does not come without a fight. Hopefully, both sexes in their intellect, recognize that there are always two ways of seeing.

Scripture says, "We overcome, by the Blood of the Lamb and the Word of our testimony". What this means is that we need to have contrite hearts, willing to be humble and to speak the Truth. Additionally, we need to be able to receive forgiveness for times when we miss the mark. We must continually place our missteps at the foot of the Cross, so that they no longer hold any power over us. And finally, we need to share our testimony with those around us.

We can be overcomers, to help others along on their way. And each of us has a choice to make. How will we use our voice today? Will we speak up for the benefit of all? Will we participate and share our Truth and help someone share theirs? We can make this world a better place by being brave. It's a choice. So choose to lead in Love today, and use your voice for good.

August 17

No Condemnation In Christ

God loves you, all of the time. He knows your innermost desires. He understands your needs and knows every matter in your life that has led you to where you are today. Additionally,
God is not mad at you. His desire is for you. To lead you along to a better place, than you were yesterday. So please do not feel bad about yourself, for the times when you may have been rebellious or contrary. Restoration and healing is a process that does not come overnight.

Our lives are multifaceted and there are times when Spirit filled people can come under condemnation, for not being perfect and sinless. Plenty carry guilt that hinders their joy. However, living with purpose, hope, and resilience comes with the belief that we are accepted and loved completely by God. Knowing this, we are able to rise above feelings of unworthiness and insecurity. This empowerment enables us to overcome challenges with confidence.

God doesn't sweat the small stuff and neither should you. His Love is perfect and not predicated on human merit. This is a free gift to all who place their faith in Christ. When we repent and bring our failings to the Lord in prayer, He wipes the slate clean. Now with no condemnation, we have security that strengthens our relationship, as we trust the Lord to meet our needs.

Scripture says, "I will supply all of your needs according to His riches and glory in Christ Jesus". So we can count on His supply daily, to live unburdened by the shadows of the past. Further, His supply in our lives is not dependent on our being perfect and sinless.

God sees your beautiful heart and wants you to enjoy a relationship with Him. And you need to enjoy who you are completely. So don't turn away, but enjoy the Holy Spirit as your loving friend. This is a true Love story. Not a story of condemnation. So be your loving self today.

August 18

In The Moment

The older we get the more we seem to value the time we are given. But at any age, time is of the essence. We never know the length of our days, and because of this, we need to live in the moment and give all that we can, to whatever it is that we believe we are here to accomplish.

How we use our time is important. And being lackadaisical in our efforts can jeopardize our happiness. Have you noticed how procrastination causes discontent? Maybe you have struggled with procrastination, yourself, or you know someone who has? Procrastination steals away joy from the present moment. And it can snatch from future moments too, because whatever was needed to be accomplished, still exists today. Consequently, the tasks become compiled.

And we see things happening in real time. Changes, announcements, product launches, businesses, services and more sprout up like wildflowers in the hot summer sun. And society appears to value multitasking and constant connectivity. However, when we slow down and engage in the moment without dwelling on the past or worrying about the future, we reap numerous benefits for our well-being, such as reduced stress, improved focus, and enhanced emotional resilience.

Moving forward in the direction of your dreams, there is a reward. So, live in the moment and pay no mind to the results. Do what you are committed to doing, the thing you envision is important. It is your service to the Lord. So, follow your heart and do not wait to make your mark. It would be a tragedy to wake up one day and see that time has passed you by, along with your dreams. So, do the thing you dream of, in the moment, but remember that the clock is ticking.

And finally, we are impatient people, but it's important to stay in the moment and not get ahead of yourself. In the moment, there is no blur of distraction. Here you can create meaningful experiences, where the Universe oversees who is watching, listening, and benefitting from all you do. So don't wait to use your gifts. Harness the power of now, in real time, for efficiency.

August 19

Reach For The Brilliance

The definition of brilliance is, "intense brightness of light". And in our world, light is a natural agent that stimulates sight and makes things visible. Light illuminates everything. And as we look around, we see this energy in the sun, the moon and the stars, and it also lives in us.

Many people claim to see the light in meditation when they close their eyes. Some have had near death experiences where they come awake to a testament of following or seeing a brilliant white light. Furthermore, we define "enlightenment" as understanding a problem or a mystery. And when understanding comes to a person, we see it in their facial expressions as they evolve. It's a mystery at best, but it's amazing when someone says, "I saw the light" and you can see it in their face.

Now, emotion is built into our beings. And if we are not free to express our emotions, we can lose our sparkle. Repressed emotions affect the light we allow to shine through us. And repression changes our countenance and shows up in the eyes and face. Please do not risk losing your sparkle and brilliance due to fear of feeling your emotional pain. Holding emotional pain within, can cause disease. And drugs also can put a damper on human brilliance. So, if you can, opt out and feel your emotions. Get to the other side of the issue. This is where you will find freedom.

It would be great if we never had to experience stormy nights or hazy days, but they come to each of us, from time to time. And music helps to open the floodgates of emotion and break down the walls. Naturally, people try to avoid pain. But, things happen in life that cause pain and when situations occur, it is best to reach for the brilliant light and seek clarity by feeling and embracing emotions. It is ideal to seek out the root cause of the pain. And when we do this, we are refreshed.

Scripture says, "Cast your care on the Lord, for He cares for you". This is The Way of health and vitality. Find a private space and purposefully go to God and pour your heart out. You will notice that your stress is relieved, your brightness and brilliance returns, and your clarity is restored.

August 20

Love Is Understanding

We need people to walk alongside us. Family; whether blood relatives, or friends, are very important to our personal wellbeing. And difficult relationships can really stress us out! So we must continually work on our ability to communicate and help others along, in doing the same.

Love equals understanding. And every person, whether knowingly or not, desires to be understood. Therefore, we must take our minds off of ourselves, when another person is speaking and confiding in us. This is the high path that requires humility. Also, it is putting yourself into another person's shoes. And when we become good listeners, we can walk alongside each other better, to shoulder the joys, along with the burdens and the trials that arise.

Generally, when people share, they are not asking for others to solve their problems. They simply desire expression. And mostly, they strive to feel close and connected and not so alone, as many sometimes do. Further, sharing matters can go one of two ways. People can either walk away feeling better, hopefully edified and encouraged by being heard, or they walk away feeling worse. And when a person walks away feeling worse, it's likely because they did not feel understood. There was a breakdown and someone was not being a good listener, or worse, lacked empathy.

Supportive people have an encouraging word and a listening ear. And people tend to gravitate towards those who make them feel understood. One of the greatest things you can say to someone in a situation is, 'I hear you' or 'I understand.' Alternatively, you might say, 'I can't fully comprehend what you must be going through, but I recognize how challenging (or wonderful) it must be.

So, through engaging in meaningful communication, we foster understanding, which leads to Love. And when humility is absent in our communication, we often unintentionally distance others. This is problematic, because what we genuinely seek is connection and understanding. Finally, we can set an example, by prioritizing the other person over ourselves, selflessly. This act of sacrifice lays a solid foundation for Love to flourish and is something each of us can cultivate daily.

August 21

The Healing Path

Our experiences mold and shape us. And the stories we tell to one another are important for personal growth and healing. Ideally, we have enough experience, to enliven compassion.

Jesus was a gifted healer and miracle worker, who lived through injustice and intense pain. He was referred to as the Hound to Heaven, and went through situations that every person is potentially faced with and will suffer through in life. Some of the situations were brutal.

And many of us go through injustice and intense pain. We know what it feels like to be injured, backstabbed, or wounded. Perhaps, misunderstood, alone or needy. Broken and despised... These are situations where we understand what it feels like to hurt. And until we understand the pain, we are less likely to "feel" for others deeply. But when we have been through it, we know how it feels.

Being a listener and having an open ear to another person's broken heart, is surely a privilege. And as our world turns and gets more challenging every day, we can be thankful for the many experiences that help us to stay on the healing path. This is good for us and others.

Healing is a privilege for the brave. It is for the soul that is unafraid to go deeper. And healing really shines in those with a rich experience. These are empathetic and compassionate souls, because to help others heal, requires sensitivity. And although we may wonder why we step into matters that affect people and our well being, it is necessary at times, because we must go through things in order to really understand how to connect and champion other people.

Are you a healer? Have you suffered injustice or pain that feels unbearable? You will make it through with a testimony that can change the lives of those around you. So don't give up! We do not know God's higher purpose in every situation, but we can trust that our actions toward healing will help others. So move ahead knowing that your path is valuable. And do not discount that healing can and will be painful at times. Visiting the places where you have been wounded is not fun, but it offers the rewards of wholeness, as "all things work together for good".

August 22

All Things Work Together

All things work together for good, for those who Love the Lord. So look up today and take the high road when issues of life cloud your sight. There is an astounding Grace that exists to carry you to the next level and you are moving up through the trial, as you go from Glory to Glory!

Grace weaves throughout our lives, for our benefit. And adversity is an inevitable part of our existence. Every individual will encounter challenges with personal setbacks that will test their resilience and perspective. It is during these moments of hardship, where the scripture and concept of "all things work together for good" provide solace and a renewed sense of purpose.

There is a divine plan at play. And it's not about denying the existence of pain or difficulty, but rather reframing these experiences in a way that fosters our growth and transformation. When trouble comes, we learn that we can trust the Lord. And we discover more about ourselves.

Additionally, challenges produce increased empathy and the development of inner strength.

When you experience a setback, it's good to think of it as a set up. And whether it be in your career or your personal life, there is an opportunity for redirection that ultimately leads to greater fulfillment. So rejoice and do not allow a spirit of disappointment to steal your joy. Instead, celebrate a time of self-reflection and personal growth. And be prepared for an increase!

Sometimes the outcomes of our challenges may not always be immediately apparent or straightforward. However, embracing uncertainty is a part of living. And we develop faith through the twists and turns. Also, experiences, both positive and negative, contribute to the betterment of society as a whole. Your personal challenges invite innovation, and problem-solving that weaves together, in a meaningful narrative, larger than our individual experiences.

Scripture says, "where sin abounds, Grace also abounds that much more". (Romans 5:20). So there is this interlacing of mercy throughout our lives. When we fall and experience failures, and when times are troublesome, we can know and remember that good is also coming.

Are you looking on the bright side today? Stay focused on the good that comes from your challenges. And keep hope alive knowing that all things work together for good.

August 23

Cheated, Betrayed And Lied To?

When you have been repeatedly let down by people and circumstances, learning to trust can be a challenge. It can take time. And it's difficult to believe in folks, after being cheated, betrayed or lied to. Scripture tells us that God hates the lie. So we need to walk in the Truth.

We do our best to trust, yet in our world, lying is often normalized. And many of the world's politicians, lawyers, and influencers, blatantly lie and cheat. We are likely to see people lying to one another on TV and portraying it as humor. And we've all experienced the common compromise, when someone says that they are going to do something and then they don't.

Every person at one time or another has lied, even if just a white lie. Many think nothing of it. But lying is a breach of trust that is bad for your health. And there is no real power in the lie. Only confusion and an invitation to trouble. However, having the integrity and courage to speak the Truth in Love, in any situation, is the way of the overcomer. Furthermore, it's the people with integrity that have real power in this world. Because they demonstrate that they can be trusted.

We must remain committed to the Truth and acknowledge when we slip up. And we must work through difficulties with forgiveness to grow stronger. It's also important to select wisely in relationships. Sometimes we try to protect ourselves. It surely can be tough navigating the terrain. However, scripture also says that "Love always trusts". So we need to work on trusting others. A good rule of thumb is to confront the lie and strive for Truth in all interactions and relationships.

In the end, what really matters, is that we are true to God, self, and the people around us. We can hold a high standard and level of character. And to combat the issues we face daily, we need strength, but not false strength. A leader may appear strong, but when he/she lies to the people, they lose their power and credibility. Can our leaders be committed to the Truth? Every action begins with each one of us individually. For this reason, we must choose to be committed to the Truth, in word and in deed, every day, in every interaction.

August 24

Step Into The Fly Zone

Trusting can be an incredibly daunting prospect, especially when it involves risking everything we hold dear. It requires us to open up to the possibility of disappointment, betrayal, or failure. Yet, it is precisely in these moments of vulnerability that we often discover the truest and most profound connections, achievements, and growth in our lives. So we need to continually push ourselves to step out of our comfort zone and step into the fly zone!

Unfortunately, it is easy to become complacent when we do not follow our heart. This can lead to depression and especially unhappiness. Contrarily, when we take risks, we are growing. And as we set out, we certainly are vulnerable, because stepping out requires us to relinquish some degree of control over our lives and ideally, place our faith in the hand of God.

Now, if we've had mediocre results in the past, it may be tempting to cower or cave in. Especially as we age. We may decline invitations or take fewer risks in meeting new people and trying new things. However, when this happens, we experience less of life, with all of its beauty and benefits.

What is something that you have wanted to do, but have yet to? Countless people spend their entire life at the same home and in the same town. They rarely go to other places. Many do not notice the beauty that surrounds them. An example is when someone, not yet elderly, becomes fearful of driving. Maybe they have had an accident in the past. And now they don't step out. Or perhaps a choice was made, and a negative result ensued. There was a trust that something would work out, and it did not. This can be very discouraging and debilitating for individuals.

Our reliance must be on God. So start today to do something out of the ordinary. It is important to take small steps, especially if you are not one to leap into larger jumps. Choose something positive that you have been considering. And don't be afraid to go it alone. It's very important to do this for yourself, because there is a confidence and joy that comes from challenging yourself. Don't wait for someone to go with you. God is with you. Take the risk knowing that God will help you.

August 25

More Than Meets The Eye

Human beings have an intuitive communication ability. We are heightened individuals that hold the power of thought. And it's important to note that the more clarity we have in our being, the more we will experience telepathy. This is a big part of our spiritual life and it's important to embrace "mental communication" as we walk with the people we love.

We are more connected than what most of us recognize. Have you ever experienced thinking of someone, only to find out they were thinking of you? Perhaps they called you on the phone, at the same time you had them in mind? Or maybe you had someone in your thoughts and then later heard that they passed on or had to go to the hospital. It could be that they came to you in a dream. Regardless, there is more than what meets the eye, by means other than the common senses.

Each person has their own unique situations and interactions. And everyone is facing challenges. Often, people tend to focus on themselves. But when we intentionally bring others to mind and pray for them, we open the windows to heaven, facilitating powerful communication. This practice is known as intercessory prayer, where we pray not only for ourselves but also on behalf of others.

When we genuinely care about someone's well-being, we may have a feeling that they need something. There's usually a reason they come to our mind. And one of the most impactful actions we can take, at this time, is to offer a prayer for their welfare. Utilizing prayer, our intentions and thoughts, bridge a connection that energetically enters into the heavenly realms.

In the Scripture, the Apostle Paul's exhortation to Timothy specified that intercessory prayers should be made for all people. We can develop this gift of communication. When our thoughts stem from a Spirit of Love, we open up to a high level of functioning, where we experience an exciting time that allows us to see the mystery and possibility of eternal life.

August 26

Our Longings Fulfilled

What can you do when something you have been hoping for does not appear to manifest? Maybe you have been believing for many years and what you've had in mind, does not arrive.

Things rarely go the way we imagine. And if we are downtrodden or heart sick, we are not very productive. In fact, in this state of being, we tend to walk with our eyes only partially open. But when we gain a wider vision, the results we desire change, and our place in the world expands.

Each of us has a calling and a purpose. However, countless people give up and become discouraged, expecting results that never arrive. This is likely due to hope being in the wrong place. Could we be focused on the outcome? Proverbs 13:12 says, "Hope deferred makes the heart sick, but a longing fulfilled is a tree of life."

People hoping for a child, unable to conceive, know what this pain is like. So do the dreamers, the musicians, actors, inventors, and entrepreneurs who envision and continually experience rejection along with a lack of opportunity and open doors. Many walk a harrowing path of unfulfilled longings. For some, depression really sets in.

But there is a reason to not lose heart. Our life on Earth is a journey of discovery. And we have experiences that allow us to become better versions of ourselves. These experiences come to us every day, when our heart is in the right place. And as we trust the Lord, over time, we discover our longings fulfilled and our path made clear. We are open for new adventures and encounters.

If you are a dreamer and perhaps a person who has been hoping for something for a very long time, and it is still unfulfilled, it's time for a new approach. And you can fight to see a longing fulfilled, but personal strength only goes so far. Instead, put your trust in the unfolding mystery of each day. Live in the moment and let go of the results. Invite the Holy Spirit in, and have a Christ centered consciousness, which is a forgiving heart and servants' spirit. Fall in Love with the journey. Not the results or expectations. And watch the world open for you.

August 27

Peacemaking In A Turbulent World

If we live in a country that strives to have peace, we are blessed. And as we look at the world around us, we see that peace is difficult to achieve. But peace begins within each of us.

Every day we are bombarded by the news media that reveal important matters in our country and nations. Most stories tend to be negative. Learning to trust takes practice. And having peace in the storm requires a faith connection with our loving Father. In Matthew 5:9, Jesus said, "Blessed are the peacemakers for they shall see God." What a wonderful promise!

Our time on Earth is fleeting. And much of what we experience here is a mystery. You can rest assured knowing that how you go through life, really matters. When you have made peace within, and are not living in fear, you will have more stability to go through trials that come up and surprise you. And as the world appears to grow dark, it is the smaller interactions within our circles, with the people we love, and encounter, that determines our ability for peacemaking. The more spiritually evolved we are, the better we are at living in peace with one another.

Do you quarrel? Are the relationships in your life broken or lacking in communication? You can start today with your family and friends. Have you considered forgiveness? Begin here. Being a peacemaker requires humility and a humble heart. It requires not having to have your own way.

Peacemaking takes time and it requires understanding. We must want peace and purposefully meditate on key ways to work through situations to obtain it. In addition, being a peacemaker requires becoming a better listener. It involves empathy toward another person's plight.

Doing little things every day that will lead you to more peace, is where contentment begins. And our growth and spiritual development comes in stages. So don't give up on attempting to create peace. Many people are hurting. They build walls and burn bridges that are very difficult to undo. Yet still, we must strive for peace. And with Jesus in the center, there is hope.

August 28

The Still Small Voice

Tune in today to the heartbeat of God, who speaks in the still small voice.

Why did the Israelites take forty years to get through the desert to the promised land? Scripture tells us that the Lord led the Israelites for all this time, through the desert, to humble and prove them. This refers to their character. The people had been slaves for so long, that they had little idea of how to live and Love successfully. They needed to learn plenty, just like many of us do.

The actual trip was said to be only eleven days when factoring in distance. But the people's hearts and minds had to be changed. And with everything that was happening at the time, the journey took nearly a lifetime. These former slaves were complaining, unappreciative and full of doubt. And because of this, their progress was labored.

Our trials and experiences teach us humility. They also help us to be aware of our character and attitude as maturing adults. Hopefully it is not too difficult to notice when negativity, fear or doubt creep in. The goal is to have understanding, enough through the trials, to recognize and discern the lies. And when these lies knock on the door of your mind, you are capable of pushing them out.

When we neglect to listen to the still small voice, we may have trouble. Have you ever been humbled? Most of us have. We do things without thinking at times. Sometimes we react or demonstrate rebellion when we don't get our own way. It's in these moments that we experience the results of our actions. Our hearts and minds are changed through discomfort and trouble.

We are in the refiner's fire, being refined. And it's tempting to feel regret or wish we had done things differently when we look back. But life is about growth. And the goal is to become Christlike. So remember to forgive yourself quickly and move forward with God, to where freedom reigns. You will reach the promised land when you don't give up.

August 29

Embrace A Life Of Change

Being free to be who you are, requires the ability to embrace change with ease. We do not need to fear new adventures when they are God given dreams and ideas. And we are pilgrims on a path. Each is unique and original. Our direction and destiny are imprinted on us by our Creator, along with those who have gone before us, as well as our belief system.

Therefore, to become all the Lord desires of us, we must bravely embrace change. We must be willing to let go and move on to where He leads. It's here, we step into Grace that goes with us, as believers in Christ. This is where we begin to see with eyes of opportunity on the pilgrim's path.

And it's very easy to become accustomed to the status quo. You may desire to break free from any mold or conditioning. To do this you must readily recognize when change is appropriate. There may be an open window. You may notice your emotions bubbling up inside. Here there is joy, sadness, fear, possibility, hope and more. All of these and everything at once.

And life challenges are real. So today, let go of outcomes and receive Grace toward change. You can begin in a small way. Something as simple as asking yourself, "what are the desires of my heart?". This is an excellent question to ask because when you pray, you are better aligned with God's will for your life. Ask God to show you the desires of your heart.

Additionally, many people struggle with the experience of working for sustenance through daily life. They feel they cannot pursue their dreams. Plenty settle and feel stuck in a relationship that is unhealthy, or in a house inappropriate and overpriced. Whatever the case may be, one thing is for sure; everything always changes and nothing lasts forever.

In Genesis 12:1-2, Scripture says, 'The Lord had said to Abram, "Leave your country, your people, and your father's household to the land I will show you. I will make you into a great nation and I will bless you; I will make your name great, and you will be a blessing."

Today, embrace a life of change and inherit this wonderful promise. Don't resist, but simply pray and ask God to show you what to do. Then follow His lead toward the desires of your heart.

August 30

Strength And Bravery

Being human, we are often faced with tough choices and difficult issues. Strength and bravery are required of each of us. And at times, we may choose to run from something God is asking us to do. We may not feel very strong or brave. Perhaps we are hesitant about matters we do not want to deal with. But we must face situations with bravery, in order to move ahead.

Strength and bravery are a gift from God. Some people have more of these than others. The most important thing to remember is that we are not alone and that our loving Father cares about our good outcome. This is a good mindset to have, because we receive better results when we believe that things happen for good. Fear and doubt only cause more trepidation and difficult learning.

Now when we look at the life of Christ, we see that Jesus was a brave individual. He was bold and able to be himself. He knew how to make a stand with those He encountered in a peaceful way. He was able to be different amongst people and lead courageously in the face of danger. And in His final hours, He faced a brutal death, with all of His faculties, in complete bravery.

When you face something difficult that needs to be done, remember to pray for strength and bravery. People in fear and doubt often avoid difficult issues. And procrastination can compound matters, making them worse. The choice is yours. Will you choose faith, or running from difficulty?

It is our right to freely receive as we get out of our own way and cast our cares on the One who cares for us. And we may be facing a physical challenge, or we may need to respect ourselves by making a stand. Perhaps it appears our future is in the lurch. Whatever the case may be, we can pray and ask for strength and bravery daily, to do whatever the Lord is calling us to.

August 31

Not Forsaken

Sometimes good people do foolish things. And even those with decent boundaries, can push past their usual strengths. The bigger the foolish thing, the greater the consequences.

We live in a fallen world. A world of recklessness and even madness. And many will do whatever it takes, come hell or high water to get ahead. However, if we depart from the Truth, we are treading on dangerous ground. Every misstep, when not addressed, compiles. So we must acknowledge our faults and correct our steps, in order to avoid greater disastrous outcomes.

All of us on occasion, in our weakness, slip up and fall into sin. Mainly because we have needs that are going unmet. And many want for something, they do not have. Some are searching for the next big thing. While others want to fall in love. Many strive to make a fortune or find fame.

And because humans are going to make mistakes, we need to understand and receive God's mercy, every day. When we continue to progress in a positive direction, we grow. We are not expected to be perfect, but we are responsible for our actions. And being in denial will only cause problems.

So learn to get back to the high road as quickly as possible. You may walk for a while and think everything is ok. It may be an interesting time that feels passionate. But if you fall into temptation, remember that God uses all things together for good, for those who love Him and are called according to His purposes. You can receive grace, even when mistaken.

Furthermore, when we are weak, we are more likely to give way to impulses. So acknowledge this inclination quickly. Do not allow sin to continue in your livelihood. The Lord is all knowing and there is nothing hidden that will not be revealed. Do not allow foolishness to compound. Instead, transcend matters with repentance and commit your way to the Truth. Do this before an issue becomes bigger, riskier, and more tragic. Stop and say to the Lord, "I'm sorry. Please forgive me".

SEPTEMBER

September 1

The Lord Will Do It!

It's pretty difficult to have faith when it appears things are going wrong all around you. Maybe you are struggling with a health issue or a financial crisis. Or perhaps a friend has walked out, a death has occurred, or you're facing a divorce. These are all difficult situations to face, but do not despair. The key is to turn everything over to God.

Within our limited perspective, it's challenging to see what is taking place for our own good. But Scripture says, "I will do it, says the Lord." I love this passage because it helps me to take my hands off situations and put my trust in God for a good outcome. And even when it appears that good is hard to find in any given matter, I can trust that good is coming.

There was a time when I was concerned about how my career would grow. I also wondered how I might become physically fit and how I would survive the artist's path. But one day, as I was lying in bed, I heard in my spirit, "I will do it," and it was as if a miracle had taken place. Those four words allowed me to let go, trust God and enjoy the journey.

How we go through challenges, especially our state of mind, is very important to our character. Every day is a gift. And when we start each day by getting right with God, we are better equipped to trust the path completely and live each day in all of its fullness. Whatever comes, there is a possibility for positivity to prevail. Most of all, we discover more peace.

This blessing is for you. Please remember that the battle is the Lord's. You are a child of the Most High God, and He is a good, good Father. You can trust Him as you go through the storm. And when it is time to say goodbye to this world, you will have the peace that surpasses all understanding. "I will do it! says the Lord.

September 2

A Remarkable Journey

Every day, most of us meet and encounter a variety of people. Personalities differ widely between individuals. However, the wiser we are and the more experienced we become at walking in Love, the more discerning we are in recognizing character in others, as well as a lack thereof.

Character is defined as the mental and moral qualities of an individual, including their basic nature and disposition. And a person who walks with integrity, kindness, justice, and Love is regarded as someone with excellent character. Generally, when we meet such a person, they are revered in their circle and usually have a glow about them.

In contrast, a person who has not developed a high level of character is not necessarily a bad person but perhaps someone who has not done the work of facing issues head-on. Experience builds character, and some individuals tend to keep moving forward without paying much attention to important aspects of their interactions. However, when matters get muddled, it's important to consider the root cause of any issue for the sake of growth.

We are born into families and we create and discover families. And most of us do not have much choice regarding the people we grow up with. Therefore, the key to improving and discerning character begins with understanding. We may meet people who come off as harsh or mean and assume they are negative and not worth connecting with. However, hidden things are likely influencing their disposition, so we must prioritize walking in Love.

Having the ability to ignite character in another person is a high calling and a remarkable journey. Many people don't even trust the trustworthy, and this often has little to do with the integrity of the trustworthy person. Instead, it usually relates to personal unforgiveness.

Scripture says, "Do not let yourselves be easily offended." When we are tempted to be offended by someone's behavior, we need to let go of the offense. There is likely unreleased pain or anger that reflects outwardly. We must remember that Love is patient and kind. It does not envy, it does not boast. Love keeps no record of wrongs. Love does not delight in evil but rejoices in the Truth.

Finally, people tend to warm up to someone who is unselfish with their mercy. And hopefully, we are in this life for a purpose greater than the daily grind of making money, and attaining success. When we understand that people are the gift, it helps us to be a light in the darkness.

September 3

Tap Into The Source

When you tap into the source of your energetic and loving spirit, you can build bridges and dreams that will go farther and last longer. And this source begins as Truth within you. The path requires clarity and a conscious choice to go deeper in order to soar higher.

It's easy to go through life not paying much attention to the spirit within. You might turn to the planets and science, which only show what we are made of—dust, light, energy, and darkness. However, there is a power at your source, which is Spirit, flowing from either Love or hate, faith or fear. And although we possess both in varying degrees, we need our focus to be on what produces more strength, light, and intelligence.

Even amidst pain and turmoil, with a little willing effort, we can go deeper and experience a profoundly meaningful journey. The first step is to humble ourselves and seek the Lord in prayer. We need to invite the Holy Spirit in daily and consciously share our concerns. Meditating "in" power, having clarity of vision, and maintaining a clear conscience can be immensely rewarding.

You can make a difference in your destiny and in the lives of those around you by honoring and considering the first and second commandments in Exodus: "You shall love the Lord your God with all of your heart, with all of your soul, and with all of your mind. And you shall love your neighbor as yourself."

When we set our priorities straight and let go of pride, we can live in and encounter true freedom that only comes from knowing Jesus and what He did to set us free. If you feel you have walls up or blocks, simply send up a prayer and ask God to remove them in faith. Begin by saying, "Come in, Holy Spirit," and show me more in the way of Love. God will do it. So, tap into this powerful source within today, and victoriously achieve personal greatness.

September 4

Freedom From Oppression

Are you feeling free to follow your heart and your unique path today? Maybe you need to take a clear look at what is holding you back. Are you under someone's control? You may need to stand up to an individual or quietly distance yourself while surrounding yourself with encouraging people. If you feel stuck, it's very important to contemplate self-respect. Because when you respect yourself and stand up to oppression, you are free.

Living in freedom requires keeping your eyes wide open. It's best to use all of your senses to avoid falling into oppression. People sometimes oppress themselves, but we can also be oppressed by others, especially when faced with certain controlling personalities. People who live free from social norms, particularly non-conformists, are highly susceptible to others' attempts to oppress. This is because those who are not free often have difficulty with those who are.

Oppression is defined as prolonged cruel or unjust treatment or control. It is a wrongful and merciless exercise of authority and power. This could be a person or a spiritual situation where someone or something is controlling you. It can also be a mental state or an addiction, like cigarettes. Another form of oppression is believing untrue things about yourself that keeps you from living your best life and receiving freely in God's will.

It is a sin to oppress ourselves and to oppress another person. Sin causes lack and disease and does not bring any good things. So pay attention to where you stand today and be the type of person who sets at liberty the oppressed. This is a sure-fire way to happiness and true victory. You cannot encourage and be an oppressor at the same time. So get used to encouraging people. Listening is a great way to encourage those who desire to be understood. You can choose to be the kind of person who helps others find their way to betterment.

The Bible speaks plenty about oppression. For example, Psalm 9:9 states, "The Lord is a stronghold for the oppressed, a stronghold in times of trouble." Isaiah 1:17 says, "Learn to do good; seek justice, correct oppression; bring justice to the fatherless, and plead the widow's cause." Proverbs 14:31 says, "Whoever oppresses a poor man insults his Maker, but he who is generous to the needy honors him." Finally, Luke 4:18-19 says, "The Spirit of the Lord is upon me because he has anointed me to proclaim good news to the poor. He has sent me to proclaim liberty to the captives and recovery of sight to the blind, to set at liberty those who are oppressed, and to proclaim the year of the Lord's favor."

September 5

You Can't Take It With You

What does it profit a man if he gains the whole world, yet loses his own soul? (Matthew 16:26)

In the hustle and bustle of our modern world, the pursuit of happiness often becomes entangled with the relentless chase for more—more money, more possessions, more status. This insatiable hunger for material wealth can lead us down a treacherous path, blinding us to the true essence of a meaningful and contented life. And you can't take it with you, so why choose greed?

Your time on Earth is important, and if you are given the means to make money and have more than enough, why not live generously? There is a profound liberation that comes with embracing freedom from greed and selfishness. When we are giving, we are better able to connect with our deeper emotions and the world around us in ways we may have never imagined.

And greed has a way of distancing us from those we love. It can turn us into workaholics, obsessed with our careers or businesses, and in doing so, we neglect our family and friends. However, when we break free from the clutches of greed, we are better equipped to nurture our relationships and be fully present with the ones we love, cherishing the moments we share.

It is good to contemplate whether we are raising young people to be entitled or greedy? Or to live in poverty? The bible tells us that it is good to leave an inheritance for your children and grandchildren. We must be in balance. And when we free ourselves from the relentless pursuit of material gain, we create space for serenity, gratitude, and tranquility to enter our lives.

How can we help others live a better life? The best way to combat greed is to become a giver. We can fully enjoy the fruits of our labor when we generously share our material possessions with those in need. If you have stored up possessions, why not pass them along or donate them to a cause that helps the needy? Freedom from greed leads to a life of fulfillment. It allows us to focus on the things that truly matter: our relationships, our passions, our personal growth, and our contributions to the greater good. Such freedom results in a life filled with purpose, gratitude, and genuine happiness.

September 6

Press On And Through

When the going gets tough, it can be challenging to be kind to yourself and others, especially when you are hurting and have a need for change. Emotional pain is very real, but we need not be overcome. Instead, we need to press on, pick up the pieces, and press through to what is ahead.

Challenges can feel insurmountable and life can deal serious and major blows to each of us. And when the going gets tough, we need both strength and courage because this is where true character is revealed. Also, the key to progress is to stay functional and balanced. We don't need to let our feelings take us too high or too low. Nor do we need to deny our feelings or our pain.

And pressing through matters involves confronting difficulties head-on. Growth and progress come from tackling the hard things. Therefore, when we go through something, we need to take notice of why we feel a certain way. By releasing our cares to the Lord in prayer, we clear the way to victory. The goal is to have an overcoming spirit and a positive mindset, in the midst of the storm.

Humans experience a myriad of emotions, including sorrow, anger, fear, confidence, joy, Love, hatred, longing, emulation, and pity, often accompanied by pleasure and pain. Some emotions, such as anger and fear, may arise without our conscious choice. However, being a child of God and a believer in The Way means trusting the One who leads you. And when you do, you grow in your ability to handle any situation, including fear, successfully and with resilience and faith.

Peace comes when we place our life in God's hands. By letting go and trusting Him, you are better equipped to accomplish your purpose and fulfill your mission in the world. Press on today, despite the pain and trials you may face. Do not let difficulties defeat you. God resides within you. Tap into this divine source, connect with it, and find the power to correct any challenges.

September 7

Selfishness - The Sin Of Today

People have a natural tendency to focus on themselves. Each of us experiences life with a unique reality, often centered around family, friends, work, entertainment, health issues, and more, while desiring a good time filled with success and adventure.

However, selfishness is a prevalent sin today, with many people overly focused on themselves. It's not difficult to discern those who think more of themselves than others. You can tell by their conversation. A few dead giveaways might be: Are they good listeners? Do they honor you as an individual with a unique point of view? Can they empathize?

An abundance of grace is received according to a person's openness, and a closed-minded person may hinder their own growth. Furthermore, it's likely true, people are not happy when they think only of themselves. True fulfillment comes from embracing generosity and empathy. And when we open ourselves to the needs and experiences of others, we invite a deeper sense of connection and joy into our lives. Letting go of self-centeredness and cultivating a heart of compassion, not only enriches our own lives, but also contributes positively to the world around us.

Have you ever had a conversation where you felt unheard? Or encountered a hard-hearted person who won't empathetically listen to something important you have to share? Someone closed-minded and unforgiving? Such experiences can be deeply frustrating and isolating, highlighting the challenges of meaningful communication and understanding.

When we are unwilling or unable to engage with others' perspectives, it not only stifles connection but also impedes growth. Do you know a selfish person? Do they know God? Are they having a personal relationship with Jesus Christ? When we are mature, it is nearly impossible to walk with the Lord and be selfish at the same time. This is because charity and selflessness are virtues of serving the Lord, emphasizing the importance of putting others before yourself.

Having a generous heart and being aware of what another person may be going through is key to growing in Love. Therefore, if you want more joy, one way to invite blessings is to conquer and destroy the negative influence of selfishness by being selfless. Take the focus off yourself and keep it on what you can do for others. It's not always easy, but you can do it!

September 8

The Winning Edge

Do you ever find yourself wishing? Saying "I wish" when referring to your hopes and dreams? Perhaps, "I wish this would be" or "I wish this would happen"? We all do this, from time to time. But wishes alone do not bring results. However, there are two primary things that can deliver a winning edge to whatever it is you hope for: perseverance and integrity.

When we have perseverance and integrity, much good can come from our efforts. This is how dreams are achieved. Our heart's desires come true not by wishing, but by being a person of Godly character, who persists daily, in small ways, toward a larger goal and purpose.

Do you have trouble sticking to your decisions, listening to your heart, or following through on your word? It is essential to get honest with yourself so that you become a reliable person. It's important to align what you say with what you do. Does your yes mean yes? Does your no mean no? This is very important and requires a good level of Godly character.

Navigating relationships successfully requires establishing healthy boundaries. These boundaries are essential for maintaining strong and effective connections. Ignoring people or leaving situations unresolved can create negative dynamics. Therefore, when you genuinely care for others, you stand by them and remain true to your choices, while also honoring your commitments.

Love and emotional strength come from the source, who is God. So, trust yourself through difficult times and stand for what you believe in. You will grow strong. And when you slip up, receive the forgiveness and mercy that comes from your relationship with Jesus Christ. Perseverance is healthy for success, and integrity requires being true to God and yourself. So keep it real and commit to honesty at your core. This is essential to holding the winning edge, especially when failures come.

September 9

Everything With Excellence

We are not perfect, but being mindful of how we handle the small things is crucial. It's important to be diligent, especially when pursuing big dreams, goals, or visions. Each day presents tests of our ability to manage various situations. By being dependable and detail-oriented in the small matters, we prepare ourselves for greater opportunities. So, how you handle your responsibilities matters.

The more you commit to integrity, excellence, and doing what's right, the more you'll find doors opening to new possibilities. And excellence is the quality of being outstanding or extremely good. Some people fall into big positions with less-than-stellar performance efforts. But in any position, how we do things is a reflection that speaks volumes about who we are and what we believe.

Most of us have noticed big players who self-destruct at one time or another. Why does this happen? It is likely due to a careless mindset. Motives make a huge impact on our performance. Furthermore, many people fall into disaster when striving for power. Also, it could be an inferiority complex that causes destruction. This is the state of feeling less or lower in caliber or position.

Perhaps your sphere of influence is within your family and friends. What steps are you taking to excel in your role? In every challenge, whether big or small, aim to act with the highest standards for the greater good. Are you pursuing greatness as you navigate various trials? Do you have a grand vision to make a difference? If so, commit to doing everything with excellence.

We all get lazy from time to time, and sometimes our bodies do not cooperate, and we take shortcuts. That's okay; just do not make the shortcut your way of life. Get back to excellence in the small things and keep striving for higher living. Your conscience will reward you.

Finally, choosing kindness is also a form of excellence. And there are times when being kind is not so easy, especially when you are hurting. However, you must continue to strive for excellence. And as you choose the more excellent way, you will notice and experience a sense of accomplishment, which further blesses with an increase in self-respect and preparation for leadership.

September 10

No Fear In Love

Many people are afraid of silence. For some, paying attention to their thoughts and relaxing in their own presence can be a challenge. And countless, fear going it alone and solitude.

In today's society, there is a constant need for attention-grabbing stimuli. Are you glued to your phone every minute? Many are. Plenty have the television on. These distractions become habits that can be difficult to break. For some, the emptiness of thought is frightening. There are those who jump from relationship to relationship, seemingly needing someone near constantly. Solitude can be daunting. Especially for those who prefer to avoid confronting their own thoughts.

The Spirit and the soul can be terrifying when we haven't explored within. Many struggle with self-doubt. Yet, when we come into this world, we are a single soul, and when we leave, we are a single soul. So, facing our fear of being alone is an important step we must take. We want to get to the point where there is no longer any fear in being alone or in solitude.

We certainly do not want to quench the Spirit that flows through us. Our inner world is complex and often misunderstood. And acceptance plays a crucial role in our successful living. Avoiding silence and not paying attention to our fears can lead to greater aloneness. As Job 25:5 states, "What I always feared has happened to me. What I dreaded has come true."

We are meant to do great things and lead fulfilling lives! And to achieve this, we need to reduce our dependence on distractions and maintain a healthy balance of input, contemplation, and rest. This includes faith and reliance on God for daily living. Also, accepting our circumstances without denial is essential to living victoriously. We can face dependencies and fears to have greater peace.

So stay the course and do not fear. Balance is key in all things, including time alone and time with others. This is The Way of the Master. And initially, detaching from our comforts can be very challenging, especially when habits have formed over many years. However, for growth to occur, we need to let go of these habits. And remember, there is no fear in Love.

September 11

Like A Child

When we are born, we arrive at the onset, to grow and learn. We don't know much, but with every day, month and year, we develop and continue to grow through each stage of life. And hopefully, we become better equipped to handle the challenges that come our way.

In 1 Corinthians 13:12 Scripture says: Now we see but a poor reflection as in a mirror; but then we shall see face to face. Now I know in part; but then I shall know fully, even as I am fully known.

Our living reality, brings innovative wisdom and modern evolution, to spiritual understanding. We may know much, but when we look toward our heavenly Father, we remember who we are—God's children. Therefore, we need to come to the Lord in prayer to embrace our full potential. We may be fully mature and spiritually evolved, but without daily time to listen, we may struggle to flourish.

Living and dying are about growth and understanding. It is wise to recognize that answers to questions are coming, along with the revelation of big mysteries. And even though we are grown, childlike qualities remain. Look inside at your thoughts. Do you feel young? Can you recognize an inner childlike quality? You may be older and wiser, or foolish and unlearned. But as you come near the end of your days, hopefully, you notice that you are still young at heart.

In Matthew 3:18 Jesus said: "Truly I tell you, unless you change and become like little children, you will never enter the kingdom of heaven".

So, enjoy your life today and embrace a playful spirit. Stay young at heart and free from burdensome oppression. Never lose your childlike qualities. And even though our bodies are deteriorating, don't be so irritated that you lose your joy. Keep growing and be excited about what is ahead. Now, as a child of God, you know in part, but soon you will know in full.

September 12

Unity In All Things

Politicians and people in government, activists, professionals, union laborers and individuals in general can be very opinionated. Each person believes their way is the "right" way. And often people attempt to make others think or believe the way that they do. Furthermore, when folks do not choose to believe or agree on a situation or subject matter, they become divided. This happens often in our world today. And it is not good. Because a house divided will not stand.

One of the most significant ideas to contemplate is that we do not know everything. None of us has all the answers. We are faced with questions every day. And the choices we make are often difficult. And we learn by the results we experience along "The Way".

Socrates Paradox says, "The only thing I know, is that I know nothing." And in 1 Corinthians 2:2, Paul said, "For I decided to know nothing among you, except Jesus Christ and him crucified."

Life is much too complicated to figure some things out. So it is good to not have to have all the answers. It is a humble place to be and a merciful space to stand in. There is a depth here, when we dig deep to see. And we are not always able to comprehend all that is happening behind the scenes, as well as, what may occur with our outcomes and choices.

Not knowing and having all the answers, keeps us dependent on God to reveal the responses. And as we meditate and contemplate Love into every equation, the answers come in time. So it is good to say, "I don't know". Because when we do, we place our trust in the Lord, to reveal what unity looks like. We see the Lord's will for all spiritual understanding, knowledge and wisdom.

So don't let anything divide you from the people you love. Some may think they know it all. And there may be disagreements because people are not always going to see eye to eye. However, watch, listen and pray. And wait for God to reveal the answers you seek. You will have unity in all things when you believe and put into practice humility that comes from following Christ.

September 13

When Chains Break

How real are you? Do you put on a persona for friends and family, or do you try to be someone you are not? It takes courage to be yourself and not be affected by what others think. We need not live as an expression of someone else's ideas, especially concerning what others think of us.

Our world is full of conformists and folks putting on a persona. People who pretend to be someone they are not. So be yourself today. You can be zany, funny and wild. And you will go farther and make more people smile, when you decide to be who God made you to be. You were born for this! And at every stage of your life, your experience portrays to the world, who you are uniquely.

Many individuals feel internally constrained, lacking the freedom to express themselves or to fail and fall when taking risks. Do you feel ashamed when things do not go right? Does this stop you from trying? We are our own best teachers and must learn the truth about ourselves.

The best way to break any chains is to follow God into uncharted territory.

When chains break, real people shine. And it's a joy to watch souls become free, because they look better. Their faces appear relaxed and calm. And those who are authentic are inviting to be around. They tend to be accepting of other people and are welcoming while understanding real struggles.

You were born to be free and to experience self-actualization. Whether you are young or old, it's never too late to be true to yourself. So, embrace how amazing you are. By choosing to be authentic, you demonstrate incredible strength, fortitude, and courage. Keep pressing forward. And if you battle with being true, ask God to help you. Invite the Lord in by saying; "Take me as I am Lord, and lead me in becoming my true authentic self, with everything you have for me."

September 14

Our Brothers Keepers

We are meant to take care of each other, as there is no greater calling. When we stand together to do what's needed during difficult times, we demonstrate the power of Love working through us.

Ephesians 3:20 says, "Now to Him who is able to do exceedingly and abundantly above all that we ask or think, according to the power that works in us." So we know that God is here to help us, to bring an abundance of good from our actions and efforts, when we have the right motives.

We are our brothers' keepers and must believe we have what it takes to do hard things. Helping someone in need demands being a peacemaker and walking in humility. It requires us to be better listeners and take the time to truly hear others. Helping someone in need also requires understanding and putting others' needs above our own. Moreover, helping others isn't always about monetary giving; some of the best gifts we can offer are comfort and peace to a worried soul.

Life can be very hard, and most people are hurting emotionally or physically in some way. It's also apparent that those who are hurting tend to hurt others and often push people away. Therefore, to make a difference, we need to be very intuitive and walk in humility. We are our brothers' keepers. And this is how we convey openness toward healthy interactions. Instead of being prideful, arrogant, or full of ego, we practice non-judgment. How will you help someone today?

When we let go of our selfish ambitions and motives, we can enter a room full of people and instinctively recognize where the needs are. In this state, we are awake and in tune with our purpose. By unselfishly caring for others, we bring restoration and revelation, stirring things up for the cause of Love. It's very exciting when this happens! Our lives elevate, and a sense of purpose ensues, making the living and dying we see all around us very worthwhile.

September 15

Live For Today!

There is a beautiful person living inside of you, and there is no better time than now to shine. Your story is unfolding like a motion picture, with today's reel playing out before you. Trust this moment, for you are exactly where you are meant to be.

Our time on Earth is precious, and today is all that is promised. And when we focus on the past we miss out on the day's blessings and joy. So it is imperative to seize the day and not get stuck in the past. You can live joyfully in the moment! Embrace each day with gratitude and purpose, cherishing the present and letting go of worries about the past or future.

When we fix our eyes and thoughts on the future, we often fail to recognize what we have at our fingertips in the present. Our sight becomes limited, as we wait for a future day, or the "right time," which may never come. So, live for today because tomorrow is not promised.

Procrastination is another moment stealer. When we procrastinate, we cause ourselves dissatisfaction, adding more to our plate than necessary. Don't wait until tomorrow to do what you can accomplish today. By tackling tasks promptly, we free ourselves from unnecessary stress and create space for more joy and fulfillment in the present moment.

Finally, fear can be debilitating and steal moments of joy. The fear of the future or dread can be overwhelming. So don't let dread rob you of your happiness today. Instead, pray and place all of your fears at the foot of the Cross of Christ. Rest in His promise that He will never leave you nor forsake you (Hebrews 13:5). Your story is unfolding, so embrace this day fully. Stay present in your circumstances and savor every moment! This is your time, so live for today!

September 16

Press Through The Pain

There are times when it's incredibly challenging to keep going. Yet, we must press on and face difficulties head-on. Our bodies may ache, and our spirits may falter, but avoiding or running from problems only exacerbates them. We must confront the struggle with faith and perseverance, especially to emerge stronger on the other side of the pain. This builds resilience and not only helps us achieve our goals but also fosters a sense of pride and self-worth.

Ultimately, working through difficulties cultivates discipline and perseverance. Have you heard the saying, "The only way out is through"? It's a truth that resonates deeply, especially when dealing with pain, whether emotional or physical. No one enjoys pain, and our natural instinct is to avoid it at all costs. However, running from pain often leads to compounded issues and greater discomfort in the long run.

Resistance and oppression may try to hold you back, but leaning into these challenges and pressing through, even if it's one small step at a time, is essential. This moment-by-moment effort can lead you to the other side, where brief periods of discomfort, faced with courage and Truth, can result in significant growth and achievements. These actions teach us that true success requires sustained effort and a willingness to step outside of our comfort zones. It is good to reflect on the hurdles we overcome

Pressing through pain and obstacles is not merely about enduring suffering; it's about transforming that suffering into strength. Through this process, we often find ourselves rewarded with our greatest accomplishments, primarily achieved after overcoming adversity. So, when life presents its trials, remember that pushing through builds the resilience and character needed to thrive despite challenges.

While facing obstacles is never easy, it invariably leads to long-lasting results. Addressing the root of your pain and seeking healing is crucial. If you're ill, consult a doctor, but also remember to pray and bring your concerns before God. Jesus is known as the Great Physician, a Way Maker, and a Miracle Worker. Trust in His healing power and keep seeking His strength.

September 17

What People Think

Being true to yourself in a world full of conformists can be incredibly challenging. Self-doubt often plagues those searching for their place in the world, making it difficult to follow your own path. Yet, it takes great courage to march to the beat of your own drum, and by doing so, you embrace the evolution of your unique, God-given personality.

We start as youthful spirits, growing into maturity as teenagers and young adults. And when we are young, a "know-it-all" confidence serves us well, fueling our belief in our capabilities and visions. However, as we age, we gain a deeper understanding of ourselves through success, failure, trial, and error. This journey of self-discovery reveals who we truly are.

Many people become trapped in a cycle of seeking external validation and approval, which often leads to insecurity, anxiety, and self-doubt. However, by detaching from others' opinions, we open ourselves to genuine self-expression, allowing us to prioritize our values and aspirations over external judgments. If you ever feel misunderstood, remember that it's okay. Releasing concern over how others perceive you, enables you to be more authentic and true to yourself.

You are unique, and your self-view may evolve over time. Therefore, it's crucial to anchor yourself in God's unchanging Word, which provides a consistent definition of who you are at every stage of life. And you may find yourself as an introvert among extroverts, which can be challenging. Sometimes differing personalities face bullying or exclusion. Yet, everyone possesses unique gifts, and your individuality is valuable. So as you navigate through life's phases, stay true to yourself, even when it's painful or when you feel out of place. You are meant to rise and shine.

Understanding and accepting the Lord's unconditional love is essential. So embrace your unique path with strength and courage, and cultivate a deep relationship with God. Don't lose faith during hardships. Because perseverance builds character and deepens trust in God's plan for your life. Take comfort in this promise: "Seek first the Kingdom of God and His righteousness, and all these things will be added to you." And enjoy fellowship knowing that God's love will sustain you.

September 18

Put God First

When you were young and starting out, you were brimming with hope and vision. Everything was new around you and the anticipation of seeing how your dreams would unfold was exhilarating. And as opportunities came, you navigated the world stage with growing confidence.

Now you are older and wiser. And through trials have learned that when God is first, you find yourself blessed. Decisions come more easily, and your values are clearer. Ideally, you've uncovered a sense of calling or mission that transcends personal ambitions and material pursuits.

Are you still putting God first today? Putting God first is not just a spiritual concept; it's a way of living. And each of us has distractions, demands, and desires. So the concept of putting God first can be challenging. However, prioritizing faith is a guiding principle that provides purpose, strength, and fulfillment, where everyday your journey unfolds with a profound sense of direction.

Putting God first means making your relationship with the Lord the central focus of your life. This commitment is activated through prayer and the understanding that God is the ultimate authority and source of guidance, wisdom, and love. With more experience, our trust in God deepens, and we learn valuable lessons, including what to avoid. This brings newfound blessings.

Prioritizing God doesn't mean neglecting other aspects of your life, such as family, career, or personal goals. Instead, it provides a framework for prioritizing these areas. By putting God first, we can take a balanced approach to life, viewing all aspects as opportunities to express our spirituality and values. This leads to a harmonious and fulfilling journey.

Scripture says, "Love the Lord your God with all your heart, mind, and soul, and love your neighbor as yourself." This commandment helps us find solace, comfort, and divine support, and it strengthens us to endure hardship and emerge stronger. Putting God first will guide you toward fulfillment and a life full of meaning, as the Lord leads you for your highest good.

September 19

Who's Influencing You?

There is a benefit to *not* following the crowd or being easily maneuvered by others. And it is no secret, there are individuals who hold extreme power in select circles. But influence can change a person gradually, to become more like the group. So when we are evaluating a situation, it may seem right to follow the crowd or what society conditions us to believe. And people can be very persuasive. But anything that draws you away from the Truth, will lead to trouble.

Are you an influencer? In our world, remaining independent as an individual can feel like a lonely road. But more often than not, it is the road to safety from large missteps. Additionally, dedicating yourself to Truth and following God's leading, can in fact, make you a great leader.

Are you a person who does not follow the crowd or society's conditioning? Standing for something and influencing others for the good, takes great courage. It is not an easy path. It can be a real challenge for conformists, because group consciousness is powerful. Once an individual is part of a group, it can be very difficult to step out from the assembly, to be unique.

Obedience to God's will, over the influence of people, is the best way. When we keep our awareness of the temporal state of things and view our eternal home, we are generally better at listening to the guidance of the Holy Spirit. Furthermore, no one knows how much time there is. Every choice a person makes steers the ship. And when we get lost, we can lose ourselves. So be awake enough to know that choosing the path of Truth will lead to peace without regret.

Being an influencer for Truth can feel like going against the grain. It can be lonely. But when we follow the lead of the Holy Spirit, we avoid misguided, time-wasting endeavors. So stick with knowing who you are in Christ. It may take time to see the benefits of not following the crowd.

September 20

You Are Greatly Loved

With all of the various personalities that make up people in our society, one thing is sure; you can be yourself and trust that you are deeply loved and accepted by the Creator. The universe is yours for the making and you belong in it, for such a time as this.

And many people are so busy judging others and believing wrong about themselves, that it can be very confusing to feel a sense of belonging. But you are the creation of God, along with the animals and the sea creatures, the insects, and the earth. There is nothing about you that is not welcome here. You are understood, loved, forgiven and free to enjoy each day in the land of the living.

Always remember and believe that you are loved and accepted just as you are. It does not matter where you have been or what you have done. Christ died for ALL creation. Furthermore, there is nothing secret in the Universe. Even as we see evil around us, along with discrimination in the forms of race, sex, and income inequality, all is known. Indeed, you are no surprise to this

Great Intelligence we call God. Therefore, come boldly to the throne of Grace with your confession and receive the freedom that comes from God's unconditional Love.

The simplicity of God's Love is apparent. The Lord desires to share in your daily life, and you can trust this Love, knowing that despite your faults and the presence of both good and evil influences, you are perfect as you are. You are well-loved in creation.

Having this belief invites friendship and fellowship with the Holy Spirit. Knowing we are fully accepted by God, we can share our hopes, dreams, disappointments, and missteps, along with the Grace and profound Love that is lavishly poured out on us. So, come as you are. Be bold and invite the Lord into your journey. As you get to know this great Love that surpasses all understanding, it becomes much easier to be a more loving person. Because Love is here for your benefit.

September 21

Your Word Impeccable

It's easy to notice a falling away from The Truth in our society. Everyday we are confronted with deception and gaslighting. These situations can really let us down. However, we need not accept dishonesty, even though it is rampant. And those who desire a higher level of living, recognize the importance of being impeccable with their word.

When you look in the mirror, what do you see? Hopefully you are a person with integrity, honor, self-respect, and a clear conscience. Have you ever had someone tell you that they were going to do something, and then they did not? Perhaps they made an appointment with you, and they did not show up or call? When a person lacks integrity, we need to speak up and say something.

Gaslighting is a form of psychological manipulation where a person makes someone question their own reality, memories, or perceptions. It often involves the abuser denying or distorting the Truth, lying, or presenting false information, which leads the victim to doubt their own experiences and sanity. Gaslighting is rampant in our society today and can cause distress.

People notice the people that they can trust. And having a commitment to integrity, brings real life blessings. You are free. So respect yourself and speak the Truth in Love. Additionally, when you have a high level of integrity in your daily interactions, you welcome more success, Love, and friendship into your life. And the best part is that you trust yourself immensely.

Finally, when a person is impeccable with their word, they are better communicators. Effective communication blends honesty with respect and encouragement. Therefore, strive to speak the truth with kindness. Start by acknowledging the positive aspects of a person or situation you're addressing. For example, you might say, "I really appreciate your work ethic. However, I need to adjust my schedule before committing to a meeting time." The initial appreciation reflects your commitment to Love, while the second part conveys your truth clearly and respectfully. And when you walk in Truth, you help others to do the same. Never forget, because we lead by example.

September 22

More Than Meets The Eye

Death is inevitable. At one time or another, each of us will lose a loved one, and eventually, we will also leave this earthly realm. But there is more on Earth and above in the heavenlies than what meets the eye. And as each of us grows closer to leaving this earthly life, we can go with confidence, knowing there is more.

The human experience, with all its mystery, is ever eclipsed with wonder regarding life after death. In John 14:2, Jesus said to His disciples, "In my Father's house, there are many rooms, and I go to prepare a place for you."

Not long ago, I lost a good friend who was a devout Christian. Shortly after he passed, I was on a road trip driving across the Southwest with plenty of time to think. As I thought of him, I felt an overwhelming energy. It was as if I could feel him along for the ride, for a while anyway.

Each of us has likely experienced such moments. When they come, they can bring a level of comfort and help us understand that there is more to life than what meets the eye. Jesus embodied a powerful Love energy and pure Light, which is why He was so present when He rose from death and appeared to the disciples in transfiguration.

We know so little, especially about why we do the things we do. And believing in nothing can be an easy way to avoid taking responsibility. As creatures of the Earth, we belong to the family of God. Therefore, let us choose to acknowledge God living in us. Let us shine our light brightly and with clarity. Let us not harm ourselves or others, causing the energy of Love to diminish or our light to grow dim. We have all been runners at times, but we need not run any further.

Do you hide from God as if the Holy Spirit is not living inside you? Come to the Lord today with a heart of repentance and increase your strength and energy. Don't wait to fellowship with the living God. The more you share in God's Love today, the more you are blessed by the One who gave His life to demonstrate true Love. Finally, I once heard someone speak at a memorial and say, "wherever you are now." And to that, I would say, in one of the blessed rooms, a place prepared just for you by a loving God who knows and understands you.

September 23

Let Your Voice Be Heard

When you see the atrocities in our world, what do you think? And what can you do? Turn a blind eye? Maybe just say, "what the heck" and be far removed? Crying out to God is one of the best things we can do. We can lift our voices and ask God for specific directions to understand what changes we need to make to be the difference.

Are you a passionate person who expresses emotions easily? This can lead to a journey filled with joy. As an empathetic person, feeling saddened or angered by cruelties and injustices in the human condition does not mean we are overcome or inactive. Instead, we need to purposefully seek the way forward to lead for change, right where we are.

And many become overwhelmed by daily struggles and resist any additional stress. However, if we don't use our voices to take action, we miss the reward and opportunity for change. We need to let our voices be heard. By expressing ourselves, we are released from heaviness and emotional pain.

However, all the expressions in the world may not change a thing if our behavior does not change. Therefore, to live passionately, we need to cry out to God today, but also step out in faith and do something that will bring change into our world. Start small with something you feel is important. Listen to the Lord and your heart's leading toward Love.

Be yourself today. You can fight injustice without denying it. So, persevere and not give up. Knowing you are accepted by God and loved as you are, is one of the greatest empowerments you can experience. Let your voice be heard and live a vibrant and expressive life that demonstrates courage, particularly by putting your passion into action and standing up against evil.

Sometimes it takes a long time to see a vision come to fruition. It may take more time than you wish, but do not give up and never oppress yourself. Be free in Love and be loved passionately. Bless others radically. Press forward for your freedom, fight injustice and live passionately. There's nothing quite as rewarding as making the right decision in every instance.

September 24

Legacy: Don't Leave Without It

Our time on Earth passes quickly, so consider your purpose today. Experience brings you to a place of self-discovery in everyday living. So don't take the moment lightly. Instead, be thoughtful of time itself, and the temporal state of things. And if you are traveling the road on auto pilot and not paying attention, you may have regrets later.

Have you considered your legacy? It may have to do with inheritance, or following the patterns of your parents or the culture. But legacy can also have to do with what you determine, to be important. What will you leave behind? And how will you be remembered?

Life has its moments of glory and difficulty. For some, it's challenging to maintain daily responsibilities. Yet, to be victorious, we need to seek ways to make a difference toward tomorrows. And giving is where legacy is created. With selflessness at the center.

How do you participate in giving in your circle and around the world? Hopefully in a way that makes an enduring impact. There are great rewards when we purposefully forge legacy. The goal is to always help others to become better. And certainly, anything we do to help those who come after us, is a valuable gift to offer to anyone.

There are different ways that we can leave a legacy, and long-term developments require an insightful approach. Words of wisdom, recorded and written down, when passed along, can create lasting influence. Agreements and constitutions matter. And spiritual healing changes things. Monetary support matters, to make someone's life better. And of course, childbearing, adoption, and participation in lives through valuable mentoring and care.

Touching lives brings a sense of fulfillment to our existence in this very temporary life. So, consider legacy today, and make yours stand for something real. Consider what will last, and avoid something that will be burned up in the fire. Discover your purpose and set your sights on serving the greater good today. Don't let time pass you by. There is much to do!

September 25

Forgiveness Is Yours

Life can be difficult. And each of us will miss the mark from time to time. And when we do, it's important to be quick to bring matters to the Lord and ask forgiveness. When we are clear to overcome situations often caused by fear, temptation and/or pride, we are stronger.

And Scripture tells us that "Pride goes before the fall." So, for the most part, oftentimes, when we mess up and experience a misstep, it stems from pride. As Christ followers, we need to have a humble heart because we are called to humility. Moving between humility and pride at times is like a dance. It is not easy to get it right all the time as we go between the two. But we get better as we grow. And when we are quick to repent and receive forgiveness, we are less likely to get stuck.

Fear can be a trigger that causes us to miss the mark. Sometimes we do not even realize we are in a state of fear; it just happens. Often, we recognize it only after a misstep. Perhaps we've hurt ourselves or someone else. We may feel bad. Our failure pains us and the Lord. The

Holy Spirit is a person, so when we hurt God, the Holy Spirit within us is also hurt.

In Ephesians 4:30 Scripture says, "Do not grieve the Holy Spirit".

To grieve the Holy Spirit means to cause sorrow, pain, or distress. Recently, I noticed a level of fear rising inside me, and my actions were not on point. This fear stemmed from losing loved ones and receiving a less-than-stellar medical report. I got off course and ate unhealthy foods, seeking comfort in the wrong places. This was my learning experience; however, everyone responds uniquely when they miss the mark. So, don't wait to repent if something is keeping you from God's best. Come before the Lord in prayer and ask for forgiveness.

We are in this dance of humility, pride, fear, and trust every day. We can grow and do better, one day at a time, as we bring every action into captivity to Christ, who walks with us. Forgiveness is yours today, so turn and repent, with the goal of staying on track with clarity.

September 26

Hope with Imagination = Bliss

Have you experienced the disappointment of an unfulfilled expectation? Maybe there was a vision or dream you were dedicated to that left you feeling defeated and broken?

Life can dish out an undue share of disappointment, and most of us have felt this at one time or another. Sometimes, disillusionments and tragedies may even come in succession, compounding the impact and wearing us down. Additionally, as we age, we experience the loss of loved ones and friends. However, by keeping hope alive, we can help restore our bliss.

Scripture says, "Hope deferred makes the heart sick." This is not a thought most want to consider—it sounds depressing. However, the definition of hope is "a feeling of expectation and a desire for a certain thing to happen." Further, hope is also a state of trust. When we place our hope and trust in God rather than in situations, we are better protected through disappointments.

I have found that when I feel a sense of hopelessness, imagination is a great tool to return to bliss. Imagination requires opening the mind and thinking outside of the box. Additionally, as we open our minds and hearts with a focus on the purposes of God, the dark veil is lifted. Our footsteps are lightened, and new dreams are discovered. Here, we let go of the results and trust the journey.

Could you be inspired to place your hope in the Lord and not in the things of this world? In Colossians 1:27, Paul writes, "Christ in you, the hope of glory." This means that we are to keep our focus on being Christ-like in the moment. This is how we increase joy and satisfaction. Additionally, we become more resilient when we focus on becoming Christ-like. With this state of mind, we have right thinking and are protected from what may be and what may come.

Today, you can choose to experience bliss and walk the road primarily traveled by overcomers. Tap into your imagination and find a new vision. Even with limitations, using imagination as a tool to discover hope is a powerful way to overcome what once seemed hopeless. Are you seeing with your eyes closed? Are you using your imagination to come face to face with destiny? It's up to you. Find your purpose through the Lord in every moment. It may be how to assist a friend or family member, or perhaps your neighbor or the world at large. However, when you come like a child and place your hope and imagination in Him, anything is possible.

September 27

Strength And Dignity Is Yours

"Strength and dignity are her clothing, and she laughs at the time to come!" (Proverbs 31:25)

Can you imagine having enough freedom to be able to laugh at what is to come? This is a great ideal to embrace and practice for victory! It takes great faith and trust in God to be at peace with whatever comes, especially as we approach our latter days on Earth.

Dignity is defined as; the state or quality of being worthy of honor and respect. And dignity is the right of every person to be valued for their own sake, while being treated ethically.

But everyday people are judged for their bodies and their looks. Many people are treated disrespectfully and women especially are often considered to have less value than their male counterparts. For many, dignity can seem like a fight. This is true because the world we live in does not offer an equal playing field. Countless women remain oppressed. This is a state of being less in value, equality and leadership. But this is simply a lie and not The Truth.

Jesus stated in Galatians 3:28; "There is neither Jew nor Greek, there is neither slave nor free, neither male nor female; for you are all one in Christ Jesus."

Have you had situations occur that have eroded your vision, at one time or another? Perhaps you have felt diminished in some way? Having inner strength and dignity, is the result of an active prayer life. So be filled with the Truth every day. A woman needs to wear strength and dignity as her clothing. To put it on daily, with the mindset of letting go of falsehoods.

Finally, there are great benefits to placing Christ at the center of our perspective. By putting our trust in God alone, and donning strength and dignity before stepping into the world, we are better prepared to earn respect, which grows just as Love grows. If we slip up and make mistakes that lead us to question our worth, we can bring these situations to the Cross of Christ, releasing any insecurity or fear, and continue moving forward. This is our inheritance.

September 29

Who's Influencing You Today?

Our world is filled with online influencers. Who are you listening to? Each of us faces numerous choices in various aspects of life, so it's important to be careful in making our selections.

It's no surprise that many believe their way is the best way. Each person is unique, shaped by different life experiences, upbringings, and educational backgrounds. Therefore, it's crucial not to be quickly swayed by others, especially when we don't know their history. Instead, we should seek the influence of God, who develops our character throughout life.

Navigating our lives is challenging, and we often learn from our mistakes and poor choices. People can be very convincing, and sometimes we follow advice that doesn't work out for us, leading us astray. Influencers may use fear to persuade us, making us believe that not following their way will cost us dearly. In hindsight, we may realize there was a better path.

Consider the media and its power to shape our thoughts. When we let people, groups, or cultural conditioning direct our path instead of the Holy Spirit, we can miss out on God's best for us. It's essential to heed the still, small voice within us. Ignoring the Holy Spirit's guidance can lead to serious issues—perhaps ignoring a nudge to stay home from work or allow your children a day off could result in unforeseen danger.

Listening to the Holy Spirit is a crucial practice in today's world. For instance, in the stock market, people often lose money by following influential advice that turns out to be flawed. While this can be disheartening, we should remember to let God oversee all aspects of our lives, including our finances. By trusting God with our decisions, we allow Him to guide us in giving and receiving.

To avoid the pitfalls of misplaced trust, we must prioritize God above man, society, or any group. Trusting the Lord provides the best guidance in every area of our lives, from relationships and friendships to career choices. Finally, by listening to the still, small voice within, we can discern the right path and the ideal timing in things, for our lives.

September 30

See With Ancient Eyes

What if you could see with Ancient Eyes? What does this mean? Ecclesiastes 1:9 tells us that "there is nothing new under the sun" and that "what has been will be again." To see with Ancient Eyes means to have knowledge and understanding of fundamental universal truths, laws, and principles. It involves recognizing and applying wisdom that has always existed. By looking to our ancestors, we can gain valuable insights into the present moment.

After the Age of Reason, when it was proclaimed that "God is dead," many people feared the future. Those who struggled to connect with this new reality experienced a significant cultural clash and turned back to rituals. They gazed into crystals, sought fortunes, and consulted magicians, sticking to their accustomed practices. Meanwhile, as the West wind blew towards the East, these individuals remained like children, lacking the sign or revelation needed for reinvention.

You see, it has never been about astrology, psychic mediums, soothsayers, or magicians when it comes to discovering the future. These practices have existed in every culture for ages, but they offer no real assurance of a person's long-term security or salvation. Rituals, acts of penance, and repetitive actions may provide temporary relief to a distressed or seeking soul, but they do not bring lasting peace or freedom from danger.

When we view life with Ancient Eyes, we understand that the essence of existence has always been the relationship between God and humanity. To align ourselves with God requires fellowship with the Spirit. When we are spiritually awake, we recognize that navigating life requires freedom from falsehood. This awareness brings peace with whatever the future holds. What a great gift we have received! As Romans 5:8 states, "But God demonstrates His own love for us in this: While we were still sinners, Christ died for us.

Finally, life can end in a moment or extend over many years. Yet, when we view it with Ancient Eyes, we grasp the grand picture of God's unconditional Love for us. In this perspective, we uncover the wisdom to live in Truth. With guidance we need, along with the security and peace we deeply seek, our souls find rest. No longer do we search in countless places or walk with our eyes closed. Instead, we place our trust in the future and our eternal security in the one true God, the Lord Jesus Christ. Hebrews 13:8 says: "Jesus Christ is the same yesterday and today and forever."

OCTOBER

October 1

Dreams And Resilience

Anyone with a big dream, understands the vision and passion needed to achieve the idea. And we can use our imagination to "dream big" and step out in faith, but having the tenacity to stand, in the day of testing and failures, separates the doers from the fantasists.

A big dream is not for the faint of heart or those who give up easily. When you are committed to a dream or vision, it requires imagining yourself as a horse with blinders. With blinders on, a horse cannot look to the left or the right; they keep their focus forward on their desired destination.

Any dream worth chasing will usually take a significant amount of time, often even a lifetime. You must pull yourself up by the bootstraps, settle in, and commit to following through. Endure through difficulties as they arise. Achieving dreams successfully also requires a strong sense of purpose. Without purpose, the dream may fall by the wayside.

Persistence is the act of moving forward despite setbacks and criticisms, fueled by continual hard work. It requires meticulous attention to detail. And how we conduct ourselves with those we encounter, both personally and professionally, matters significantly. Being persistent in pursuing your dream is a character-building endeavor.

Matthew 25:23 says, "You have been faithful in little. I will make you ruler over much."

Have you ever noticed someone whose dream came true, only to see their world fall apart? This often happens when the character of a person is not properly developed. Understanding the commitment it takes to realize a dream means enduring hardships, failures, and criticism. This is how we grow resilient.

You have just one life to live, so you may as well give it all you've got. Persistence with old dreams can always morph into new dreams. Do not be afraid to follow and fail. This is how the race is won and the dream is realized. When you reach the point of having nothing left to lose, after enduring failures, trials, and criticisms, you are on your way!

October 2

For The Love Of Community

Our path has meaning in ways we are unable to fully comprehend in the present moment. We are nourished and strengthened by the people around us. The friends we meet and where we choose to live and work are important to our well-being and to God.

In community, we become intertwined with like-minded souls. Some may bring art to the body, some financial blessings, others may provide sustenance and supplies, while others teach. The secret to a successful experience with others in circles requires us to take responsibility for every interaction. There will be challenges in accepting others and learning to work together. For this reason, the community is best served with a humble spirit.

Community is for people with common interests, similar ideas and subjects, or those living in the same vicinity. In community, every person brings what they have to offer. When people come together and discern a need in their community, it is a beautiful thing.

We see ourselves in each other and are influenced by every experience and the people who help shape us. Our lives are fuller and our spirits are lighter as we journey through life with like-minded individuals. How we relate to others affects those we come into contact with. As we interact, we cause another person to consider, think, and grow.

Community invigorates Love, and no one person is the only voice. In community, each person must have integrity for whatever may come. Because personalities vary greatly, every person has something to share. We are to build bridges and not blame others for our missteps, problems, or difficulties. Some may desire perfection, but no one is perfect. We must value walking in Love and being peacemakers. When we keep this in mind and choose to respect one another, we are walking in the light in a way that only heaven knows.

In today's tumultuous times of division and fear, look around and see your integral part in the community. You have unique gifts and talents to share, and they are essentially needed. Be the person who steps out toward the fullness of Love.

October 3

Seasons Change

Most of us enjoy a good routine. We like the familiarity of the same activities, and seeing many of the same people with amicable surroundings, day in and day out.

Although change can be frightening for some, many people pursue security to avoid disrupting what is familiar, driven by fear of the unknown. However, change eventually comes to everything. While some may fear change less, it is the bold who bravely embrace it.

Embracing change requires facing fears. The Earth is changing, and so are we. The seasons roll on as we watch the leaves descend from trees. Change is where lovers meet, where winter begins anew and later melts into spring, and where the heat of the sun shines down its glare. Therefore, we need not be enslaved by fear of change and especially bad habits.

And Scripture says in Galatians 5:1, "It is for freedom that Christ has set us free. Stand firm, then, and do not be encumbered again by a yoke of slavery."

Holding tight to the familiar while playing it safe in matters, creates outcomes that have limitations. Here, compromises and significant falsehoods can occur. True progress often requires stepping beyond our comfort zones and embracing the uncertainties that come with it. There are beautiful people to meet and new horizons to see. And you can bravely embrace change and face every fear!

And Isaiah 43:19 says, "See, I am doing a new thing! Now it springs up; do you not perceive it?"

We need to trust the Lord in every season of our lives. Don't settle for playing it safe and merely existing; limiting behaviors are a trap. Instead, invite the guidance of the Holy Spirit into your heart with a simple prayer: "Lord, come into my heart today and help me see where a change would be to my benefit. Grant me the strength to embrace it. Thank you. Amen."

October 4

A Recipe For Happiness

There is something about people who bring ease and an uncomplicated outlook to everyday situations. These are the people who usually see life with a broad outlook. They don't stress over little things, or sweat the small stuff. And because of this, they tend to be happier.

The definition of simplicity is the state or quality of being simple; easy to understand or explain, in contrast to something complicated. People who live happy lives often embrace simplicity, avoiding unnecessary complications. They have a natural propensity for simplicity and are generally connective and lighthearted. As a result, they are easy to get along with.

Every person views things differently. And maintaining simplicity requires us not to be easily offended. Some may complicate matters and bring confusion, but understanding requires humility. The more we practice walking in Love and striving to understand others, the happier we are. We must desire to understand those who complicate issues or lack simplicity in their perspectives.

Scripture says, "For God is not the author of confusion, but of peace".

Therefore, the best path forward when we encounter a spirit of confusion, is to consider being a peacemaker. Being a peacemaker brings happiness. And this is the place where humility and Truth meet. We can't have peace without the two, because Truth is the center point, while humility offers the power to listen and understand and move toward our center.

Additionally, people who impart simplicity tend to have more patience. And patient people learn from each other. Proverbs 27:17 says; "As iron sharpens iron, so one person sharpens another." So difficult situations require patience as participants are sharpened in their understanding.

Yes, we will face difficulties, but when we keep our vision simplified and our time uncomplicated, we often achieve better results. It's true that a simple-minded approach can help to resolve complex issues and uncomplicate complex ideas. Also, when we are easy to work with, we impress goodness upon others. And challenges we face become solvable without much complication.

October 5

Are You Rebellious?

Rebellion is a natural response to things we fear or are unsure about. And often, rebellion serves as a way for us to get back on track. For instance, Jonah's rebellion led him to run from God, resulting in his being swallowed by a whale. This experience opened his eyes.

Reflecting on my own behavior, I acknowledge moments of rebellion. This inclination often arises in the spirit of freedom, which I have always valued. However, every act of rebellion eventually brings me back to the original issue and request.

And a keen observer will notice that original guidance and instruction do not go away. While delaying compliance only complicates matters and makes things more difficult in the long run. Also, prolonged rebellion can negatively impact our mental and physical well-being, affecting our positive outcomes. So to find peace of mind, we must understand that rebellion is futile and hinders our success in our daily life.

We are continually learning and growing. And great progress requires a certain level of maturity. Even when we feel led to act, fear of outcomes or uncertainty about how to achieve them can lead us to avoid taking action. However, true peace is found in following God's will, as He desires the highest good for each of us. Furthermore, we may not fully recognize what is beneficial for us and might resist it. Despite our initial resistance, by the end of our rebellion, we often find ourselves on the path that was originally intended for us.

Embracing God's guidance with faith and surrender allows us to overcome our fears and align more closely with our true purpose. Ultimately, surrendering to divine direction not only brings peace but also aligns us with the greater good that God has planned for our lives. The best approach is to respond quickly and affirmatively to the Lord's guidance. A simple prayer can help you today. Say this: "Lord, help me to hear Your voice and obey. Amen"

October 6

You Are Never Alone

One spiritual practice in various transcendent teachings is self-sufficiency, defined as the quality or condition of being self-reliant. This means that a person is not likely to need help from, or interaction with, others. While self-sufficiency is beneficial to a degree, we are inherently social creatures, not created to be entirely alone. We need people and help from time to time.

Ideally, self-sufficiency requires us to be connected with the Creator for guidance and fellowship. With Jesus as our example, we see that He was completely connected to God, living a life of service and quiet introspection. He may have felt alone at times, but He was never truly alone. There are moments when God calls us to follow Him into places where no one else can come with us. We are like an eagle that flies alone, soaring above the clouds. And to be a person of strength who flies victoriously, we must rely completely on God.

Moreover, every day that we live, we hold a purpose. We are always either affecting someone or being affected by someone in some way. God's guidance and blessings for our well-being often come through family, friends, and even those who serve us in different capacities. However, there is no guarantee that a spouse, friend, or family member will journey with us for our entire lives. Nor is there a promise that we won't face situations that change our perspective, reminding us of our individual paths.

Therefore, we must remember that our ultimate help comes from the Lord. We are never alone when guided by the Holy Spirit, so we should not be afraid to walk alone. Each day of life is a gift, and time passes quickly. It's important not to look back with regrets. Many people stay in unhealthy relationships out of fear of being alone. They attend gatherings with the wrong people, or make poor financial decisions due to codependent tendencies. However, codependence is the opposite of self-sufficiency. Therefore, be mindful of any inclination toward codependence, as it can distract from God's leading.

When the Lord leads you to help someone, certainly do so. Do not fear; instead, trust God and soar like an eagle. Always remember that when you miss the leading of the Holy Spirit, you miss out on the abundance of good that life offers. Whether it's fear of what others may think or dependence on someone else, know that you can find security in God's love and care. You are never truly alone.

October 7

Mountains Of Restoration

Life can be difficult. And every person has significant experiences with personal inner challenges and struggles. Some may have been bullied, abused, or even abandoned. And when people have compounded traumatic experiences, they often become guarded from future hurts, by establishing fear-based protections. These situations often happen at the onset and can cause someone to live in a compromised state of being throughout their life.

Faith in Jesus Christ, offers freedom and forgiveness. And it's important to work through issues. However, restoration can take time, when the goal is wholeness. Negative experiences must be addressed, for the personality to be restored, to no longer be broken. And healing is a quandary that only God can decode. So we need to trust the Lord to help us.

Each of us can use restoration to some degree. And when the Lord enters your life, gradually, you notice matters coming to the surface, one by one. For many, there are mountains of restoration needed. And we might be surprised, as past issues and behaviors rise up and rear their ugly head. These matters reveal themselves and appear out of nowhere. However, to face hurts head on, we need to recognize the root cause and offense. We need to look at both sides of every story; the light and the dark that holds the soul captive.

You can trust the Lord to make things right. And when you are in an emotional quandary, the mountains of stuff and fear-based protections, can be uncomfortable and likely painful. These matters are difficult to discern and face alone. So pray and do not be afraid to feel. Let issues rise up unto the Lord, in order to navigate forward, in a better way.

The Father desires for you to be healed. To live whole and free from the past and from fear. Scripture says, "We overcome by the blood of the Lamb and the word of our testimony." So, a good thing to recall when matters reveal themselves before you, is to place the issue at the foot of the Cross in prayer and trust that it has been covered by the blood of Christ. Next, proclaim the Truth with your testimony, to the praise of God, for setting you free! You can do it!

October 8

Sabotaging Your Success?

Procrastination is unnecessarily and voluntarily delaying or postponing something, despite knowing that there will be negative consequences for doing so. And there are many causes for procrastination. A few examples are laziness, fear of the unknown, and depression.

Our actions have repercussions, and the results can often be dramatic. When people procrastinate, they accumulate yesterday's tasks with today's. Indecision is a precursor to procrastination because inaction slows progress. When people avoid making decisions, they often wait and procrastinate until something forces a change, which can lead to negative emotions and a general sense of discomfort. And procrastination adds to a lack of clarity.

It's true that everyone procrastinates at some point. However, actions form habits, and frequent procrastination can create confusion that affects those around you. If you seek success, it's best to tackle issues head-on. This approach will help streamline your accomplishments.

When you choose not to procrastinate, you choose to be successful. And as the famous King Solomon quotes, "success without succession is failure." So, to be truly successful, we must make continual progress. This means that, however we define success, we need to see our actions moving forward in positive ways.

Life on this ever-changing planet requires us to be flexible and tackle daily matters head-on. When we don't postpone our responsibilities, we gain a sense of achievement. Our steps become lighter, our minds clearer, and we maintain a rewarding, achievement-oriented mindset.

Do you make commitments and then delay the follow through? This is *not* the method of an overcomer. When you miss the mark, give it to God in prayer and ask for the strength to press through to a better outcome. Don't allow procrastination to sabotage your success.

October 9

Illuminate Your Life

Living an enlightened life is a lot like driving. We need to watch where we are going and stay focused, keeping two hands on the wheel as we make our turns. This is because there are all sorts of potholes and bumps on the road that can throw us off course.

Unfortunately, we are not always able to see where we are, or what is coming until it happens. The road may be foggy and dark, but there is still light peeking through. We may have a need for a strategic move, so the more open we are to our surroundings, the better.

For most people, life lessons often come the hard way—usually through missteps. That's why we need to be careful. Social experiences often involve judging others, but when we let go of judgment, our lives become more illuminated. While we may not intend to judge, it often happens automatically when our feelings are hurt or when we feel insecure. This response is usually instinctive rather than deliberate—it just happens.

And many individuals, when slighted or wronged even in small ways, are quick to cut off communication and cooperation with others. This is not the ideal approach. Taking the high road involves communicating. And every person is navigating an unknown path. Further, when we are honest, we often realize that we have done the exact same thing. It is as if God is saying, "Look, you have done this too."

We do the best we can, but there will be times when we skid across the center line. We are spiritual beings having a human experience, and as we bump into each other along the way, mercy becomes essential. At these crossroads, we need to ask God for help. We can extend mercy and receive it for our own failings, as well as for the failings of others. One way to cultivate this is by listening well. With time, we can hope to resist the temptation to judge others.

Say this: "Lord, help me to be quick to show mercy to my family, friends and fellow man. And let me leave the judgment to you!"

October 10

We Are Warriors!

When we come to Christ, we are awakened and given all that is required to be battle ready for our world. And navigating life, with a Christ consciousness, keeps our centerpoint on the truth that sets us free. The more conflict we triumph over, the more freedom we will have.

Without the Word of God, deception runs rampant. We might be deceived in ourselves and/or by what we see around us. And, even as we are built up in God, there are matters that come against us, as we fight for love, justice, peace, and beauty in our world.

So as warriors, we need to have the Sword of the Spirit in our heart to combat the schemes of the devil, who comes to kill, steal and destroy, by imparting lies, intending to hold us captive.

Think about it: In the US women are free to fly about, have businesses, vote, and live independently. But just half a world away, they are oppressed. Their voice is diminished and many live in literal slavery. It's a real struggle, and the suffering for a woman's freedom is significant. We can learn some things from the past, but the only way out is through. So in this present day, our strength is in The Truth of God's Word.

Now the "Fruit of The Spirit" is love, joy, peace, patience, kindness, gentleness and self control. Sounds fluffy, doesn't it? One might wonder how a person would fight a battle with these character traits. But this is where our true power is. It's in the fruit.

The way we walk reflects our heart. Violence, hate, and war will never bring good results; they only bring curses, death, and heartache. And as warriors, we must impart love, joy, peace, patience, kindness, gentleness, and self-control as our foundation. Our actions demonstrate our disposition, and it becomes noticeable when something is not right.

Can you imagine if everyone had love, joy, peace, patience, kindness, gentleness and self control? God only knows the work we could get done! We are stronger people and more effective when we walk with a higher mindset.

To seek more fruit say this, "I am a warrior for truth, love, justice, peace, beauty, and grace. I am prosperous, receiving, royal and leading. A servant of the Most High God."

October 11

Faithful And True

There are moments when it can be difficult to continue believing in a God-given dream or vision. Perhaps you've stepped forward for many years and seen little progress. Growing through years of believing and commitment while staying true to God's call in your life is not easy. You may wonder, where is God in my faithfulness?

And you may hold the belief that by being faithful and true, you will see your vision realized. In your mind, the dream is for this or that. But what if the sole purpose of the dream was for character building? We need to let go of our ideas, to make room for what God is doing.

Determined to be faithful and true on the path, we might say, "I will never give up." However, sometimes we must let go of our own ideas and ask, what is the way forward? Do we truly know what God's purpose is? Letting go is never easy, but it is paramount for God to work in us and for His glory to shine through our lives.

In Romans 12:2, Scripture says, "Do not be conformed to this world, but be transformed by the renewal of your mind, that by testing, you may discern the will of God, good and acceptable and perfect."

Yesterday, you were filled with hope and promise. Everything was new around you. And you could hardly wait to see what would transpire. Your energy was boundless. However, now you are closer to the edge of existence, ready to leave the world behind. And nothing is more important than this. You are no longer ruled by fear. By faith, in Him, you live, move and have your being. So continue to be faithful and true. Not for your glory, but for His.

Also in 1 John 2:17, Scripture says, "And this world is passing away along with its desires, but whoever does the will of God abides forever."

Dreams do not always require us to push ahead in our own strength. All that will be, just is, by the grace of God. For this reason, we must hold fast to truth, and not resist the will of God. Certainly, as we remain faithful and true to the Lord, we can trust our future is secure. We may not see a complete vision or dream, the way we imagined, but God's eyes and His plan for our lives, is bigger and better than we think for ourselves. Today, live knowing that God keeps you.

October 12

The Sword Of The Spirit

Spiritual confusion stems from fear-based thinking. It's true, we can be the most faithful people in the world, but still have times when we become mentally anxious and experience spiritual confusion. It happens deep within our being. And it can be debilitating for many.

And when a spiritual attack arises, fear-based thoughts seem to whisper to the point where your head is swimming with confusion. It is at these times, we need to pray and lay our thinking down at the Lord's feet. Also, it is best not to act or move on any decision at this time. Because if we do, we are likely to experience negative results that can affect others, along with our well-being.

Mental and spiritual confusion is an attack of the enemy. The uncertainty and bewilderment can feel like fiery darts coming from every side. When this occurs, we need to recognize the condition for what it is. It is a battle in the mind. And when wrong thoughts sneak in and confuse and impart falsehoods, mistakes are made, and often, we settle for less than our best.

Fearful thoughts and insecurities are negative whispers rooted in the unknown. One thought leads to another, and confusion arises when these negative thoughts compile. There are usually many "what ifs" involved. At these times, we need to pay attention and understand that the best way forward is to focus on who God says we are. We need to keep walking, knowing that the confusion will soon pass. And clarity is near.

The enemy is known as the accuser of the brethren. So, when we experience uncertainty, and our mind is cluttered with doubt and accusations, we need to hold fast to the Word of God.

The Bible is referred to as "The Sword of the Spirit." It is one part of the armor of God. In Matthew 4:4, Jesus said, "Man shall not live by bread alone, but by every word that proceeds from the mouth of God." Therefore, our best defense in a muddled state of mind is to turn to the Word of God and learn what The Truth says about us. This also helps to clear the mind. A powerful verse to memorize and call upon when confused is 2 Corinthians 10:5, which says, "Casting down imaginations, and every high and lofty thing that exalts itself against the knowledge of God, while bringing into captivity every thought to the obedience of Christ."

October 13

True Measure Of Success

When we have experienced difficult relationships and situations that have not worked in our favor, we can become disillusioned and lose faith in people and connections in general. Repeated problems and breakups over time may lead us to no longer believe in lasting love.

Discernment is necessary when making new friends and connections. And when past experiences have been less than remarkable, it's important to remember that everyone is imperfect, and being workable in a relationship requires humility. Choose wisely and connect with like-minded individuals who value integrity and truth, as this can help improve your success rate.

Additionally, we may have habits that cause relationships to dissolve. Past hurts can lead to self-protective behaviors that result in rejecting others, which is unhealthy and stems from unforgiveness. And rejection is the act of pushing someone or something away.

Awareness of our past and mindfulness of the open path ahead, enable us to make wise choices. Everyone wants a trustworthy friend. A good place to start is to pay attention to a person's words. Honesty and openness indicate a practical approach to relationships, while a lack of integrity signals potential difficulties ahead. Some people may never reach clarity.

Healthy relationships are the true measure of success. And even when we choose wisely, disagreements are inevitable. Therefore, we must walk carefully and not reject others out of fear. Instead, we can seek guidance from the Holy Spirit on the best way forward in any given situation. Consider these questions: Are you being humble and listening to another's needs? Is each person demonstrating an equal interest in the relationship? Are you willing to show up and care about others feelings to strengthen the bonds of friendship?

No one is an island. And to have good friends, in a world with so much division, you must first be someone who is a good friend. So, don't let the past destroy what the future can be. Choose to believe and communicate. Offer understanding and compassion. And even amid difficulty, respect one another. When you are wrong or have been wronged, you can choose to forgive quickly.

October 14

Bridge A Divide

One of the best ways to give heart every day is to become a great communicator. This is because communication is the bridge between people. It is also something most of us can improve on. Additionally, it is the best way to experience deeper love and understanding.

A big part of being a great communicator, requires remaining open minded to others experiences and thoughts. We need to prefer the other person over ourselves, and learn by listening. When we listen, we essentially focus on what the other person is saying.

Communication is an art. And understanding is a gift of Love that we give to those we cherish. Oftentimes we are preoccupied by our own agenda and ideas. We may be in a hurry, or we may feel needy or self-consumed and indulgent. But this never fares well when communicating productively. So we need to offer our position in a way that does not dominate the conversation.

And there are times when we get distracted by our own thoughts when listening. This is also not good. We need to pay attention to others as we relate with them. When we are actively listening, and comprehending what another is saying, we are not thinking while they are speaking. And the more a person feels heard, by active listening, the more at ease they are to express themselves in the future. Also, as we avoid judging, when listening, we experience improved relations.

There are times we need to be the first to open up and share our heart. And good communication will bridge a divide. So we need to be free from fear. We must make the first move, by asking questions. Stopping to say hello to share a word or a smile, can make all the difference. And especially when we pay attention to the answers and the responses given.

You can embrace the art and gift of communication and put it into practice. All it takes is a smile and the ability to listen without judgment. Believe today in offering a kind word of encouragement, knowing that every word you speak has value and meaning. By being present and genuinely attentive, you will deepen your connections and inspire positive change in those around you.

October 15

An Adventurous Life

It's human nature for people to want to attach to ideas, material things and individuals. And when we have something that appears to be working, we often feel a level of discomfort in moving away from that place, to the unknown. However, by practicing non-attachment, we can experience more or what life has to offer, as we have more freedom to move ahead.

Humans love security. We all seek it, and think that we have it to some degree. We tend to choose the familiar. But nothing is truly secure and fail free. And when we attach to things, we often do not receive the fullness that God has for us. When holding on to attachments, we might turn away new opportunities, especially as situations arise that we are not accustomed to.

So the best way to have an adventurous life is to let go of attachment. And we do this by seeking spiritual guidance from the Lord. The goal is to attach to God and not be afraid to try something new. In this present time, all things are passing away. So when we let go of outcomes, and trust God, we discover new visions, dreams, friends and ideas.

In Hebrews 11:6 Scripture says, "And without faith it is impossible to please God, because anyone who comes to Him must believe that He exists and that He rewards those who earnestly seek Him."

We should not play it safe; instead, we need to be full of faith. And as believers, we have the favor and protection of the Lord when we step out and discover new opportunities. We can leap into the unknown, and expect blessings. Additionally, with any bold and courageous endeavor, we may encounter opposition. However, there is no reason to cower or retreat. Instead, we must press through the opposition and remain open to God's leading, embracing the blessings that follow.

Pay attention to your thoughts. And if you are making choices out of dread or fear, you are more likely to experience negative results. The best approach is to get into a calm state of believing. Trust that God desires to bless you, as Psalm 37:4 says, "Delight yourself in the Lord, and He will give you the desires of your heart."

Finally, as you practice nonattachment to ideas, material things and individuals, you will grow. There is no need to fear, because God is with you. And if you do feel afraid, praise Him. Because as you do, you empower yourself, by giving thanks to God for leading the way.

October 16

Can Two Walk Together?

Can we agree that every person deserves to be heard? And that every individual has a perspective? And that no relationship should be one sided? Healthy individuals understand the benefit in honoring one another. And as we grow in relationship with the ones we Love, it becomes even more important to communicate, because this is how Love grows.

When we find like minded individuals it is refreshing and beautiful, especially when we feel valued and seen. And when we are agreeable to the concept of allowing others to express their emotions and perspective, we are practicing good communication skills. This does not mean we have to agree with everything another is saying. However it does mean that we listen.

Interacting with people on a daily basis is a dance we do for Love. Have you heard the saying "let's agree to disagree"? This is a common saying where two people with a point of view, listen and respect each other by speaking from their standpoint. They may agree to disagree on the subject matter and not see eye to eye, but when there is healthy communication there is honor.

Cutting off communication and not listening, causes Love to fade. And not listening creates roadblocks that are unhealthy. It does not enable growth. So when we won't hear another person attempting to express their thoughts and feelings in a situation, we disrespect them. Think about it, if you are unable to respect another, how can you honestly respect yourself?

Countless people stuff their feelings and give up communicating, which breaks down intimacy. Do you have trouble listening or communicating? Everyone makes mistakes, and the key to successful friendship is to honor each other by listening and sharing thoughts, ideas, and feelings. And people will occasionally hurt each other without realizing it. Further, if one person is always apologizing to be the peacemaker while the other is not communicating, there is no bridge for love to grow.

So, keep your heart open today and listen well. Attempt to understand another's perspective. You may not agree with their point of view, but you can honor the communication and keep the doors open for further growth toward greater intimacy and ideally, being joined in Love.

October 17

Faith In Desperation

The path of least resistance is often the one most people choose to take. But there is another that is more rewarding. This is the road less traveled. The one that is not commonplace. It is the frightening way, the windy road and elevated pass, through valleys, hills and utter darkness.

Two of the most contrasting options we encounter are taking the road less traveled or following the path of least resistance. And it is no secret that the choices we make, shape our destinies. The path of least resistance involves choosing the safe and predictable route, this route offers stability, comfort, and security within the known and familiar.

In contrast, the road less traveled is where we discover our wisdom and innate beauty. This path challenges us, providing profound insights and remarkable growth. It offers opportunities to explore the unknown, while taking risks, and stepping out of our comfort zones.

At every crossroad, we face a choice that will define us. Will you have faith today? Faith is the substance of things hoped for and the evidence of things unseen. It is believing before you see it. Faith is the practice that will guide you along the road less traveled, carrying you through difficult times. And with long-term faithfulness, understanding will eventually shine forth.

Furthermore, a faith filled life will allow you to see both sides of things. This is where you live in the blessing and know the temporal nature of all things. You've been through the valley of lack and have seen hills of abundance. Now you recognize the futility of worry and comprehend the importance of warmth in the spirit and soul. And you cherish every day because you are free.

To have faith in an age of desperation, makes you a fortunate one. You are blessed to be a blessing. Especially when plenty are in need and despair. And although people are never approved by their works, (lest any man should boast), you are greatly rewarded by your efforts, as you serve the Lord.

The road less traveled will cause you to look around and step out and about. You are free to smile at your neighbor and look for ways to lighten someone's path. There is no reason to play it safe. You are here for such a time as this! And by faith, this is the beginning of great things!

October 18

Warm Up To Conflict Resolution

In every relationship there will be times of conflict. And when these moments come, how we go through, is a great measure of our character. So it's good to warm up to the idea of conflict resolution, because it can be a positive experience when true change occurs.

How do you feel about conflict resolution? Do you try to avoid it? It takes strength to face issues head on, and God gives us everything we need by the Holy Spirit to do so. The place to start is with humility. And listening to the voice of the Lord for direction in all things is The Way. This is important in order to have healthy relationships that bring great rewards.

When conflict arises, our best defense and solution should be to communicate with active listening. And it is healthy to work through matters versus putting walls up, because excellent communication is the foundation to any good relationship. Additionally, when people understand each other, a real change of heart can take place.

Now, it's basically impossible to resolve conflict with a person who is stubborn or selfish or prideful. This is because there is a lack of humility that is needed to listen. In addition, there may be those who tend to be all talk and no action. We know this after a few tries. When people are all talk and no action, we must see things for what they are, and walk forward.

When matters are expressed and communicated but there is no change in behavior or honest effort toward improvement, conflict will inevitably arise again. What is needed is a willingness to change on both sides, as well as the ability to listen and express feelings openly.

There may be those who want to quarrel, but that is not Love. In Love, people enjoy when understanding comes. So today, warm up to the idea of becoming a better listener. You can prefer another over yourself and try listening from a different point of view. We do not always have to agree, but we can, however, honor and listen, as we seek understanding toward restoring conflict.

October 19

Forgiveness Is A Gift

We are lovers. Lovers of something or someone. Our family, our mates, ourselves, our friends, our pets and our neighbors. Hopefully, we live for Love and kindness, and especially God. And when we understand the principles of "Walking in Love", we grow exponentially.

"Walking in Love" is the practice of imparting love principles into every action. And walking in love brings better results to our life. Further, to understand this concept, we need to ask, "What would Jesus do?" This is because Jesus was love exemplified. And in every situation, He lived purely in and for love. So, when we have questions as to what we should be doing in any given matter, we can be sure we're choosing the best way, by asking ourselves, "are we walking in Love?" And when we take the time to consider this, we are honoring creation and our Creator.

Scripture says in 1 Corinthians 13, "Love is patient, Love is kind. It does not envy or boast. Love keeps no record of wrongs. Love does not delight in evil but rejoices in the Truth".

We are in the world to serve one another and be stewards of all it contains. And all of God's creation is precious and deserves to be valued. Many think this is a no brainer, but there are those who were never shown love as they developed. Plenty of people were reared in fear-based thinking. For this reason, "Walking in Love" is a practice to be learned and mastered.

Is there something in your past where someone forgave you? Forgiveness is a gift we give to each other. And although everyone falls short at times, "Walking in Love" requires us to be quick to forgive, both when we are hurt and when we are the ones causing harm.

Consider your own personal need to be forgiven. As Christ followers, we understand the sacrifice Jesus made so that all sin would be forgiven. So, as we contemplate this goodness, we benefit by following in His footsteps. In every situation, whether big or small mistakes, when we choose to forgive quickly, we are successfully "Walking in Love".

Can you think of anyone you need to forgive today? Perhaps you need to forgive yourself? Do it now, with a simple prayer. Invite Jesus into your heart and say, "Lord Jesus, forgive me for hurting myself and others. I believe in your sacrifice at the Cross and freely receive your mercy today."

October 20

True Desires Of The Heart

What are the true desires of your heart? This is a good question to ask yourself.

Before my salvation in Christ, I struggled to understand what I truly wanted. I had experienced significant loss and grew up in an environment filled with confusion—one where I was led to believe things about myself that weren't true. I was also easily influenced by others.

I wasn't encouraged to trust myself or follow my heart. And as a young woman, I was expected to conform to what I was told, as it was deemed best for me. My ideas were frequently criticized, even though many were good. So, when the Lord entered my life, I had much to learn about discovering my true self. I needed to understand my purpose, and find the courage to follow my heart, despite any opposition.

After some time, I began to reflect on Psalm 37:4: "Delight yourself also in the Lord, and He shall give you the desires of your heart." This verse made me question what the true desires of my heart were and whether I was delighting in the Lord.

My primary desire was to serve God and be who He called me to be, although much of it was still unclear. And after some time, pressing through, many who knew the "old" me, noticed a big change. I had a newfound confidence in believing. I also better understood my heart's desires.

Each of us has unique desires and choices to make. We may seek to help others, desire loving relationships, strive for good health, or hope for a challenging career or better education. Perhaps we want to make more money. But it's important to dig deeper. Our desires evolve over time, and every day, we can continue to discover what our hearts truly seek.

To gain clarity on the desires of your heart today, meditate on Psalm 37:4. If you find yourself on the wrong path or confused about what's truly important, ask the Lord to reveal the desires of your heart. It's never too late to find yourself in Him. God knows what's best for you in every moment. Although His timing may differ from yours, He delights in fulfilling the desires of your heart.

October 21

What Can We Expect?

When we are following the lead of the Holy Spirit, what can we expect? Do we expect radical blessings? Guidance? Perhaps success? Maybe we expect our daily life to go well. Perhaps we expect to receive more strength in facing the day?

Expectations are defined as a strong belief that something will happen or be the case in the future. And it's good to anticipate positive outcomes, but we must be cautious with our expectations because none of us can predict the future. We can be disappointed if things do not unfold as we anticipate.

There also may be times we feel a prospect of fear or dread. And when this happens, we need to recognize that this is not from the Holy Spirit. In 2 Timothy 1:7, Scripture says, "For God has not given us a spirit of fear and timidity, but of power, love, and self-discipline."

So dread is expecting something bad to happen. It is fearing, with a sense of impending doom. It is an oppressive and overwhelming force that sucks the joy out of life and smothers enthusiasm for new experiences. And when this feeling comes, we need to slay it with the Truth of God's Word. These types of feelings are the work of the enemy.

Yes, we can expect great blessings, spirit filled guidance, strength, and success according to the Lord's plan for our lives. And we can trust the Lord for whatever may come, knowing that God has our best interest and His will for our lives is for the highest good.

But each of us will have to face difficulties, trials, hills and valleys, to get to the mountain top. So expect great things, but learn to trust God for whatever comes. Do not fear going forth and doing good. When you pray first and have eyes wide open, you welcome the guidance of the Holy Spirit, who always has your good outcome in mind.

October 22

"I Will Do It, Says the Lord!"

Humans are often self-absorbed. And most of us do our best to be self-sufficient. So, when it comes to relying on others, and especially God, it can be a challenge. We may struggle with trusting another for our benefit and welfare. Often, we have real fear about what could happen or how we will achieve certain things, with big dreams and visions.

However, there is only One who can make The Way for us as we venture forth. And the Lord knows every part of the equation. He knows the people we are to be in connection with, the places where we will travel and what is needed for the journey.

And when we come to the end of ourselves, we recognize that we need plenty of help and guidance daily. Mainly because we are always evolving. It can be especially difficult to know where to begin, along with what exactly is needed to move forward through uncertain times.

Have you ever felt blind sided by life? Attached to ideas about things and the way they might work out to be? Perhaps you've been living for God, working to fulfill responsibilities, only to be let down, defeated or completely headed in the wrong direction?

When we are attached to specific outcomes, things rarely turn out as we expect. We might get excited, find romance, and believe that what we see is exactly what God has planned for us, only to realize that the entire experience was a significant teaching moment. At this point, we often feel let down and discouraged.

Also when we have a dream, our ideas and vision may differ from what God has for us. Therefore, we need to let go of our way and let God work. We must take our hands off the wheel. And a good place to start is to say, "Lord, not my will, but your will be done."

Finally, fear can be debilitating. It can keep us from walking in clarity. So, remember, "I Will Do It" says the Lord. You can let go of worry, striving and expectation. In Isaiah 46:8 Scripture says, "I have spoken, and I will bring it to pass; I have purposed, and I will do it."

October 23

God Changes People

There are many who have had born again experiences, where their lives have been changed and turned around by a power greater than themselves. And some may never get into the Word of God for further discovery of His magnificent Glory. While countless have yet to understand what it means to receive Christ. But this does not discount their journey.

When the Lord awakens the Spirit, we are usually at a place of openness to receive. We are offered a choice to follow and believe. Or not. Often lives are changed significantly, but every person's path is unique to the individual. So, we need not discount others for having their exclusive experience. And we need to practice non-judgement when sharing ours.

God is changing lives and touching people in His way. And Scripture says in Matthew 28:19, "Therefore, go and make disciples of all the nations, baptizing them in the name of the Father and the Son and the Holy Spirit." So, the best thing we can do is pray with our brothers and sisters as they come to know the Love of God.

We can share the Gospel if we are fortunate enough to do so, but it is our actions that will impress others who are finding the Truth on The Way. Telling others what they should or should not do is unproductive, because people are generally rebellious in nature. Preferring to learn things on their own and oftentimes the hard way.

After making enough mistakes and missteps, most people come to understand the significance of a Christ consciousness. We recognize the need for the Cross as we lay down our lives to follow the Lord's will. And whether we need healing, forgiveness, or something else, we come to realize our need for redemption.

Reading the Gospel is a blessing, and we should be grateful for the opportunity to do so, especially as we grow and mature. We must show Love to our brothers and sisters and inquire about how the Lord has touched their lives. And avoid judging or claiming that one denomination is superior to another. Instead, demonstrate open arms of encouragement and a willingness to grow in Love.

When we live by example, practicing forgiveness and integrity, we become living epistles. So talk about Love today. And demonstrate Christ with people. Lead by example and show how and why He became the center of your faith. This is The Way of Love.

October 24

A Commitment To Truth

Are you committed to speaking truth? When we are committed to The Truth, we are equipped to express experiences freely. We have good results in business and home life when we pledge to have integrity. When our words line up with our actions, the outcome is greater responsibility along with prosperity. This is the best way to grow in godly character.

By speaking our truth, we reveal to others an honest agenda and are able to look at the things we do with improved satisfaction, understanding, and personal growth. Walking in integrity, we know just what is necessary to flourish. And if we are confronted regarding what we are doing, we have no doubt about the questions or the answers. We are clear about what is true.

Having the courage to speak the truth reveals maturity. When we are not willing to face Truth, we experience deception that affects our life's goodness. So, the words we express must be spot-on.

This world is filled with deception. Many people will lie, cheat, or steal to be regarded as someone "in the know." Additionally, plenty say whatever it takes to look good. Many take the easy way to get ahead, a little fib here and a fib there. But for every action, there is an equal and opposite reaction. A breach of truth will reveal itself eventually., because every lie, big or small, potentially catches up to the doer. So, the best thing is to make yourself beyond reproach.

When lies are told, we are not making progress. Instead, we are holding ourselves back. It takes courage to have a commitment to the truth. In Scripture, Proverbs 6:16-19 says, "There are six things the Lord hates, seven that are detestable to him: haughty eyes, a lying tongue, hands that shed innocent blood, a heart that devises wicked schemes, feet that are quick to rush into evil, a false witness who pours out lies, and a person who stirs up conflict in the community."

Yes, every person has fallen from the truth at one time or another. But this is not the way of a spiritual warrior. When we commit to truth, we heal, prosper, and experience increased self-esteem and personal joy. So adhere to the truth today, in all things. Stay committed and walk in the light. And remember that if you miss it, you must repent and bring it to the Cross. Jesus is The Truth, The Way, and The Life!

October 25

Little Whispers

The Lord leads us by the Holy Spirit in small whispers that go tap, tap, tap upon our hearts. At times, we do not hear or pay attention, but listening to the still, small voice is necessary for guidance, protection, and abundant living. Therefore, tuning in is helpful.

Are you listening to the Lord's voice today and putting God first? Every day we are faced with a multitude of choices. We can rise, or we can fall. Each daily challenge brings unique results to every individual. And the Lord is continuously speaking to gain our attention. He communicates in these little whispers that lead us with guidance, vital to our well-being.

You may believe that you know what your heart desires. And you may even believe you know how to fulfill those desires. Perhaps you seek what you feel is important—financial success, relationships, or material things. However, the desires of your heart are deep intentions that exist in your subconscious. And these desires change as you walk through different life stages. What you may have desired at one time, may no longer be what is needed today. Therefore, it is important to pay attention to what the still, small voice is saying to you now, in the current season.

Tuning into the leading of the still, small voice takes practice. Our thoughts can become very busy. A good place to start is to clear the mind by first giving thanks for provision and guidance. Sending up praises to the Lord is the best way to combat inner chatter and bring clarity to the mind. This is where to begin. Praise invites and activates the Holy Spirit to speak and lead.

Revelation 3:20 says, "Behold, I stand at the door and knock! If anyone hears my voice and opens the door, I will come in!"

When we live authentically, we come to know the true desires of our own hearts better at every turn. We desire to receive all that God has for us. When times become noisy and the world appears to have trouble on every side, we will make better choices and experience improved results when we listen and obey the little whispers. You can hear where God is speaking.

October 26

God Is Our Lifeblood

Have you ever felt like the hammer was about to fall, as if something bad is going to happen just because you're enjoying life? This feeling often stems from trauma, a common situation for many. When a person is told they are wrong for doing good, it's no surprise they grow up confused. Healing from this takes time and requires addressing every concern to enjoy the journey.

Childhood trauma can drain the lifeblood out of a person, with significant damage and lingering negative effects into adulthood. Insecurity and fear often dominate, especially when taking risks or following the heart's pursuits. And only God can heal these deeply rooted wounds.

As a child, I was frequently scolded for things out of my control, like spilling a glass of milk. These instances made me feel that my parent was unhappy with me. Over time, I internalized these reactions, believing that even minor mistakes were signs of personal failure. It left me feeling anxious and afraid of doing anything wrong.

Did you know that childhood trauma falls into the PTSD category? It causes post-traumatic stress situations that need to be confronted. And when we become confused and blame others and ourselves, we are adding to the problem. This is futile, because everyone is faulty. Therefore the only way out is to forgive those who hurt us and forgive ourselves for not trusting the Lord.

Proverbs 3:5-6 says, "Trust in the Lord with all your heart and lean not on your own understanding. In all your ways acknowledge Him, and He will direct your path."

Lay down your pain at the foot of the Cross and trust God to bring recovery to your heart today. Jesus is the healer. Therefore, begin with forgiveness. Don't be afraid to commit your way to the Lord and break the cycle of abuse. Our human experience is to grow and overcome, and holding onto animosity does not help our recovery process.

Through the blood of Jesus, we have victory. There is no reason to fear that something bad will happen when you are in the Lord's care. Yes, you will have trouble, but God is good and will not harm you. He will guide you to safety, where you can stand in joy, when you trust in Him.

October 27

Guard Your Heart

It's not difficult to assess that the times we are in are complicated. We are busier than ever, and it's easy to be distracted. Additionally, danger exists everywhere, so we need to guard our hearts and listen to the still, small voice within, for protection and direction.

Technology has rapidly transformed our world, bringing both advancements and potential dangers. And as we face increasingly perilous times, we must recognize the threats posed by technological and political forces. Despotic rulers and nations with advanced weaponry can cause unprecedented destruction, and many new weapons can go undetected. Therefore, we must remain vigilant and prepared to move to safety at a moment's notice.

Power and control are not the ways that the Lord wills for us. And just as David was guided by the Lord to remain and wait under a tree while his enemies pursued him, we too need this guidance to stay safe and flourish. Zechariah 4:6 says, "Not by power, nor by might, but by my Spirit, says the Lord." Therefore, we must be adept at listening to and following the Holy Spirit's direction. The better we are at hearing and obeying this still, small voice, the more guided and protected we are.

For some, discerning direction can be a real challenge. Diversions slip in and can lead astray. Sometimes, we can get confused. And if we are not careful, we might uncover a dangerous journey where real-life issues quench the Spirit. Therefore, we need to remain prayed up and rely on God.

Additionally, we must guard our hearts, which means being careful about what we let in. We must be right with God because we are in a spiritual battle. This is the place to start. Especially when you do not know the way to go. You need God to flourish because everyday challenges appear from virtually nowhere. They just happen. So, make sure you are joined with God every step.

Finally, learn about the wonder of Christ and receive forgiveness along with the miracles that come from believing. Hold fast to The Truth. Furthermore, a great way to experience more guidance is to lead others to The Truth. This is how to hold a hedge of protection that Christ alone can bring.

October 28

Facing Conflict

People will often disagree. And many have a natural inclination to avoid conflict. But conflict is what brings resolution. And because each person is different, we need not fear the process. Instead, we can become better communicators and welcome "working" solutions.

People often avoid and dislike conflict because they've had negative experiences when expressing their perspectives. And poor communication can leave people feeling misunderstood. When this happens, conversations tend to escalate. And when conversations heat up, trouble can ensue, and many often say things that they don't mean. In extreme cases, physical violence may occur.

But what if we preferred others over ourselves? What if we put listening first, to allow the person with the issue to feel understood? Resolutions are found when individuals demonstrate mutual respect along with listening skills. We need to honor each other's unique perspectives. And a good way to de-escalate a heated debate, is to repeat what the other person is saying. This accentuates understanding, where the person expressing the thought knows that you got it.

We live in a divided world where our nation and people have fallen prey to building walls instead of bridges. However, we have the power to make a difference by refusing to succumb to division. We have the power of understanding on our side. There is no reason to fear facing conflict, especially when we can demonstrate that we can handle conflict in an upright way!

So today let us be the change and give another person a chance to tell their side of things. And when they do, let's repeat back what they say, in a simple way. Like, "so what you are saying is...."this or that." And then let us share our view with the same precision. We can choose to participate in thoughtful and precise communication that builds bridges of understanding.

October 29

For Your Good Outcome

Life is a challenge at any stage, but as people progress and grow older, the difficulties appear to mount. What is required is a great deal of faith and courage to face each test head-on. God has a way of making the impossible possible. He is Love, and His desire is to Love you well.

There is nothing too hard for God. So, as you seek Him for daily guidance, there is no reason to stress about the future or the past. You may face significant testing during difficult times. And if you have struggled with fear for a while, walking by faith might take more effort and be a significant challenge. This walking by faith implies that we must hold the substance of things hoped for, along with the evidence of things not seen. For this reason, trust can feel like a roller coaster.

Jeremiah 32:27 says, "Behold, I am the Lord, the God of all mankind; is anything too hard for Me?"

Fear can cause people to make poor decisions, and living in the past does not allow freedom for what the future holds. Therefore, we need to take life one day at a time. No one knows what a day will bring. What we do know, however, is that God always has our best interest at heart.

When we honor the Lord, He honors us. As we age, our best solution is to trust the Lord for a good outcome. Being self-motivated can lead to a plethora of negative results and situations that humble us. It's better to be humble first. We need not lie or walk in ways that deter God from working in our lives with a high level of grace and clarity. Also, keep your word impeccable; this is important.

Trust, trust, and trust some more. Consider starting your day seeking the Lord's direction for your life. Remember, as the Lord's Prayer says, "Give us this day our daily bread," we can focus on the day alone. And God will make the path straight amidst great challenges. Seek first His Kingdom. When you take your hands off the wheel, matters will work out well, for your good outcome.

October 30

Accepted And Loved As You Are

Have you ever felt you were not accepted for who you are? Perhaps by family or friends? Many of us experience a feeling of unacceptance with ourselves. We somehow feel unlovable for something we have done or just for the way we are, and this prejudice really hurts.

Maybe the kids in school bullied or made fun of you. Criticism can mess with a person, and it can take a lifetime to overcome. Growing up, I was expected to be what society and others wanted me to be, not my true self. This happens in many cultures, especially to women. Today, with social media and body culture, it is easy to feel as if you don't measure up. Many of us feel different.

But when the Lord touched my heart and soul, everything changed. I began to see myself through God's eyes. At this time, I chose to accept myself. I would trust God to lead and heal me, knowing that wholeness was my destiny. I was finally accepted for being me. In addition to the unique physical qualities I was born with, my personality was very headstrong. I had challenges with like-minded people. To walk my path, I had to separate myself from those who would judge me.

When we accept Jesus Christ as Lord and Savior, we become children of God. Hopefully, we put God first and are free to grow in truth and beauty. And what others think of us no longer matters. We soon learn that the only One who can influence our destiny is the Lord.

Do you struggle with self-acceptance? You can be free from mental oppression, flaws, imperfections, and any deceptive ideas. So, trust the Lord today. With salvation comes relief. And the world does not provide acceptance as we need. However, there is comfort in knowing that you are accepted by God. It is also good to know that you are never alone on your journey. God knows everything about you. He knows your weaknesses and your strengths and is by your side.

Please don't forget that you are fearfully and wonderfully made. And there are no mistakes in you. You have a purpose. And the Lord knows how to heal your brokenness. Also, there is nothing that can keep you from the love of God in Christ Jesus. This will help you to live judgment-free, to overcome, and be yourself. Finally when you have the Word in your heart, you will live with power in the inner man or woman. So, take the scriptures to heart and allow The Truth to set you free.

October 31

Change... Get Navigation Savvy!

When change comes, the moments we experience can be both exhilarating and frightening. Choices produce different outcomes, which is why we must become adept at navigating change. We may do our best to follow our hearts, but without the Holy Spirit guiding our steps and leading the way, we could have regrets later, wishing we had done something different.

Often, we are surprised when an unplanned change comes. We experience stressors beyond the norm, and if we are not relying on anyone, it can be especially trying. But this is where dreams are made and our courage is fulfilled. Through trials, we learn to navigate matters in a way that brings great joy, or at least a sense of peace, as we walk by faith.

And often, we may find ourselves under pressure, needing to make a quick decision. And if we get ahead of God, we can make mistakes. We are more likely to act impulsively and do things we wish we had not. Therefore, the key is, to remain calm through any changes that need to take place.

2 Corinthians 3:18 says, "And we all, with unveiled faces, beholding as in a mirror, the Glory of the Lord, are being transformed into His image from glory to glory, just as by the Spirit of the Lord."

We are being changed into God's image. And when we put God first, we discover an entirely new realm of adventure. With God, we can see better and brighter things. And if we are afraid of what lies ahead, we need to allow more time to "cast our care" on the Lord. We need to take time to pray and seek guidance, laying our burdens down. This way, we can be sure that when matters arise, we are making the best decision for the future and the time we are in.

In 1 Peter 5:7 Scripture says, "Casting all your care upon Him, for He cares for you."

Finally, it's true that hindsight is mostly 20/20. And hopefully we can look back and see that our choices were good. We are rewarded when we become navigation savvy. And we learn to navigate change successfully through practice. Therefore, dream big, seek first the Kingdom, and watch good things come. You are about to embark on something exciting and new! So, put God first!

NOVEMBER

November 1

Out Of The Fog

There is something very beautiful about fog. When we see people walking in fog, it is impossible to discern who they are or what they are doing. There is mystery here. Fog can feel frightening and exciting, even exhilarating, as if anything can happen. Everything is unclear. And as the light shines through, the fog dissipates, and all is seen. Everything becomes clear—people's expressions, their actions, and who they are—all revealed. Every blemish, every fault, and every dark mark, unveiled.

Because of this clarity, there is room for judgment. This may be why some people choose to keep their head in the fog. Many individuals live a life that feels a bit muddled or even hidden, where a simple float through the day's journey will suffice. And humans in general, fear being judged. Many do not even realize that they hold this fear, but it's true that people generally care what others think. We are culturally cultivated to conform to society in ways that reinforce this reality.

All of this begins when we are young and increases over time. However, when we invite the light of Christ into our heart, we are able to let go of all judgment; of others and ourselves. Thankfully, there is no condemnation for those who are in Christ Jesus. (Romans 8:1)

So, when we have the Light, we do not fear God's judgment. We can bring our concerns to the foot of the Cross daily. Our past, present, and future sins are no longer in the way of judgment. Because of Christ, we have complete clarity as we walk in the Truth that shines forth from within.

Life is very temporary, and every freedom we have ever hoped for comes from the cornerstone of what Christ did at the Cross. Believing in Jesus as our sacrifice for sin, allows us to walk with purpose, and to experience greater freedom daily. And especially freedom from fear.

So, come out of the fog and into the clear today by coming boldly to the throne of grace. (Hebrews 4:16) And although you may need to face fear from time to time, you can do it with clarity and freedom from judgment. The Lord delights in leading you through.

November 2

Don't Give Up

When you come to know Christ as Lord and are following the leading of the Holy Spirit, you receive spiritual gifts suited to your unique personality. Your vision is on point with important confirmation, and your path aligns with the gifts you receive. You are awakening.

It is an exciting time, however, when opposition comes, along with resistance, you will need to dig in and not allow anything or anyone to steal your gifts and vision. There will be challenges. So, be on guard and do not compromise your good outcome.

You may notice accusations in the mind and also from people. This is because the enemy of your soul is also known as the accuser of the brethren. And this force comes to steal, kill, and destroy. Also, you may have expectations. But keep going and don't give up. Because with every new direction and each step toward the prize; obstacles will occur and issues will rise in opposition.

And because of this, there may be times when a break is needed to re imagine yourself in a new way. Especially if you have had a vision or dream which has not transpired the way that you thought it would. Only remember, that failure is not the end, but a sign that you may need to re adjust your sails.

There is a force that is against producing love in this world. Therefore, hold fast and seek first the Kingdom. In other words; remember that God is in control. And when accusations come, you can see exactly what is happening. Do not allow the situation to obstruct God's good plan and will for your life. Also, people can be mean, and haters will hate. So do expect persecution and don't let outside chatter steal your joy.

You are rising. And whatever it is the Lord is asking of you, hold on to your intentions and do good. Keep going and do not give up. The path will evolve. And where you start out is very different from what will become as you follow. The Lord will bless you, when you believe, and you cannot reverse it. So, don't give up!

November 3

Walk In Victory

When we fall into sin, a contrite heart often brings an urgency to do better—especially if we have been walking in the light for some time. Slips can steal your joy and rob you of self-esteem. And after making a mistake, you might find yourself dissecting why you missed the mark, but often, that analysis doesn't lead to any real solution. The mistake remains, and it can feel like a significant disappointment.

It's true that we all slip up from time to time, often because we are hurting or longing for some unmet need. Maybe you've experienced a big disappointment and now feel vulnerable and weak. Perhaps you think that a moment of compromise will make you feel better. Unfortunately, it always leaves you feeling diminished. These struggles are closely tied to our emotions. So, what can you do better? And how can you walk in victory?

First, if you fall and miss the mark, don't beat yourself up. Instead, get back on track and be quick to forgive yourself. Can we do good deeds to make ourselves feel better? No, good deeds won't erase the mistake. Can we punish ourselves with negative thoughts for a few days until we feel we've served some form of penance? No, that only steals precious time.

The best thing we can do is bring our mistakes to the Cross of Christ. We need to confess and recognize what led us to stumble. Talk it out with the Lord and acknowledge your sin. Then ask God to strengthen you and help you walk in victory. Believe that you can do better in the future. We are all growing, and as long as we have life, we will continue to grow.

So, what can we do better? We can remember God's grace and His great mercy. We remember that He has a plan for our lives and that He orders our steps. And most importantly, we remember that He loves us. We don't need to act out when we are hurting; it's pointless. Only God can bring healing to our hearts and lives, and only He can change us. Remember, it's not that we first loved Him, but that He first loved us.

November 4

God Understands

We all have a handicap in one way or another. We may have a physical handicap, such as a weakness in our body, or perhaps we feel unqualified mentally for some reason. Maybe we have an emotional bondage. Something that makes us feel less than 100% of what the ideal is for us. But God knows every hair on your head, and He understands your weakness.

A handicap makes you feel needy and disadvantaged in an area of your life. Paul had a thorn in his side that God did not remove. But this did not stop Paul from doing the work of the Lord. In fact, Paul pressed through this weakness in God's strength and not his own.

Having weaknesses can be painful. And no one likes to feel less than their best. However, we need not invite further pain. We need to understand that the Lord's strength is made perfect in our weakness. So when you are weak, rely solely on God to accomplish what you need to carry out. He understands you completely. And you can trust Him to strengthen you daily.

It's comforting to know that you are never alone and that every human has weaknesses. You are fearfully and wonderfully made and uniquely fashioned. And there is none like you, with your set of gifts, abilities, strengths and weaknesses. Every fault and every muscle in you is utilized in the grand scheme of things, so you can flourish and fulfill your purpose.

Therefore, keep pressing through weakness and do not give up. When opposition comes, and you face all sorts of challenges, that's when it's time to pray and ask God to guide and strengthen you. You will have increased blessing and clarity for daily living, when you acknowledge that your achievements are not of yourself alone. "I will do it!" says the Lord.

November 5

Crooked Places Straight

The Lord is all knowing. He goes before you and understands exactly what you need, at every turn. And moment by moment, He makes the crooked places straight. Therefore, you can walk in freedom today, knowing that progress is being made.

Sometimes, when faced with multiple issues that need healing, we notice a repeated resurfacing of problems and wonder when we will ever see an end to them. You may question how to become the person you envision yourself to be and ask, "How will I overcome?"

The road can be treacherous. And on this crooked path, we need to keep Christ as our focus. When we have our hope in the Lord each day, we recognize the Holy Spirit working. And although there may be all sorts of tangled paths and troubled waters, our faith remains that God will bring it to pass. There is no way around it! We must go through things to get there.

The goal is to completely trust Jesus. And God's Love for you is of great importance. So hold on and believe what Jesus did to set you free. He gave His life, to heal you. Our walk on the narrow path is not something we do in our own strength. And the changes we see in the inner man/woman, go beyond what we can do for ourselves. It is surely supernatural.

God gets the glory on this path of healing and comfort. It is the path of restoration. Restoration from hurts, disappointments, injustices and sin. So take your hands off every situation and outcome. Give all to God and cast your care. For He cares for you and will see you through.

One thing you can do on the crooked path, is to pray to become more disciplined. And as you grow in faith with a humble disposition, in due time, God will restore you. He goes before you and knows just what you need and when you need it. The main thing is that whatever you do, don't give up. He makes the crooked places straight, so you don't have to.

November 6

Purpose In Trials

As we journey upward to the place where we truly belong, we have much to give. Yet, at various times, we experience discomfort and difficulty in applying our gifts. In our efforts, we climb toward the mountaintop and do our best along the way. With each step, we strive to make a meaningful difference.

However, there may be times, we experience a failure of some sort and arrive at a basin. Perhaps the vision we hold in mind, is not what we are seeing come to pass. Maybe we have suffered a loss. At this point, it's not unusual to run out of energy. We may experience a level of discomfort. And discomfort can increase difficulty. Yet, don't give up. Your reward is coming.

Sometimes, we get thrown off course. However, the Lord wants to bring you to a place of solid ground. He wants you to be level and believing, firmly planted in a foundation of faith. And if you are not relying on God and bringing your cares to Him, on a regular basis, you might experience bigger troubles. Therefore, it's important to understand that where there are places with highs and lows, there is usually discomfort. And this makes us desirable for a path that is level.

The Lord has called you to His purposes and does not desire for you to live with ups and downs. His will for your life is a peaceful and steady walk. And He may want you to climb a hill, but climbing is rarely without struggle. It's not a comfortable experience. In fact, you may feel a temporary high from achieving something, but for peace and continual care, steady is best.

There is purpose in our trials. And there will be peaks and valleys, however, how we go through circumstances is a testament to God's goodness. So even though there is much going on, there is no need to accomplish or achieve perceived goals in your own strength. You must have faith. And faithfulness brings comfort in difficult circumstances. This is the prize we must strive for.

Have you ever found yourself in the valley of darkness, only to wonder, where do I go from here? Take time to pray and ask God to direct your path. He knows The Way forward for you.

November 7

Our Great Intelligence

Feeling out of control can be unsettling. With so much happening around us, it's difficult not to be affected by world events from one moment to the next. Everyone carries a level of pain, facing private and personal challenges. And because so much is beyond our control, we focus on managing what we can. While exercising self-control in our speech and actions is beneficial, we also need to release the matters happening around us, trusting that God is ultimately in control.

The Lord is our Great Intelligence. He is all-knowing. And isn't it comforting to know that we don't have to know it all? God knows exactly what we need and when we need it. This Great Intelligence understands everything about us and how the world works with us in it. For this reason, we can let go and turn our will over. We do not need to perceive our way in everything.

When we are uncomfortable, we are moved to action. And pressure often prompts us to grow through situations that feel out of our control. It may be that we need to change something or step out in some way. Circumstances may even be frightening. But this Great Intelligence we call God, knows what we can handle and is changing us within, especially as we let go and trust.

We cannot manage all things and oversee all outcomes. And when we hold on to control, we are not trusting. Instead, we demonstrate distrust toward our Creator. And we overcome the world, through storms and challenges. God blesses us amid our struggles. Therefore, we can face issues head-on, knowing a greater power is at work for our best outcome and benefit.

And through it all, we are becoming more Christlike. Especially as we face matters head on. Furthermore, most people would prefer God to run things anyway. We recognize that our wisdom does not measure up to the miraculous wisdom that created the Universe and everything in it.

Scripture says in Jeremiah 29:11 "For I know the plans I have for you," declares the LORD, "plans to prosper you and not to harm you, plans to give you hope and a future." So, remember today, that you can let go of control because a greater intelligence is at work for your good outcome.

November 8

The Anxious Heart

God changes us on the inside and after some time, we notice it revealed on the outside. And as the Lord works on the inner man/woman, we grow to become enlightened and stable.

Have you ever said something you never thought you would say? Or done something that shocked you, all by your own actions? How do we change the actions and thoughts that seem to occur outside of our own will and awareness? The ones that seem to just happen?

Our soul is mysterious in many ways. Habits formed in childhood, along with personality traits we are genetically inclined toward, shape us. And inside the soul, we are pulled by both light and dark forces. As we grow and mature, we experience an unfolding of these forces daily, moving us gradually toward a better version of ourselves. At least this is our hope.

Change is uncomfortable for most, and people generally prefer comfort. Rarely do we heal ourselves completely.

We may work to make changes, like quitting a bad habit or starting something positive, but the outcome and timetable are supernatural, because they belong to God.

Have you ever felt an insatiable craving for something or found yourself wanting a bit of relief so you could relax? Feeling needy is unpleasant and not a good place to be. And if we struggle to change ourselves, we may notice we feel anxious. This is an indication that it is time to pray.

God understands and heals the anxious heart. And our struggle is for the sake of His glory, so the timetable belongs to Him. He pours out a blessing that alleviates our discomfort as we trust Him.

What does it mean to be pardoned? It means to be forgiven of sin. God is merciful, and when we feel troubled, anxious, unsettled, and needy, it is important to remember that God knows and He is working inwardly for our benefit. We may not know exactly what our soul needs or is calling for in the exact moment. It could be unconfessed sin or a selfish motive that needs to be addressed. But the Holy Spirit is our comforter, and Christ died to set us free. To release us into perfect peace.

November 9

Love With Contentment

How often can you honestly say you feel content? Hopefully, a good portion of the time. Yet, many live with a silent sense of discontent. And discontent often manifests as a desire for more—especially for something beyond a person's current circumstances.

And while many live with expectations, they also carry ideas and beliefs about their role in the culture. At our core, humans generally desire to be admired and loved. However, countless people strive for a form of admiration and contentment that is fleeting and falls short of the ideal. Navigating "The Way" amid various influences can lead to contradictions and conflicts. Therefore, it is essential to have a grateful heart that appreciates being alive to follow your heart, dreams, goals, and visions.

You are here for such a time as this, with a uniquely distinct purpose. To be content, you must understand that you are welcomed, loved, and accepted as you are by the Lord Jesus Christ. Your words, however, can cause discontent. So, learning to say what is needed, when it is needed, is crucial to maintaining contentment. Recognize the importance of choosing words wisely. When you are not mindful of your expressions, and too many words are spoken, trouble is bound to arise.

Learn to speak the Truth in Love, and avoid justifying situations after the fact. When we speak the Truth in Love, we can trust that the outcomes will align with the highest good, according to the Lord's will. There is no need to defend a position that speaks for itself. Along the path, rejoice in the Truth and The Way that God is leading you. Avoid getting caught up in conversations that muddy the water with unnecessary explanations as you become more true to who you are.

And to experience more contentment, you need three primary things: First, know that you are greatly loved by God and redeemed by Christ's sacrifice. Second, be grateful for what you have. And third, watch your words! You can do it!

November 10

Blessed To Be A Blessing

The path of least resistance is often the path we take. This is the easiest way. But there is another that is more rewarding. It is the road less traveled. A road that is not commonplace. This is the road for extreme personal growth, knowledge and mystery. It is a frightening and unknown windy path. An elevated pass, above the fray and full of light, that travels beyond any dark valleys.

When you have been faithful for a long time, you learn to respect the temporal nature of all things. And with this, it is easy to cherish every day because you are relatively free. Also, you understand the challenges of pressing into the resistance to determine yourself to shine forth. You have gone through it and now you are strong. And after multiple trials, peaks and valleys, you are able to uncover mysterious wisdom and natural beauty. In this circumstance, you find yourself seeping with experience and magnificence. Is this not a wonderful state of being?

Today, wisdom allows you to recognize the significance of keeping God in the center of your life, along with the importance of loving others. At this point, you are at the beginning of great things! Hopefully you have lived through the valley of lack and experienced the hills of abundance. Now you are able to recognize the futility of worry. And you understand the need for warmth toward your fellow travelers. You are capable of loving deeply, in soul and in spirit.

We are the fortunate ones who are blessed to be a blessing. And many are in need and despair. Often, the times we are in, feel desperate. So we must pour our hearts out, with no expectation of anything in return. And although we will never be approved by our works, lest any man should boast; we are greatly rewarded by our efforts to serve God, in giving what we can today.

So look around you, knowing that the greatest joy is in giving. You are blessed to be a blessing and can give your time, your talents, and your treasures. Look for ways to lighten someone's path. And smile at your neighbor. Because this is where bliss begins. Blessed to be a blessing.

November 11

The Spirit That Flows

We are created beings, who are creative people. And we are meant to do great things. Each of us has something beautiful to bring into existence. However, oftentimes, we are distracted. Especially with technology at the forefront of our world. Plenty of individuals are addicted to tech and it can be enthralling. Now machine learning is finding out about us!

What we give and produce is deeply connected to the condition of our heart—our spirit. In today's world, our devices often control much of our attention and actions, causing many to become disconnected from their innermost feelings. However, we achieve great things for the benefit of our world when we look within and spend time getting to know God, our Creator, and ourselves.

We are a hungry people. But hungry for what? When we say yes to the Truth, we gain guidance and understanding. We may wonder why we do what we do. And we may hunger and thirst for more and still have much. However, anything that becomes more important to us, than the spirit within, is troubling. There may be a lack of satisfaction. And yet we strive and attempt to fill up on things like technology, sex, drugs, money, and materialism. Even though these quench the spirit.

Within each of us, Love exists. And this Love goes beyond our comprehension. A good way to pay attention to your heart condition is to be aware of your motives. It may take a bit of digging to uncover motives, but you need to do this so that you do not compromise the gifts you are given. In no way, do you want to stifle, ignore, snuff out, or wound the spirit within you.

Loving your life and the Creator, requires you to check your heart daily. And as a child of God, your soul and spirit are the most important thing that you have. Especially as you venture out and explore your purpose. What you do and what you think, and who you rely on for your daily satisfaction, is very important to bringing great things into this world, creatively.

So remember that the joy of the Lord is yours daily. And as the world evolves, rely on the creative genius that is God. Fear not and don't quench the spirit that flows through your soul. With God as your guide, anything is possible. And when you allow God to be the leader in your daily life, nothing can stop you in your creative purpose. A great prayer to pray is the Lord's prayer. Especially, "Lord, thy Kingdom come, thy will be done, on earth as it is in heaven".

November 12

Freedom - You Can Do It!

When you have lived a life of captivity and been stifled by situations out of your control, it can be quite an experience to work out your freedom. But you can do it!

Perhaps you need to relearn everything about being yourself and being brave because you were not allowed to be yourself as you were developing in this world. Maybe you were heavily criticized for things you believed or ideas that you had about this or that. And now you struggle to express your thoughts and follow your heart.

When we are not encouraged in our dreams and ideas, we can experience a state of confusion and sadness. We may feel mistaken. Because of this, we don't know how to follow our hearts and change. Also, peer pressure or intimidation from family members, clergy, friends, or co-workers can be devastating. For this reason, it takes courage to overcome and be bold and true.

The important thing is to not waste any more time being oppressed by others or repressed by your own actions. Your success in the end will be sweeter, now that you have overcome the hindrance of being oppressed, to hobble along.

The people who appreciate freedom the most are those who never had it. And when they experience freedom, it usually comes as a God moment. It is like a new birth. In other words, when the Lord enters in, the only choice that remains is to be true. No more lies, no more compromises. Only the freedom to be. And it's true that those who have been in bondage and then set free are the ones who shine the brightest in many ways.

Nelson Mandela spent many years in jail and was released after a very long time. He had to forgive the people responsible for stealing his freedom and his time. The same goes for many individuals convicted of crimes they did not commit.

Freedom that comes from forgiveness is the sweetest freedom there is. And what remains is the Truth to follow your heart with clarity. Here, many discover a new lease on life. And you can too. Jesus is The Way, The Truth, and The Life. His great Love and Mercy are all that you need to be set free. It will be scary at times, but you can be brave.

November 13

The Lord Builds The House

As we set out on a path to do something great, we need to remember, to not get ahead of ourselves or God. The thrill when starting out can be very euphoric. It is as if you are experiencing a high. Endorphins kick in and motivation takes over. And mostly, we're thrilled and excited at all the possibilities. We make plans and begin to develop them. But it's essential that we walk in a way that does not waste time or money.

Maybe you have a desire to create something one of a kind and new. If you are wise, you will seek God first. Primarily because there is so much to do that it's quite easy to get lost in the muddle, and carried away by your own desire to grow and achieve. Therefore, it's important to remember not to strive in your own strength. Because, unless the Lord builds the house, the workers labor in vain.

Taking life one day at a time and putting one foot in front of the other is the most effective way to grow. Who wouldn't want to see their dream realized with the fewest missteps and mistakes? Every endeavor involves numerous factors; some efforts will succeed, and some will fail. However, there are always valuable lessons to be learned along the way.

And there may be times when you feel anxious because you see growth and want to keep it going. When this happens, it's easy to push or pull in ways that create more work and expenses than necessary. For example, investing in expensive technology one day, only to find it obsolete not long after—even shortly. In such cases, it might have been better to wait.

Building a dream can take a lifetime of effort. And as the Lord orders your steps, you do well to create *with* Him. So walk in a way that trusts God for your success. Each day, take in balance and remember that it is the Lord who builds the house.

November 14

A Good Father

It's easy to get caught up in the daily news and the challenges of life. If we are not careful, we can lose our joy and feel as though we are constantly fighting for survival. We find ourselves hoping for the best in a world full of lies, while navigating hopes and dreams, doubts, and fears. The Lord knows all of this. He is all-knowing and invites you to come to Him like a child, embracing a childlike nature in following Him.

Children are trusting. They are non-judgmental, and for the most part, kind. Particularly if kindness is modeled toward them. And kids are wide eyed and innocent, with imaginations along with dreamy dispositions. Most toddlers have a twinkle and sparkle in their eye.

Additionally, children are in the moment with their emotions. When they feel something hurt, they cry. When something is funny, they laugh. When they don't get what they want, they scream. However, as they grow older, many disengage from their emotions in the moment. Blockages arise and individuals experience less joy.

Mainly because they are not releasing their emotions in the moment and their feelings get hung up inside. When this happens, the eyes grow dark.

However, as children mature and develop, some lose their childlike sparkle because there is pressure adulting. Somewhere along the way, the child's nature was pressed down because of life's challenges and judgments. And when adults are regularly faced with troubles, aches and pains, and other stressful issues, their childlike being might lose awareness of their good Father.

Many don't feel safe to express emotions. There may be fear of ridicule or being criticized. Perhaps one fears that someone will think less of them, perhaps that they are weak in some way. But this is not how God wants us to be. He wants us to be in touch with our emotions and to feel every feeling as it rises. We need to express it, and then release it, in order to let it go.

The Lord is our comforter. He wants to comfort us in our emotions. He is a good, good Father and we are his children. So be like a child today. Release your emotions to the Lord and regain your sparkle. Take back your innocence. Rest at His feet. You can trust Him because He is your Father.

November 15

Get Up And Go

Life changes rapidly as we evolve through time. And when we need to move on and get up and go, we may feel inclined to panic. We might feel like we have come to our wits end. But it is here that we are at the beginning of a new dawn and our own wisdom.

It's easy to form attachments. We get hung up on ideas and people. Individuals may show us good and enduring things. While others may demonstrate that they do not have what is needed to go the distance for the time remaining. We may have formed certain ideas about how we thought things would pan out. It can be very difficult to let go and move on when these attachments are formed.

Most people have a level of beauty and goodwill, and when you have a heart of love, it can be especially difficult to let go and move on from people, places and things. This is because you can see the good in everything. It is also very easy to recognize the potential in souls. You may relate to people and ideas that have brought much into your life. Then the time changes, and there is a new direction needing to take place. For this reason, we need to stay fluid.

We need to cast down our own ideas and imaginations. Because when we attach to God and are committed to Him, we see that some of our situations are not meant to go on the next journey. Perhaps the connection was made for a time, so we could learn from one another. But now the time has come to get up and go. And because no one has the full knowledge of the future, attaching to our own ideas and imaginations is not the best way. Also, when we take too much time holding on to things that we are meant to let go of, we miss out on new blessings and opportunities ahead.

So, remain close to God and guard your heart. And get up and go forward today. Listen to His voice and attain wisdom. It is good to stay open minded, outgoing and friendly at times like these. And always be kind. Love never dies. So whatever you have had with a person or an attachment to an idea, it may not be part of your future, however, it will always be part of your life treasure.

November 16

Take Nothing For The Journey

When we have been in the same place for quite a while, it can be difficult to let go of material things, as well as familiar faces and places. However, the best way to experience God's blessings, is to let go of attachments and take nothing for the journey.

There are times God calls us to new frontiers and we need to be free to go where He leads. When we are burdened and held down by material things and mental attachments, we can become overwhelmed. So remember that as a Christ follower, you are free. And the Lord delights in your freedom! You can go where He is leading you, as God speaks.

You may need to start anew. And being heavily burdened is no way to live. Many people get stuck not knowing how to move forward. They feel restricted and struggle with letting go. Have you noticed folks with garages full of stuff? Or people that have a house full of clutter? There are hoarders who have so much stuff that they barely get around in their own home. This is sin. These individuals are greatly weighed down and held in a form of captivity. God does not want this for us.

God's perfect will is to meet your daily needs. So take nothing for the journey. The future is not promised. And when we carry a heavy load, we experience the weight of concerns that come with it. There's more work, along with added responsibility and stress. This can waste time and steal joy.

When God led the Israelites through the desert, He provided manna for the people to eat on a daily basis. And when you pray the Lord's prayer, you say "Give us this day, our daily bread". Therefore, don't waste your time with nonproductive attachments that aren't a blessing. Take nothing for the journey. You have everything you need inside, when you have the Holy Spirit.

November 17

Wisdom And Holiness

Life is a journey and we are meant to change as we march the road. And on the pilgrim's path, if we are the same person we were yesterday, we need to ask ourselves, why?

Humans evolve and grow. And if we are not developing and advancing into more wisdom, toward holiness, it's time to wake up before it's too late! We need to ask God to adjust our sails, so that we develop in the right direction to make better choices.

When we have been faithful for a very long time, we may feel we could really use a miracle. Forces come against us. And perhaps we have held onto hope and felt very alone. But it is in trials that we are changed to become Christlike. And just as the potter molds and shapes the clay, we are being formed into beautiful mature beings. Strengthened to withstand the storms and pressures of the day. So, the most important thing is to not give up.

Challenges can sometimes feel overwhelming. And hard times will come. Job was faced with losing everything when he said; "Though He slay me, yet will I trust in Him." (Job 13:15). And Habakkuk 2:3 says, "For the vision is yet for an appointed time, but at the end it shall speak, and it will not lie. Though it tarries, wait for it, because it will surely come; it will not tarry."

So, when God gives a dream or vision, and you have been keeping faith for a very long time, the thing to do is to focus on building godly character. No one knows what is to come on the path that is ahead. But what we do know is that our spirit requires holiness. And deep within, we know that the right thing to do is to change. Therefore, follow your dreams, above all else. And change to become more holy. Grow in Christlike nature and become beautiful on the inside. Do not focus on anything else. God will do the rest. He will bring to pass His purpose and will for His glory.

In the world, there is plenty of temptation with evil and sin all around. But as you walk through the fire, trust that your inner man/woman is being fortified. This is the most important thing to focus on. And finally, it does not matter how far you have come. He loves and accepts you as you are. So if you feel stuck, like you are not changing, or fearful of taking a leap of faith, ask God to help you.

November 18

The Abundant Life

Having an abundant life is a heart thing. One must have plenty to give, in order to live an abundant life. Because abundance isn't all about receiving. It is about giving.

Being awake to the temporal nature of things, most desire to share and make a lasting impression. And many struggle for daily survival. Countless people live on very low means and find it hard to forge ahead, let alone live with a spirit of abundance. But abundance is not a hard thing. It exists within the condition of our hearts.

With a giving heart and mindset, there is no way to avoid being blessed. However, it can take a great amount of faith to continue giving amid difficult circumstances. We may give once or twice and then feel the struggle and wonder why keep giving? But it is the one who does not ask why, but continues to give, who discovers abundance.

Now it is essential to look at motivators. Our intentions in doing something, is important. What is motivating you today? You can give your time, talents, or treasures. And when your heart is centered on being a blessing each day, you have fullness, and will find ways to abundance. However, when your heart is centered on lack, having an abundant life is going to be very difficult.

Have you heard of prosperity preachers? These are those who teach giving to get. And many blindly follow this lead, even though it does not work in the long term. Additionally, this does not produce real and lasting joy. When giving, we must let go of expectations and determine to give without expecting anything in return. And when we give with the right motives, perhaps to uplift another person or simply striving to bring a smile, we make the journey a little lighter.

Live the abundant life and be sure your spirit is willing for the right reasons. There are all sorts of ways to bless, as you offer a helping hand. Expressing gratitude to others is also a great way to give. Ephesians 3:20 says, "God is able to do exceedingly, abundantly, and above all, that you could ever ask, imagine, or think, according to His power working in you. To Him be the glory." Therefore, sow into the lives of others today and be the difference maker. Choose to live an abundant life.

November 19

Every Day To Give

Generosity is the best way to fight depression. It is also ideal for confronting lack and low motivation. Generosity is spiritual warfare and an important ingredient to the abundant life.

Did you know that when you are generous with your time and resources, it is nearly impossible to feel down, condemned, bored or useless? Isaiah 32:8 says, "Generous people plan to do what is generous, and they stand firm in their generosity." Another version states; "He who is noble, plans noble things, and on noble things he stands."

We can take these words to heart and live our best lives, when our efforts and energies go toward the highest good. Generosity must be given without expectation of anything in return. And it's important when we choose to be generous, that we are not doing it with a selfish spirit. In other words, to advance our own causes or purposes.

And science has shown that practicing generosity triggers a cascade of positive physiological responses. It reduces stress by lowering cortisol levels, boosts mood through the release of endorphins, and even fortifies the immune system by promoting the production of antibodies. Generous people often experience lower blood pressure, with decreased risk of depression, and increased longevity.

There are many ways to be generous and give in our hurting world. You can offer a kind word. Maybe provide help to a neighbor or friend with a needed task. Or even offer sustenance to a hungry soul. All of these are good. And generosity begets generosity. It works a bit like the game of tag. One generous act inspires another. So let go of control and give something today.

The act of giving, whether through time, resources, or kindness, acts as a tonic for your health. Nurturing not just the soul but the body as well. So give generously because each of us has good things to bring into this world every day.

Finally, let us not focus on the negative news of the day, or what may be lacking, for us individually. Instead, let us be generous with one another in ways that produce real fruit.

November 20

An Eternal Difference

Have you wondered what truly endures in this world? It is said that it takes three generations to lose an idea. And for most people, time passes quickly. Life is but a breath and then it is over. So, what really counts toward longevity and an enduring legacy?

Legacy is where life stories live on. And what really counts toward longevity, is the difference we make in other people's lives. This is what has lasting power for eternity. Buildings and land developments can last for a time and do make a difference in producing more comfortable living along with a pleasing worldly appearance. But they have less importance than touching the soul, for the sake of Love, which makes the eternal difference.

Are you aware of the impact your words and actions have on others? The good that you sow into the lives of others and the world around you, is what matters most. And you have influence to affect someone's soul and even their will and emotions. And when a word is given that changes someone's trajectory, to the glory of God's Love, you are on the right track to what makes an eternal difference.

People tend to remember a person, culture, or tribe, that makes the world a better place. Negative stories are generally uncomfortable and do not last. These stories may be in the news for a moment before they are gone forever because people don't want to go back and review negative stories and remember things that they would rather forget.

So remember all the beautiful stories. Remember sweet memories, beliefs and opportunities where beauty prevails. When we do everything unto the Lord to make an eternal difference, we are building a timeless legacy. And the best way to make an eternal difference, is to see a soul comforted, changed, and secured by the blood of Christ. So lead on today, because what truly endures is your every action motivated by Love.

November 21

Settled And Established

One of the best ways to live in freedom is to address any challenges you may have with others in the present moment. Make sure you have done everything you can to bring resolution to every interpersonal situation. Where there has been disillusionment or a break in a close friendship or family relationship, you are not truly free until there is resolution. And if you contribute to a conflict and then leave it unresolved, there will always be unfinished business.

It's not mentally healthy to continue forward without working through things as time marches on. We may believe that we are over a situation as we bury it deep down. However, this can cause conflict in our own personal freedom. Mainly because unsettled relationships can also cause us to move away from God, as unforgiveness settles in and builds a wall.

God settled the relationship between us and Him, through Christ and now calls us to settle our relationships with each other. Therefore, to live free, we must work out our concerns, so that there is forgiveness and if possible, positive closure. There may not be a future relationship, however, going forward, we can have peace.

It takes a humble heart to walk this way, because forgiving people who have hurt you, while owning up to instances where you may have hurt another, is not easy. But it is the secret to personal freedom. Additionally, this is how we build deeper relationships, for a future that brings us closer to God. The goal is always to have a clear conscience with no regrets.

A humble heart is a healing motivator. And many often live surface lives. Plenty rarely experience the joy of the Lord and the freedom that the Holy Spirit brings. And people are not moved by those filled with pride. So don't be afraid to embrace humility. It is one of the greatest gifts to bestow.

God settles our relationship with Him through the death and resurrection of Christ who gave His life for the sins of the world. When we believe, we lose the weight of mistakes and troubles locked within the soul. We rejoice because we are free. For this reason, we are to do it for others.

November 22

The Dreamers Journey

In a fervent dreamer, the dream takes precedence over much. This is because dreams have a way of possessing the dreamer. They motivate, lead, and direct a person's path in a way all their own. And often the route reveals passages where the dreamer has little control.

The dreamer's journey is complex and difficult for others to understand. They live authentically. If you are a dreamer, you will need plenty of faith and discernment. Quite often, the dreamer stands alone. And being authentic means that you are the only one responsible for your happiness and dreams coming true. There is no one to blame when a dream does not come to pass.

Living an authentic life requires you to do what you enjoy doing. There is no need to place cares in what other people think. Also, there is no need to count likes, or strive for false gains, or allow anyone or anything to talk you out of, or stop you from believing what is in your heart and the vision that God gave you. These are your dreams! They are a gift to you. And they are attainable in this life. So follow the dreams in your heart. Let the Lord lead you through.

Cherish the unique place dreams play in developing your authentic self. Give your authentic self as an offering to the world. And when haters and opposition comes, rest assured, they will fall away. All that will matter in the end, is that you gave what you were motivated to give, in order to follow your dreams. What will endure is the truth and all that you have mastered.

You are an authentic human being, unlike any other with your own God given dreams. So trust in following your heart, because God knows how to grow your authentic self in a way that nothing else will. The Lord knows every hair on your head. He understands what you need, just when you need it. He knows the best place for you to thrive.

Let your dreams help guide your experience and don't succumb to unbelief, or put up a false narrative. Additionally, taking shortcuts can lead to defeat. So be your authentic self. Look the naysayers in the eye and say, "This is me! And today, I will follow my dreams!"

November 23

Jesus Saves

There are times when we feel that our wounds are too deep to overcome. Maybe we were traumatized or experienced a devastating loss. We may have suffered abuse and now recovery feels insurmountable. Often, we may wonder how things will ever change?

Our walk on Earth is a training ground. And we need to face our root issues head on, and not turn away or become dull to the healing that needs to happen. We do not want to be hindered in living out all that God has for us. The goal is to attain wholeness and fullness of joy. And we are here to learn and grow and overcome defeat.

God delights in your good outcome and is always working on your behalf. And the Lord knows every intricate part of your life. So, if you are struggling with fear, pain or defeat, call on God for strength. And remember, as long as you have breath, there is hope for transformation.

Isaiah 59 says, "Surely the arm of the LORD is not too short to save, nor his ear too dull to hear!"

Stay close to God, especially when the painful feelings come. The Lord is calling you home and will bring comfort when the mountain feels too big to climb. And when the road is rocky and you feel you will never make it, trust God's perfect timing. His desire for you is to live free from chains. He works in you and around you and through others. He will bring recovery to the broken places.

We demonstrate maturity when we lift others and are patient, understanding and kind along "The Way". So lay it out in prayer and walk knowing that you are justified by your faith. Remember that the times when you are overwhelmed with hopelessness, the Lord is working on your behalf, for the highest good.

Remember, it's not over until it's over. And there are times, the journey can feel like it has taken longer than you could have ever imagined. You may feel as if your dreams and the vision you were given will not come to pass. There may be a level of brokenness that remains after a very long time. Perhaps there was hope for a loving relationship, or a position of leadership and now it feels as if it will never happen.

Remember Jeremiah 32:27 where Scripture says, "I am the LORD, the God of all the peoples of the world. Is there anything too hard for me?" God can do it and He will.

November 24

Inspiration Leads To Freedom

Inspiration leads to freedom. And our path takes us on a journey of learning many things, including what is right and wrong for each of us. And because knowledge is power, when we are inspired, we experience energy, as we uncover the subject of our inspiration.

The word origin of inspiration stems from Middle English and Latin "inspirare". Meaning "divine guidance". So, a good place to begin is to recognize that when we are inspired, there is divine guidance available. What inspires you? This is a good question to ask.

There is an unfolding that takes place when we are inspired by something. And when we study and learn a subject, we discover freedom to understand greater things, for the greater good. Likely, we experience more exuberance in living, because we are seeking out understanding and knowledge.

A smart way to overcome depression while having more liberty and freedom daily, is to pray, and ask the Lord for a new vision. Especially to do something creative because inspiration is the process of being mentally stimulated to do or feel something. This reminds us we are alive.

When these feelings come spontaneously, it is ideal. They strengthen our faith, as the spark of inspiration that unfolds naturally provides valuable insight. However, there are times when we need to actively seek out inspiration to break free from doldrums, hopelessness, or depression. So, if a life of freedom and liberty is what you desire, seek out inspiration.

Uncovering inspiration is complex. And as we pass through different stages, there are times we are raring to go. We may feel alive and on fire and surely recognize that we do not know everything. In fact, so much of our time on Earth is a mystery. This type of inspiration is truly divine. But after walking through the forest of living, with successes and failures for some time, we may wonder what inspires us now? Now that we are at a new place and stage in life?

Perhaps we don't know how to move forward. Maybe we are not excited by life any longer. It is here we need to pray for divine guidance. Now is the time to press in and seek inspiration again, which leads to freedom. You are here today until God calls you home. Don't get stuck in doldrums, hopelessness, or depression. Instead, seek divine guidance and ask the Lord for new inspiration.

November 25

Resolution With Repentance

Repentance, reparations, and recovery are the three R's for resolution. And we will never receive the recovery our soul needs, or all that God has for us, if we have not repaired our missteps. Moreover, we are not truly free without repentance.

Repentance is a turning away from sin—a contrite heart before God. In other words, repentance means acknowledging the error of our ways and choosing to change course. We must turn away from the sin that has ensnared us. And a contrite heart may also reveal that reparations are necessary for the sake of abundant blessing.

Repentance and reparations are not easy. Many people choose not to go there at all, to their detriment. When the Lord shows you that reparations are needed, there is healing. It's true that when we are in pain, our faith is tested. However, if we are unwilling to confront and lay aside our self-induced rebellious nature, we can miss out on the fullness of joy and the abundance of goodness and peace that could manifest throughout our lives.

Having a desire to please God by avoiding disobedience in the first place is the way to go. But in life, we are often desiring to go our own way. So repentance is a profound acknowledgment and sincere regret for one's past actions or behaviors that caused harm, pain, or injustice to others or oneself. It involves a genuine desire to change, seek forgiveness, and make amends.

When necessary, reparations encompass the actions taken to repair the damage caused by past wrongs. This involves tangible steps—whether through restitution, compensation, or active efforts toward reconciliation and restoration. Reparations go beyond merely acknowledging fault; they involve actively working to rectify the harm done while aiming to restore dignity, equity, and justice to those affected. Together, repentance and reparations represent a commitment to accountability, healing, and the pursuit of a more just and compassionate society. And addressing issues at their onset is the best way forward.

November 26

An Abundance Of Love

Do you have a problem with loving people? Some people can be difficult to love. While others are easy to adore. And although loving people in our world can be a challenge, due to the many differences and judgements that cause division; we must choose to pursue Love.

Countless people tend to profess to not liking or loving people in general. They have great mistrust of others and rarely make an effort to get close to others to know them deeply. Often there are hurts that appear insurmountable. Are you someone who is once bitten, twice shy?

Recognizing how much God loves you, and how well you are loved by the Creator, is an important first step to an abundance of Love. And being conscious of the limited time you have on Earth, helps to inspire you to become better at giving Love. When we recognize the value of the moments we have, we understand and know that each second and minute is a precious gift.

Further, when we understand the Love of God that's in Christ Jesus, we should expect to become more loving people. And it's easier to Love others, when you choose love over selfishness, pride or anything that interferes with the bountiful Grace you've been given.

Life is a breath, a dream and a chance for beautiful souls to meet. So remember to be strong and of good courage. Love requires you to be a loving person, who is not afraid to take action. If there are hurts or unforgiven moments, don't wait to bring them to the Lord in prayer and repent.

Take action to do something good for someone today. There is much to give and receive. And there is no better time than now, to demonstrate and speak love towards the people you care about. Whether it be providing an encouraging word, or filling a need of some kind; The reward is yours toward abundant love.

November 27

Testing Your Faith

Have you ever felt like screaming; "Stop this ride! I want to get off?" This is the way many of us feel at times. Life can be very trying. And we're all faced with matters that are out of our control and often devastating. Yet we carry on and carry through.

God's purpose propels us forward, along with our natural propensity to fight for survival. And as we grow older, we are faced with traversing a slippery slope. Often, we'd rather stay the way we are, instead of moving forward with what lies ahead.

James 1:2-18 says, "Count it all joy, my brothers, when you meet trials of various kinds, for you know that the testing of your faith produces perseverance."

Why was Jesus, going to the cross, called His passion? It was because of Love, and the realization that there is nothing more important than doing the Lord's will.

Suffering is not fun and it can feel like a decline. A withering away. And yet we are to count it all joy? Jesus did not want to go to the cross. He prayed and asked God if it was possible to remove the cup of His suffering. Yet, this was His passion and what He had to walk through and experience in his final hours on Earth. It was certainly horrendous.

Does this mean we should approach life with passion? I believe so—even when we are hurting and things don't look good. We can be an example to others by expressing great love through our trials. We don't need to lash out with derogatory comments when we are in pain, nor do things that cause us more suffering in the long run. Instead, we need to press into the abundance of strength that the Lord provides.

Love will fill us and reveal the miracles we hope for when we take time to pray and seek God's face. God honors those who honor Him. In doing so, we gain the understanding needed to flourish with passion, even in difficult times.

November 28

The Body Of Christ

Life is complicated. And profiling any group is wrong. Only God knows the heart and we are not to generalize about any group because we do not have the entire story. Every person is different. And everyone's heart is unique.

Many people think that Christians are a group. But they are not a group. Instead, they are the Body of Christ. Freedom fighters who choose to follow the leading of Christ as an example. Christians are interdependent people, independent of any group. And in the body, there are no carbon copies. Every Christian stands in their own unique place.

People are fickle, and the heart is difficult to discern and basically carnal and wicked in many ways. So it's impossible to say that all Christians are this, or that. People can say one thing and do another. It has everything to do with the condition of a person's heart.

However, Christ came to seek and save the lost. And He shows up brightest, in hearts that have been broken. These are the ones who haven't always had it so good. He clearly arrives in an open heart that has been emptied of self.

God shows up quietly in everyday lives. And He shows up in the ones who have much power too. The people who are on the front lines for change in our world. And because there is good and evil in every person's story, it's necessary to not be swayed by foolish rhetoric. There is a battle for the soul of man. And Satan is the prince of the air. So we need wisdom, discernment and loyalty to know, "not by might, nor by power, but by my Spirit, says the Lord".

Being part of the body of Christ, means there is independence. Independence to worship and pray, at a time all of our own. And there is freedom that comes with independence to be you. This independence does not have to follow a crowd or group. We simply ask "What would Jesus do?" This is what it means to be a Christian and a part of the "Body of Christ".

November 29

Thankful In All Ways

It's easy to be thankful when we get what we hope for. But it is challenging to give thanks when struggling or in pain. Like when our health is compromised or there is no money to pay bills, buy food or maintain a home. When provisions are thin, why be thankful?

When we do not receive what we believe we should see, being thankful is an exercise that requires a level of discipline. And it may be difficult to get words of praise out. We may not even truly believe what we are saying, as we attempt to give thanks while suffering. But it is important to continue, because after a time, the sentiment sinks in.

Thankfulness can change a person's happiness, health and outcome. And being thankful helps to counter negative feelings in the midst of trials and tribulations, because as we give thanks, we release positive energy throughout our bodies.

There are times, we need to start from scratch. From the very minimum. So we may need to remember to be thankful for something as simple as water or sunshine. It's the little things that help us to appreciate the journey, especially when we are hurting for something we feel we may need.

Scripture says, "speak those things that be not; as though they are" (Romans 4:17) So there is power in the spoken word. Which means to praise and use our words to claim what we do not see. As we speak hope, even though we have yet to see what we hope for, we speak forth power in that area. And we know that God is in control and if it is His will, it will come to pass.

Finally, to be thankful in all ways means to be content whether abased or abounding. This means with little or much. And the fact that we are alive for another day is a gift worthy of thanks. So remember to give thanks for the little things and the big things daily. Give thanks for the dreams you hold in your heart. And trust the Lord who hears you and listens.

November 30

God Is Our Protector

Our God is protective. And when we choose to give the Lord our heart, we learn to trust His will for our lives. He knows what is for our highest good, in every moment. And true followers of Christ can expect protection, because the Lord is a God of justice and fights for His own. When evil people mess with believers, they will account for it.

God knows what would be a determinant to the believer. And the beloved of God receive not only protection, but favor in much of what life offers. However, because of God's great Love for us, there will be times that we are chastised. We will experience trials. However, we can expect supernatural outcomes through situations, knowing that God works all things together for good.

Now, as born again believers and children of God, we can expect healing not only in our health, but also in the emotional realm. This is the spirit. The inner man or woman. And even though it may appear to be taking time, the work has begun. God Loves you with an everlasting

Love. So continue to trust, and keep walking forward. He will fulfill the promise of bringing wholeness.

When we are truly walking with Christ, there is peace about what is to come. The road is not promised, or easy. It may be treacherous. But we have the Lord's protection. Therefore, we are not afraid. In 2 Chronicles 7:14, Scripture says, "If my people, which are called by my name, shall humble themselves and pray, seek my face and turn from their wicked ways, then I will hear from heaven, and will heal their land."

This tells us that God is calling us to be humble and repent. And this call signifies acknowledging our limitations and imperfections, while recognizing a power greater than ourselves. Repentance is the pathway towards spiritual growth. It's an invitation to approach life with a willingness to learn and grow. And by doing this, we have protection.

DECEMBER

December 1

Help Is On The Way

Finding peace amidst the storm can be challenging. When the world seems to come crashing in and we face extreme difficulties, peace can often feel out of reach—even when we pray. We do the best we can, but every challenge becomes a training ground for God's purpose and goodwill to shine through. In these moments, it's crucial to check our hearts and reflect on who is in charge.

And most of us desire peace to navigate daily challenges, big and small. We often find peace more attainable in smaller issues, reasoning there isn't as much to lose. Yet, our God is a Way Maker through everything. Therefore, as believers, we are learning to trust the Lord, knowing that through any storm, He will work all things together for our good.

Sometimes, extreme situations arise to capture our attention. Could it be that we've been ignoring signs and walking in the wrong direction? The Lord is always calling us to follow and trust Him for our good outcome. Sometimes we listen; other times, we don't. But when we finally come to the end of ourselves and realize we are not in control, we find the help and deliverance we need through the most difficult situations.

No one enjoys difficulties and painful experiences, although they are a part of life. And bigger challenges awaken us to the idea of perfect peace through trust in God. When we put issues in their rightful place, we do better. We are not God; we are simply sojourners needing guidance, direction, covering, deliverance, and, most importantly, peace through the storms.

We have only so much time on Earth and these changes lead us to our eternal home. In the twinkling of an eye, our time is up. We can choose to embrace the process, knowing our path is laid out before us in perfect Love. There is no need to be afraid. Help is available for every situation when we pray. And we can find peace by resting in the mighty hand of the Lord.

December 2

The Hardest Part

Tom Petty had a famous song, "The Waiting Is The Hardest Part". And he captured what many of us feel. Waiting is difficult. Whether it's waiting for progress in our home life or business, waiting for a test result, or a loved one returning home from overseas, it's never easy to wait.

The idea of delayed gratification is not a pleasant concept for most people. We crave immediate results and we want instant satisfaction. Sometimes, the struggle of waiting can be painful, even agonizing. It challenges our natural inclinations. However, waiting builds trust and godly character.

And when you think about it, waiting and discipline go hand in hand. The better we get at waiting, the more disciplined we become—and the more disciplined that we are, the better we become at waiting. Dieting requires waiting. And quitting a habit like smoking demands it. In these instances, moments once filled with familiar actions, are now filled with longings and cravings.

Another challenge of waiting is the mental battle that can ensue. We often overthink situations, making them seem bigger than they are. Additionally, we may choose to ignore our feelings and seek instant gratification elsewhere in an attempt to fill the void. However, waiting with patience and discipline is the ideal. True self-control lies in the ability to wait well.

So, how well do you wait? Are you able to see the bigger picture as you go through the fire? When you let go and trust the Lord in your seasons of waiting, you become better at maintaining discipline, while also treating self and others with grace. And although waiting is often uncomfortable, it is a valuable experience that we need to pay attention to.

Choosing instant gratification often leads us to poor choices. So we must learn to wait without unrest. And waiting can be likened to fasting. When we know and understand that it is a challenge, and that the discomfort we feel is healthy—we can go through better. And waiting produces Godly character. In our waiting, we become more aware of our disposition, along with our level of trust, and our purpose. Yes, the waiting is the hardest part. Yet, it is also an important part of maturing.

December 3

Our Ways Are Not God's Ways

Every person has a story. And most people are driven by their ideas and dreams, which shape and propel their lives in unique ways. Our thought life, subconscious mind, and spirit, guide us in creating our living reality. Additionally, we are influenced by those around us—family, friends, and the culture we live in. And due to many outside influences, having a direct path to our unique vision is highly unlikely. We must be patient as situations unfold and trust God to guide us through.

Jeremiah 29:11 reminds us: "For I know the thoughts and plans I have for you," declares the Lord, "plans to prosper you and not to harm you, plans to give you hope and a future."

God is omnipotent. And He knows you intimately. His desire for you is good. And along the way, there are often circumstances that make the way seem crooked and steep. Often, poor choices lead to chastisement. When this happens, we must take responsibility for our actions and accept the forgiveness that Christ offers. By doing so, we stay on course to receive God's grace and unmerited favor. If we choose to rebel or walk away, we face delays and tougher lessons ahead.

Life can be intimidating, and difficulties are inevitable. But we need not be fearful. As children of God, we can trust that a good outcome is guaranteed. We have everything we need to succeed on this journey. However, realizing a dream requires character—especially if we want to maintain the success of that dream. It's crucial to be aware of this, as it is a tragedy to see someone achieve a dream only to sabotage it and lose the blessing they once strived for.

Furthermore, a person's journey may reveal that there are other important things that God is doing. So stay flexible with the original vision. Receive healing in trials and find peace as you continue to pursue the vision in your heart. And God's grace and unmerited favor toward you remain.

Therefore, call on the name of the Lord Jesus Christ every day and especially if and when you fall, to be restored. You may need to adjust your sails as you grow with experience. The important thing is to never give up. Especially when you fail or fall. Do not be afraid to step out and follow your heart's desires. This is how to discover God's will, His way, and His blessing.

December 4

Omnipotent And Benevolent

To be omnipotent and benevolent would be extraordinary. Omnipotence means having unlimited power—the ability to do anything. Benevolence, on the other hand, means being kind, compassionate, and caring. Our God embodies both omnipotence and benevolence.

People love power and constantly strive for it. The more power they obtain, the more they desire. And when people believe they have power, it is easy for them to forget just how powerless they truly are, as the sin nature works to justify a fragile reality.

There are indeed powerful people in our world—rulers of nations, those with great wealth—and others who control much. But they are not omnipotent. In an instant, a tornado, earthquake, or another natural disaster can strip everything away.

Zechariah 4:6 reminds us, "Not by might, nor by power, but by my Spirit, says the Lord."

When God's Spirit flows through people, we see benevolence in action. This is power, with Love. And when we witness power combined with God's Love on Earth, we recognize the work of the Holy Spirit. All this good, is from our God of Love, whom we serve.

How many powerful people do you know who are truly benevolent? While some display a level of compassion and caring, all are still influenced by a fallen nature. God is the only being who is both omnipotent and benevolent. He can bring about anything He wills.

Therefore, it's important to consider that no one can serve two masters. It is crucial to look inward and examine your heart and motives. Who are you serving? When you ignore God and strive in your own strength for power, money, or fame, you miss out on the grace of God in your life.

And when we act with selfish motives, without regard for others, our souls are in danger. We are setting ourselves up for a fall. However, when we walk humbly, knowing that God is all-powerful and works through us by the Holy Spirit, we experience the kindness and love that surrounds and flows through us. We encounter the grace of God, which empowers us to do great things in the world, all while making an eternal difference.

December 5

Go Deeper To Rise Higher

It takes practice to recognize God's presence. Some feel things deeply, while others not so much. And there are those apathetic and unenthusiastic. Happiness feels distant, and sadness seems like an old friend. This does not have to be. You can overcome. You must go deeper to rise higher.

God is always with you, however, you must learn to tap into His presence. This is the way to be set free from emotional hindrances. By going deeper, we can rise higher. And the best way to experience God's presence is by not avoiding your emotions. Feelings matter—especially sorrow and emotional pain. Therefore, we must allow ourselves to express what we are feeling at the moment. The goal is to release present and past events, and even deep-seated trauma.

Do you avoid your emotions? You can rise higher and find more joy in your daily life. Have you noticed that after a good cry, you sometimes feel like laughing? This strange experience tells us something important about feelings.

That we gain clarity, and can experience and learn more as we go deeper into the root of our emotions—the good, the bad, the joy, and the sorrow.

There may be hidden things to uncover that are necessary to look at in order to break free. Matters like forgiveness— for ourselves and others. These are critical for the journey. We need not fear. And when we feel numb or listless, we must intentionally sit down, meditate, and pray to understand the root cause. You can choose to press in, go deep, and live fully moving forward.

It's often uncomfortable to confront the root causes of hidden pain and hurt. Some issues may have been buried for a very long time, and today, there may be a dullness that makes life feel boring or even not worth living. But this is not a permanent condition. And when you face the broken things you have been afraid to see, God's presence becomes more profound.

Is there something hindering you today? You have a role to play in your journey toward healing and joy. When you face your emotional struggles head-on—including depression—and choose to rise above, you will discover a new spring in your step. It is possible to no longer be weighed down by past hurts. However, you must partner with God, by faith, and bring your experiences to the Cross.

December 6

Tumultuous Times Ahead

Do not be surprised by tumultuous times ahead, but hold fast to the goodness of God.

Our world is changing at incredible speed. And every moment brings new discoveries, technology and more information to process. We are evolving through it all. Many are consistently tuned into the media, bombarded with frightening and negative noise.

Like a rudder that steers the ship, we must remain fixed on the Truth that lives in our soul. Let your faith not fail. Hold fast, knowing that you have purpose and are fiercely loved by God today and always. Whatever comes your way, you can handle it. Only remain focused on the fact that you have a role to play in serving your fellow man. Pay no mind to the distractions that attempt to throw you off course or create fear.

Your focus determines your destiny. So, become like a horse with blinders. Hold fast to the simplicity of knowing that this day is precious and ripe for giving. Do not look to the left or the right; instead, fix your gaze directly ahead. Pay attention to where you are and where you are going. There will be traps—avoid them at all costs!

Be forewarned, that when you lose faith and do not stay focused on God's purposes, you walk blindly and risk becoming part of the problem. Belief and focus are essential to achieving great things. You may feel invincible, young, or timeless, but the Truth will reveal that life is but a breath—you are only here for a short while. For this reason, value your time and who you are.

Hold fast to the Truth and make your life a grand adventure. Always keep your focus, and remember not to be distracted by things that can steal and destroy your good outcome. There will be tumultuous times ahead, and so for the goodness of humanity, hold fast to Love.

December 7

A Sheep Led To Slaughter

When we stand for something we believe in and step out in faith to make a difference in our community, we can expect to face resistance. Whether it's launching a new business idea or initiating something to help the planet, new challenges and endeavors often bring counteractions.

And pursuing a dream or vision can be a lonely journey. Opposition primarily comes to those who believe in something and strive to achieve it. Mainly in the form of criticism and other challenges. There may be struggles in accomplishing certain tasks. Or working with others who do not share in the vision. At times, it may feel like you are a sheep led to slaughter—mostly because others don't see what you see. And when your vision involves being in the public eye and putting yourself out there, it takes a tremendous amount of courage to overcome the naysayers. You might feel exposed and ineffective, but these are natural feelings that you must go through, in order to overcome.

Reaching the goal and achieving the prize, requires facing the world head-on. This can be taxing due to our imperfections. Perhaps no one is cheering for you. Don't be discouraged. Instead, be brave and keep pushing through the resistance, to reach the other side. Remember, that the path is rarely straightforward. For sure, it would be easier to avoid it altogether! However, when you understand that these challenges are all a part of the journey, you are equipped and headed in the right direction. You know the signs are leading you on purpose.

There is nothing that we must endure that Jesus did not already endure as our example. And when walking a distinct path, it can indeed, feel lonely—much like going against the grain. However, once we face these difficult challenges, we emerge on the other side, where blessings reveal themselves in powerful ways. We are stronger, knowing there is no gain without some level of pain.

So, pray, stand strong, and walk on today. The pain you feel can manifest as physical exertion, emotional challenges, or the sacrifice of time and resources. Do not forget that it is through these trials that you build resilience, and learn valuable lessons, to ultimately achieve your desired outcomes. Persevere through these difficulties with the understanding that the rewards of your efforts are likely proportional to the challenges you face. Thus, while the journey may be arduous, the resulting growth and the accomplishments, make the effort worthwhile.

December 8

Interdependence In All Things

When we place all of our focus on one person, we risk forgetting the importance of reaching out to others. Many people become codependent, missing out on valuable friendships and connections. We are meant to meet the needs of others in this life, and when we direct all our giving toward one person, we fail to spread love and support, as we are intended to.

There is a flow you can live in freely. And if you are codependent, you hinder your ability to reach your full potential. Imagine if each person reached out to a handful of others nearby without becoming overly attached to any one person—what would happen? Perhaps we would cover the planet with a web of Love!

We are social creatures, born to embrace, love, and support others. Yet, people everywhere feel lonely and helpless. If we remain open, we discover that our circles are always changing and expanding, constantly reaching and surrounding. The solution is to sense the direction we are meant to go and move toward it.

Interdependence is mutual dependence between things. When we focus on just one thing or one person, our existence becomes limited. In contrast, when we walk in love and remain open, we talk to people and notice the needs that are around us. We are not confined to any one person or thing. And The Way forward is through mutual interdependence among all people and things.

We all need love, but what can we learn from relationships that dissolve and break apart? What about the connections that break our hearts, or those relationships that do not last? Let us not fall into habits of obsession or attachment. Instead, let us put God first and practice interdependence with one another—for the good of all people and the planet.

Moreover, let us not remain in relationships just for comfort. Comfort now may lead to discomfort later. Instead, let us embrace a little discomfort now and be courageous in recognizing and welcoming our interconnectedness.

December 9

Extreme Faith

We experience conflict and fear in every season of life. Therefore, we need to cultivate persevering faith through times of trouble. We must hold fast to the Truth because difficulty will inevitably come. And when it does, we can walk through in victory.

Often, those who have faced the most trouble and challenges demonstrate the greatest levels of faith. This is likely because they have survived intense pressure and persevered through trials. And people who have come through many difficulties, reveal a depth of trust. They know what it is like to walk on the edge. And often their accomplishments and inner strength are great.

Having a strong faith, especially as we mature, is crucial. Life's troubles and challenges can compound over time, and as we experience the loss of loved ones, health difficulties, or financial crises, we must hold fast to what is truly important.

And when we endure challenges, while surrounded by others, we can let our light shine as an example of endurance for all those around us. Having the faith and strength to face difficulties with steadfastness actually encourages and uplifts others in their struggles.

1 Peter 5:10, Scripture reminds us: "The God of all grace, who called you to his eternal glory in Christ, will himself restore, establish, strengthen, and support you after you have suffered a little while."

Don't be discouraged when you go through hardships. Instead, focus on trusting God and exercising unwavering faith. You may suffer for a time, but after you've endured, God will restore you, allowing you to experience growth, to do great things. You never have to lose your childlike innocence as you grow in faith. You are His child. He will be with you, to lead and guide you.

December 10

The One Who Changes Not

It's amazing how people change over time. Truly, we are evolving every moment. Our appearance shifts, our actions transform, and our responses to situations evolve. Some may think they haven't changed much and feel that everything is as it has always been. But even when we seem to coast along and appear to stay the same—whether we fall, rise, or climb—we are always changing.

How does all this change truly matter? Some might say that none of it matters—that all the changes are merely a part of life and a predicament. However, every change shapes who we are becoming and influences the path we take, guiding us toward growth, wisdom, or perhaps even greater understanding. And as we let go of what is behind, we embrace strength in who we are becoming.

Do you enjoy the challenges you face? Embracing who you are in the present moment is valuable. What matters most is your relationship with the Creator. The Lord walks with you and delights in you through every change.

Each challenge is an opportunity to grow closer to Him and discover more of the purpose He has for you.

It is good to take both the good and the bad from the past, to shape our present. Walking with the living God in fellowship and friendship is the entire purpose of our salvation. We are marvelous, exquisite, and beautiful beings who hopefully grow in character as we mature. And as we reflect on our actions and their outcomes, hopefully, we gain clarity to better understand our spiritual nature.

You are never alone. And when you truly grasp this, you can face any fear and find more peace, in navigating difficult life challenges. It's comforting to know that you are loved unconditionally as you are being transformed inwardly. You are God's beautiful creation. And every step of the way, as you go through change, presents an opportunity to fellowship with the One who changes not.

The Lord is always walking alongside you—today and into eternity. The more you experience His presence in your daily life, the more you evolve to reflect His glory at every stage. So, share your heart today. If something stands in the way—perhaps a block or a wall—invite the Lord into your heart again. His love knows no bounds. And if there is a need for repentance, don't hold back or be afraid to come as you are.

December 11

The Highest Calling

Many people feel removed from helping others in times of distress, often unsure of how to be of service or what exactly to do. However, helping those in need is one of the highest callings.

As children of God, the Holy Spirit guides our path, offering signs and suggestions for ways to make a difference. Yet, when trouble arises, it can be challenging to discern how best to assist others. What is needed is a sense of urgency and selflessness.

Do you want to experience true magnificence in life? Then embrace selflessness. Being selfless means prioritizing the needs and well-being of others above your own. Acts of kindness can make a profound impact. Consider the story of the Good Samaritan: a man was left by the side of the road, and while many passed by, one person stopped to help, lifting him to a place of healing.

Do you need a miracle? A powerful way to grow is by shifting from selfish thinking to reaching out with selflessness. Even with limited resources, there is always something you can do to help another person or find a place to serve. Perhaps a neighbor needs a ride or their lawn mowed, or maybe a friend needs encouragement, or someone to talk to.

Would you help your pets but not your neighbors? Many people do. They lead limited lives and feel powerless to make a difference. But if everyone viewed their existence as an opportunity to serve humanity, the world would be a much better place. We would witness an abundance of selflessness rather than the prevailing selfishness we see today.

Stepping out to make a difference requires energy, vision, and drive. Love is inherently selfless, and communities thrive when they look beyond their differences and focus on meeting the needs of others. This is where wonders occur, and life becomes truly sweet.

Ultimately, we are not justified by our works, but there are rewards for having a helpful, giving spirit. Great blessings and peace come when we prioritize others over ourselves and practice selflessness. Selflessness is the path to excellence, creating hope in others for the sake of Love. It requires a balance that only the Holy Spirit can bring.

Are you feeling trapped, unmotivated, or depressed? Tap into selflessness. This is where true life force energy resides. And let go of expectations for rewards.

December 12

Where There Is Hope

Hope is the joyful expectation of good. It can be a dream, a wish, a promise, or a desire. Yet, after repeated disappointments and failures, believing in the possibility of good—and maintaining hope—can become challenging. It often requires practice and resilience, especially after heartbreak.

Many people find themselves in a state of "come what may," accepting life as it comes. However, when we place our hope in a loving God, we gain purpose and peace, transforming our journey into one of positive and lasting fulfillment.

As we age and face more difficulties, maintaining hope can feel elusive. Yet, learning to trust in the Lord becomes easier with practice. Over time, His faithfulness becomes more evident, revealing His protection, guidance, and blessings in hindsight.

Our faith should grow stronger each day. To build confidence, take time to reflect on where you've been and how you've been guided and protected. Recognizing God's past goodness reinforces your assurance that He is still at work in your life. This awareness fosters hope in His provision and direction, equipping you for whatever challenges arise.

Hope is essential for a fruitful journey as pilgrims on Earth. And since life is short and Love is vast, focusing on Love—both from God and towards ourselves and others—is paramount. When we place our hope in God to direct our path, we attract more of what we desire.

Whether it's a promise, a dream, or peace through a storm, hope is rooted in trust. Ultimately, as your love aligns with God's will, you can expect more blessings and, especially, more hope. As you mature and grow into who God has called you to be, your love for others deepens and reflects your personal faith and state of mind. Remember this: where there is hope, there is trust.

December 13

Reaching New Heights

There is a flow and guidance that comes from our thoughts, ideas, and dreams. To reach new heights, we must be aware of our thinking and speech. We need to center ourselves in every action with a sense of purpose to achieve greater outcomes. Ideally, we should continue pursuing excellent accomplishments, dreams, and visions.

Our ventures typically have a "why" behind them. We might say, "I want to do this" or "I want to go there," but understanding the deeper "why" uncovers our true motives and purposes. This clarity makes the path forward more direct and purposeful. Discovering why we choose one path over another helps us learn more about ourselves, ideally leading to growth rather than settling for the status quo. And when we understand our motives and reasons for an action, we gain practical knowledge.

Purpose is a powerful driver that leads us in ways nothing else can. Parents often say, "This is my child, my reason for living." Pet owners find purpose in caring for their beloved animals. Friends help friends and siblings, while grandparents often pass on wisdom and grace. Everyone senses purpose at some point. And most people who reach new heights are motivated by something greater than themselves.

We develop bravery when we act with a sense of purpose, especially when we tackle challenging tasks for significant reasons. This approach brings more satisfaction and less discouragement in life. So when you're ready to open up your world, first bring your thoughts and ideas to the Lord for important understanding on where to go from where you are. Pray with a sense of why to determine your purpose and examine your root motivation. This brings clarity to the forefront and improves outcomes.

Reaching new heights often requires stepping beyond our comfort zones and embracing both challenges and growth. It demands a clear sense of purpose and unwavering faith. By aligning our actions with our deepest motivations and seeking divine guidance, we unlock the potential for remarkable achievements. As we rise to meet our goals, we inspire others to pursue their own aspirations, creating a ripple effect of progress and fulfillment.

December 14

Unrelenting Faith

Life can be a hard climb. The path is never straight, and each person has a route to take with a windy breeze that blows through corners and turns. And to experience the biggest blessing and available grace, you need to have a constant and unceasing, abiding faith.

Many challenges come to those who dream and pursue their vision. And when there is a goal in mind, it's helpful to be relentless. We do not need to compromise purpose. And the walk is not for despair, but toward contentment and the realization of what we strive for.

Therefore, our faith must be a constant directive that drives us through challenges. And every day is a day for unrelenting faith. Additionally, perseverance is required in the face of defeat, discouragement, rejection, and broken dreams. Being relentless means reaching for the prize.

Often we struggle with the feeling of being alone from time to time. And every person will go through hard things. So don't detest trials, but instead, become relentless in the pursuit of your faith. When you choose to accept the difficulty and press forward to not shrink back, you overcome obstacles and experience the miracles that come with belief.

God works in mysterious ways and on His timetable. There is no human timeline in God's plan. So don't stop believing, however long it takes. Many receive their blessings and promises later in life. Furthermore, the journey builds Godly character and demonstrates the miraculous working power of God. So the important thing is to not lose heart through the challenges.

If you struggle to keep moving forward in any area of your life, remember to be relentless. Take a stand and abide in faith. And believe that God can and will do it. Do not give up on your dreams. You must believe that when God gives you a dream, it is because He has given you everything you need to see it come to fruition. For this reason, it will come to pass.

Habakkuk 2:3 says, "For the vision is yet for an appointed time; But at the end it will speak, and it will not lie. Though it tarries, wait for it; Because it will surely come. It will not tarry."

December 15

Sing A New Song

You've heard that old saying, that when life gives you lemons, make lemonade? Well, a good way to make fresh lemonade is to start by counting your blessings. You can give thanks! This is how we begin to sing a new song. And having a new song in your heart is akin to a new attitude. It is a great way to avoid being stuck in negative circumstances.

In Scripture, Psalm 96 says, "Sing to the Lord a new song; sing to the Lord, all the earth. Sing to the Lord, praise his name; proclaim his salvation day after day. Declare his glory among the nations, his marvelous deeds among all peoples."

We should focus on the positive things we can think of and express our praise to the Lord. Music is particularly effective for this, as it can uplift and transform your mood. However, even if you're not musically inclined, you can still praise the Lord by cultivating a thankful heart.

When you go through hard things, it can take effort to be thankful. Yet, we need to always find something to be grateful for. And whatever it is, that you find, can help you from being sucked into a dark place. When you freely give thanks and sing a new song, you avoid getting "stuck".

Another sure way to create something new, and sing a new song, is to reach out in kindness toward someone else. Sorrow and tears may come for a night, or even a season, but joy comes after a while. So, sing a new song and rejoice that everything changes. And that this too shall pass.

You are not alone when you are grieving. Everyone suffers from time to time. For this reason we must press through the pain, to grow in hope for a new day. Please don't run from the pain, but instead feel it and let it go. Find your hope in the Lord, because as long as you are alive, there is something you are meant to do. A reason to sing a new song.

You have an important purpose in the gift of today. So give thanks to God for the experience of living. Give thanks and praise Him, especially to harvest new hope and strength. This is spiritual warfare and a significant way to fight defeat, depression, and hopelessness. When you vocalize your faith and express yourself, especially your hope, you gain strength for the journey. So, don't give up, but sing a new song. A song that is medicine to your soul.

December 16

Wild Diamonds In The Rough

People often go to great lengths to avoid pain and suffering. No one enjoys experiencing discomfort or hurt. Some may numb their feelings with drugs and alcohol, while others might avoid situations or relationships that cause emotional pain, such as making amends with family members or deepening connections with loved ones. However, when we confront and make peace with our pain and suffering, we grow stronger and more resilient through the process.

In Scripture, 1 Peter 5 says, "And the God of all grace, who called you to his eternal glory in Christ, after you have suffered a while, will himself restore you and make you strong, firm and steadfast."

And what does it profit a man if he gains the whole world and loses his own soul? We are born into this wild world of human existence, to be transformed into spirit bodies along "The Way". Therefore, we need to approach life with a humble nature. And why not? We are frail and very miniscule when we look at the big picture. But God is Great.

No one can run from pain long, as it has a way of catching up. And like wild diamonds in the rough, we are being transformed into shiny jewels. And it's good to know that the path of pain and suffering is temporary. We don't need to deny our feelings or spiritual side to protect ourselves.

When we embrace the journey, knowing that the substance of our challenges will manifest toward something greater, we make incredible gains. Therefore, cast your care on the Lord and be willing to listen to the Holy Spirit, in order to be restored, made strong, firm and steadfast.

Fix your eyes on Jesus. Nothing compares to the peace of God. If you're hurting and going through a difficult time, avoid the temptation to self-medicate or to project your pain onto others, as this only leads to more suffering. Instead, bring your heart and trials to the Lord. Move forward slowly, trusting that, in time, you will be renewed and made strong again.

December 17

Focus On The Fruit

When we place our faith in God, we trust the Lord for everything that we need. He knows where we are, and where we are to go, and never leads us into something we cannot handle. And when we have maturity, we are ready to be greatly used.

Time moves forward, and the future remains a mystery. Some days may feel like progress is slow, but remember that God is omnipresent and omnipotent, and He knows all things. As we trust Him and move through our journey, we should focus on cultivating the Fruit of the Spirit to aid our progress. The Fruit of the Spirit includes Love, Joy, Peace, Patience, Kindness, Generosity, Faithfulness, Gentleness, and Self-Control. These qualities reflect the presence of the Holy Spirit in our lives, distinguishing those who are in Christ. If you find yourself feeling uncertain or confused, turn your attention to the Fruit of the Spirit in your daily life.

You may have a big dream, a new relationship, or a business idea. Perhaps you are not sure what to do? With a focus on the Fruit of the Spirit, you are positioned to become the best version of yourself that you can possibly be. And having Godly character, provides clarity as you walk and trust further that God is above all, ordering your steps, especially as more challenges come.

There are people who will bring out the best in you and those who tend to bring out the worst. Some will lead you to harm. Having the ability to remain even keeled through it all, is a sign of maturity. Are you trusting God and His leading? Are you walking in Love toward those around you? Are you being kind to yourself? Do you have peace when you lay your head down at night?

The Lord leads us into new places. And often when we are faced with trouble, it's from our own poor choices. Prayer helps to sort things out. So, if you desire more blessings, pray and ask God to fill your need. He delights in giving you the desires of your heart. And as you wait in faith for Him to direct your path, know that His plan is good. To bless you and pour abundant Love upon you.

Fix your heart and mind on the Fruit of the Spirit and get ready for a blessing. Always remember that your steps are ordered by the Lord. And never forget that God has the great power to do exceedingly and abundantly more than you can ask, think or imagine.

December 18

The Signs Of Our Times

Every generation develops its own language and perspective. Over the centuries, people have observed the signs of their times, and as societies evolve, they face various choices and perspectives on pressing issues. Determining the best course of action for the highest good requires practice, with the ultimate goal being the pursuit of Love.

When we choose the most ethical and compassionate path, we are rewarded. Current signs of the times include messages such as "Stay 6 Feet Apart," "No Entry Without a Mask," "Say NO to Gun Violence," and "No Human Being Is Illegal." Other expressions that reflect our era include "My Body, My Choice" and "Black Lives Matter." These statements capture the essence of our contemporary social landscape.

Determining what is truly good for us is of utmost importance. Sometimes, we may pursue our desires only to later realize that our preference was not the best choice for the highest good. With hindsight, our vision becomes clearer. Experience can be a valuable guide, and ideally, after making mistakes along the way, we learn to make better choices by considering both sides of a situation.

We are fortunate to live in a culture where individuals have the freedom to choose who and what they love. In contrast, in many countries, choices are made for people by others or by the prevailing culture. As we navigate life, we should strive to make loving and thoughtful decisions. Our actions inevitably impact others, so it is important to model excellence for those around us.

Always remember that you lead by example. Be vigilant in considering both sides of every situation. If you are uncertain about a decision, take your time. A good indicator that you have made the right choice is when you feel a sense of peace about it. There is no need to follow the crowd, as many have done so to their detriment.

Pay attention and make decisions with care and thoughtfulness. Pray first, then wait to discern the Lord's will. Making the ideal choice from the outset, will help to avoid future regret and lead to a more fulfilling life.

December 19

God Will Make The Way

When you have suffered a broken heart, it's nearly impossible to be restored and made whole without a humble disposition. It's also very rare to overcome addictions and past trauma without humility. Healing requires a spirit of forgiveness, for the process to flourish.

Restoration and humility go hand in hand. And when a person is in a place of humility, God is in the midst. Additionally, you can tell plenty about a person by the words they speak. Where there is pride, there is a separation from grace. Additionally, the human heart can be fickle and unpredictable. And because a person's heart condition determines their words and actions, plenty have good intentions, but many find overcoming complicated.

Scripture says in 2 Chronicles 7:14, "If my people, who are called by my name, shall humble themselves, and pray, and seek my face, and turn from their wicked ways; then will I hear from heaven, and will forgive their sin, and will heal their land."

We need to remember who oversees our path. God knows everything about us; nothing is hidden from Him, and He desires the best for us. He does not want us to remain stuck in our flaws, whether they are addiction, pride, deceit, or self-importance. His wish is for us to experience a fruitful, joyful, and fulfilling life. To achieve this, believers may undergo pruning to remove hindrances that prevent spiritual growth and true fulfillment.

When we are truly children of God, we understand the necessity of having a humble heart. We recognize that the Lord desires to heal our souls and acknowledge that chastisement is part of this process. We often notice corrections in our lives through problems and difficulties—perhaps an addict faces arrest, a friendship ends due to pride, or a financial crisis occurs. These challenges can serve as wake-up calls, leading us to confront our errors and come to the end of ourselves.

We are humbled not to be punished, but to begin anew. Each lesson offers the opportunity for grace and forgiveness. God loves you and desires for you to be whole. He will heal the broken parts and guide you towards better days, fulfilled dreams, and your ultimate destiny. He does not wish to harm you, but to lead you. Invite Him in and trust Him to show you The Way.

December 20

Love Energy And The Source

Life is a mystery with many unanswered questions. And when we consider the ambiguity of this world and all that is in it, it is easy to conclude that anything appears to be possible.

And human beings are miraculous and amazing. We are given dominion over all the land and animals, the fish and the sea. And with much intelligence, since our prehistoric beginnings, we recognize that we have evolved at record speed. Surely, we are fearfully and wonderfully made.

Scripture says in 1 Corinthians 13:12, "For now we see only a reflection as in a mirror; then we shall see face to face. Now I know in part; but then I shall know fully, even as I am fully known."

Christ came into this world as the son of God. He was and is God. He led a pure life of Love, with submission and miracles, so that we would come to know the height and depth, the width and length, of God's Love for us. This is the story and meaning of Christmas.

The Love of Christ that lives within us through the Holy Spirit is truly powerful. Each day, as we grow and our souls are transformed toward eternity, we experience this change. When we align ourselves with God in Christ, we gain clarity. This pure energy of Love flourishes and expands through our beliefs, words, and actions. Christ exemplifies how to walk in unity with one another, highlighting the importance of forgiveness and humility—key elements for Love to flow freely.

As we reflect on our evolution, let us embrace the wonder-working power that shows us that anything is possible. Scripture tells us that after our time on Earth, all will be revealed—miracles, restoration, healing, abundance, gift-giving, hope, and timeless change for the good of all mankind. We have the opportunity to collectively manifest Love in our world, beginning within each of us.

Take a moment today to tap into this source of Love energy by praying and inviting the Lord into your heart. This experience is ongoing, and we need to refresh our senses from time to time. Ask God to forgive any missteps and guide you on the path forward. Embrace this process, as there is purity and strength that come from humble submission to the will of God.

December 21

A Love Song For Every Person

I used to think that if my music moved many people, I would be healed. That all the pain I had ever felt would go away, and everything I had gone through would be reconciled. I believed the writing was curative and the presentation of the message would help others.

Much of this is true, and what I learned over time, is that it is not about accolades, fame, or glory. Instead, it is about this great Love song that lives in our hearts. Another thing I discovered when writing, was that the words were actually Love songs to me. It's the song that sings, "you are deeply loved, just as you are and in the midst of suffering."

Greatness often arises from a deep need for change, healing, comfort, and encouragement. Motivators such as the desire to overcome pain from loss, abandonment, and brokenness have led to remarkable accomplishments throughout history. Self-expression is vital, and each of us has a unique Love song to sing from the heart. What matters is our willingness to connect with this song and story. By sharing your own journey, you can help others discover their own. Do you believe that God understands every tear you shed and every need you have? His presence becomes evident when you invite Him into your heart's cries of pain and praise.

No one is perfect and we are going to make mistakes. Sometimes we will go through painful situations that we have no control over. These may be things that we did not instigate or bring on ourselves. Yet, in our suffering, we bring about further hurt and agony when we are prideful and unwilling to listen to the Holy Spirit guiding our path.

In Luke 19:40 scripture says, "If my people remain silent and do not praise me, even the rocks will cry out!"

God has a unique Love song for you to discover. Even if you feel stranded in circumstances beyond your control, remember that you are not truly stranded. God is near, and He will work all things together for your good. So, ask God for help. There is hope for freedom even in suffering.

December 22

Happy Joyous And Free

What makes a soul happy, joyous, and free? To be happy, joyous, and free, requires some life experience. We need to understand what we do not want. While some people may naturally possess a freewheeling personality, for many, achieving a state of happiness, joy, and freedom requires a thoughtful approach.

People often base their happiness on external factors such as circumstances, successes, and the love they receive from others. And when relationships change, or people leave or pass away, some fall into darkness. Similarly, when happiness is tied to achievements or financial status, changes in these areas can lead to feelings of depression and hopelessness.

As emotional beings, we experience and need to process a wide range of feelings. Remember times when you cried so hard it felt almost like laughter? Life involves tears, and every emotion holds significance. For true freedom, it's important not to avoid difficult situations and emotions. Instead, we can confront and address issues as they arise,

734

or at least before the day ends, so we can start each new day with a clear and unburdened heart.

The devil comes to steal, kill, and destroy, but Jesus offers life. This means we will face temptations—temptations to make poor choices, to harm ourselves or others, especially when we are hurting. We might also be tempted to pretend everything is fine, but ignoring issues and pretending they never happened only invites more trouble. However, there is a path forward.

Christ came to free us from any curse, and this means we need to repent daily for our missteps. It's important to confront emotions as they arise, rather than suppressing them, which can lead to passive-aggressive behavior and outbursts later. We must take up our cross and follow the path of humility each day, recognizing that pride can obstruct our freedom.

Life experience teaches us that our pain often stems from not allowing grace, mercy, and forgiveness to flow freely in our hearts. And as we receive these gifts from God, we are called to extend them to others. This is the way to true freedom in Christ.

Micah 6:8 says: "He has shown you, O man, what is good; And what does the Lord require of you? But to do justice, to love mercy, and to walk humbly with your God." This is the true secret to happiness, joy, and freedom—and you can achieve it!

December 23

The Wisdom Of Love

It's often difficult to understand why things happen the way they do. There may seem to be no rhyme or reason, yet there is a wisdom to Love that we cannot always see—at least not until we've traveled further down the road to enlightenment and glory.

Life's circumstances can leave us feeling confused or unfairly treated. We may question a parent's actions toward a child, feel disillusioned by a friendship, or grapple with betrayal from someone we love without understanding why. Yet, the wisdom of Love ensures that we never endure more than we can handle, even when things seem like a mess. Though suffering may leave us speechless and our hearts broken, we can trust that we are destined for great Love.

As we mature, wisdom gradually reveals Truth in our lives, reminding us that our ways are not God's ways. We often cannot see the big picture until we walk along the path to gain understanding. What we do know is that God is Love, and He knows what is best for us—what we need and when we need it. Love will often slay our selfish nature, preparing us to receive more magnificent blessings in our lives.

The wisdom of Love works through people, as only God knows the heart. He alone understands what each of us is thinking and what we may need at any given moment. His ways are higher than ours, and the purpose of our earthly journey is to grow fully in grace. The wisdom of Love cultivates and produces the fruit of the Spirit in our lives.

As Scripture says in Galatians 5:22-23, "But the fruit of the Spirit is love, joy, peace, patience, kindness, goodness, faithfulness, gentleness, and self-control." There is no use in resisting God's work. Instead, we must accept that a greater power is at play, and the wisdom of Love manifests to instruct us and foster growth. Though situations may be upsetting, Love permits them for our ultimate good. When troubles come, we are called to maintain an open and honest outlook.

The wisdom of Love always dismantles self-importance, and we receive an abundance of grace, knowing we are meant to walk together toward the light. In time, we will understand what it all means, but for now, we move from glory to glory in Christ, with His forgiveness at the center. This is the wisdom of Love—everything we experience is used to bring about God's best in our lives, shaping us into powerful soldiers of grace.

December 24

Birds Flying In Formation

It is exciting to watch birds flying in formation—they are a beauty to behold! Studies show that the wind from their wings makes flying easier and provides support for the group. As each bird flaps its wings, a rotating vortex of air rolls off its wingtips, creating lift and reducing air resistance for the birds behind. Additionally, researchers believe that birds possess a kind of biological "radio," allowing them to communicate intricate patterns and actions instantly. Each bird hones in on the signals of the seven closest to it, enabling them to act as one, moving up, down, around, and to the side in perfect harmony.

And just like birds who gain strength flying in numbers, we do well in community. We are not meant to be alone. We rise highest when we have the support and love of our families, friends, neighbors, and team members. However, in today's tumultuous society, people are becoming more isolated. Many stare into their phones and have lost a great deal of social awareness and niceties. Additionally, facetiming on social media does not replace the experience of sitting in someone's presence. We need others around us.

In community we gain powerful connections and support. In community, we recognize that each person has a unique gift and something specific to share and bring to the table. We do not need to compare ourselves to one another. Everyone is made with different abilities, gifts, and talents. And we experience a level of intimacy that brings strength and meaning to the journey when we spend time getting real and sharing ourselves and interests with one another.

Live life well. Don't wait for someone to come to you—step out and be the first to take action and enjoy your community. Reconnect with group meetings, whether at church, school, or wherever your interests lie. Be smart and safe, and do not fear. Holding someone's hand or giving a hug to embrace another will strengthen both you and them.

You will fly higher and go further as you step out of your comfort zone and open your heart. So don't let the fear of intimacy or disease hold you back. It's time to fight the resistance. And like birds flying in formation, you can overcome the temptation toward isolation.

Scripture says in Hebrews 10:25, "Not forsaking the assembling of ourselves together, as the manner of some is; but exhorting one another, and so much the more, as the day approaches."

December 25

Healing For Mental Health

When do we learn right from wrong? Do you believe there is a sense of conscience even in young children? What if every time we hurt someone or missed the mark, we addressed it immediately? Would this lead to fewer mental disorders? One thing is certain: when we do wrong and don't address it, issues can compound, leading to greater depravity in our lives. There are different stages of consciousness: certain conscience means being convinced without doubt that an action is good or bad, while doubtful conscience occurs when one is unsure about the right choice. Given the deception present in society today, we can conclude that repentance is essential for mental health.

People desire to be accepted and loved, but they also make mistakes and often replicate the negative behaviors they encounter. For many, it's easy to fall into a "monkey see, monkey do" mindset, especially without supportive family or friends to demonstrate a better way. This is why it is crucial to model good behavior and positive habits—to lead by example.

Coming to Christ can cleanse the soul. Scripture tells us in Acts 3:19, "Repent therefore, and turn, that your sins may be blotted out." And in 1 John 1:9, "If we confess our sins, He is faithful and just to forgive our sins and to cleanse us from all unrighteousness." Therefore, we must face issues head-on and address situations that are unpleasant. When we avoid or ignore our failings, the conscience becomes seared and detached, leading to confusion and even personality disorders. Over time, a "dam" of unresolved transgressions can form, making it difficult to process negative experiences.

Place your life at the foot of the cross, believing that Christ died for you. Here, all sin—past, present, and future—is forgiven. You may need to revisit certain painful experiences to let them go completely, and this may be revealed further as you receive the mercy Christ provides. This process is ongoing as you daily, monthly, and yearly remember and acknowledge Christ's sacrifice.

There is no need to beat yourself up. You must forgive yourself and keep moving forward. Sin, when compounded, becomes disorder. So it is vital to repent whenever you "miss the mark." Don't simply gloss over it and move on. Bring it to the Cross and experience the true freedom Christ offers today.

December 26

Birthing New Dreams

Scripture tells us that without a dream a man dies. Dreams give us something to hold on to. And our dreams go hand in hand with hope. They walk with us and propel us forward. And all of us have had a dream that did not come true at some point in time. Many lose hope when this happens. However, most dreams come to pass in a roundabout way. For instance, you may be walking in one direction, only to uncover new provisions.

Just because your dream hasn't come true in the way you imagined, don't give up. There is a difference between striving for a dream and receiving provision for a dream. As we mature—often after much striving—we discover that dreams come true as provisions for our lives. They become the sustenance that remains after everything else has failed. These dreams are birthed through multiple attempts and failures and are a re-creation born from renewal and refinement.

Some choose to indulge the mundane. The daily grind. The idea that what has been, will always be. And this is the "Boulevard of Broken Dreams". But God does not want us to live this way. The Lord delights in giving His children the desires of their heart. He also knows what we are able to handle at any given point in time.

So keep hope alive by focusing on the Lord today, to become whole in your soul. Wholeness is the key to manifesting greatness. And when it appears that much is failing in the way of your dreams, pray and ask God to give you a bigger vision.

Remember, we do not see what God sees. And when it seems the whole world is falling apart around you, focus on wholeness again. When you keep your eyes on manifesting greatness within you, the greatness is sure to manifest outside of your circumstances. Just don't give up. And if you are walking in the wrong direction, turn around. It's never too late to get right with God and to understand what is important. You can make the difference.

December 27

God's Timing Is Perfect

Life is a faith walk, unfolding moment by moment, step by step. Just as the Christ child came at the ideal time, fulfilling divine prophecy, the moments in your life are also destined to arrive in perfect order. Trust that every season, every challenge, and every blessing has its purpose in God's greater plan for you.

Have you ever noticed how solutions often come at the last minute? Whether acquiring a home or a space to rent, or getting the job we hope for, or perhaps being accepted into college or school; the answers always seem to come at the end of much waiting and wondering. They seem to show up at the last minute. And just in time. Mostly when we are at our wits end.

When we learn to trust the Lord, we understand that our situations matter. Where we go and what we do, who we meet and how we fit in, are all important to our life's journey. So we put our feelers out, and seek to find. But it is God who orders our steps. And learning to trust the Lord while finding our way is not always easy.

When we understand that God's timing is perfect, we can relax and truly enjoy the moment. Scripture tells us in Proverbs 3:5-6, "Trust in the Lord with all your heart and lean not on your own understanding; in all your ways acknowledge Him, and He will make your paths straight."

God's timing is perfect, and we often grow through trial and error. Sometimes, we rush ahead of God, trying to make things happen in our own time, acting impulsively or hastily. When this happens, we may face more cleanup and consequences from poor choices, potentially leading to greater costs and complications. However, with time and hindsight, wisdom can develop.

Waiting for important issues to resolve is a wise practice. Trusting and waiting require self-control. So, don't be in a hurry; instead, learn to trust God and pray along The Way. You may find yourself rescued from difficult circumstances by not forcing your own will. Trust in God's guidance, even through uncertainty and challenges.

December 28

Visualize Healing And More

Prayer and meditation are powerful practices that help us live our best lives. And when we add visualization to the mix, we begin to see the things we hope for manifesting in our lives. Taking the time to center our thoughts and petitions allows us to find clarity and strength, especially during difficult moments. These practices help us connect with a higher purpose, maintain inner peace, and cultivate a positive mindset that supports growth and fulfillment.

There is great comfort and possibility in the practice of visualization. If it is your body that needs healing, you can pray and visualize, focusing specifically on asking God to touch the area where you hurt. This focused intention can aid in quicker recovery and may even open the door to miracles. Visualize yourself as whole and healed, trusting that God's will is above all. The key is to be specific. If you are seeking a better job, picture yourself walking through the doors of your new workplace and experiencing that reality in your mind's eye. This focused visualization helps align your intentions with your desires, bringing clarity and direction.

Many simply pray for God's will to be done. And most are not accustomed to being specific in prayer using visualizations. But our thoughts precede our outcomes. So, it is important to become familiar with visualization, because of the benefits that come with seeing. As we tap into imagination by the Holy Spirit and visualize, we obtain improved results.

The mind is powerful, and God is all-knowing. When focusing on healing, you might visualize blood flowing through muscles, expanding and strengthening, or imagine a warm light entering an area of soreness or infection. Combining prayer with visualization, rather than merely petitioning for something, can enhance the healing process.

Remember, change and healing are inside jobs. Use the tools provided by the Holy Spirit to aid in your progress. Invite Christ in and receive the Holy Spirit. Learn to pray with intention, knowing that it can only help and never hurt any situation. Ultimately, trust that the Lord has the final say on the outcome.

December 29

Choice Equals Destiny

It's amazing how one choice can change the trajectory of our lives. And because we have many small and larger choices to make, choosing wisely is important. Additionally, there are times we may feel we don't have a choice. But how we deal with every decision matters.

People face all sorts of trials and it's true, everyone falls short sometimes. We will occasionally make foolish choices. Some avoid choosing altogether and procrastinate until the walls come tumbling down. However, not choosing is also a choice. And most often pride is at the root of every foolish choice that can potentially change one's destiny.

Have you ever told a lie and not realized it until you were caught in it? Perhaps it was a white lie and the thinking was that it was not a big deal. Motives often hide within the subconscious. And it's good to wonder, what is the motivation behind this?

A contrite heart is one that sees the big picture. When we are aware that pride is the root of most sin and failure, we can choose to remain humble and stay on track. You may have overwhelming motives to do good in the world, but there may be another motivation that takes precedence when failing. Hopefully one poor choice does not change the trajectory of your future and destiny. And it is a choice we make, to not destroy our good outcome.

When we Love God, we desire to please Him. However, the spirit is willing but the flesh is weak. So to grasp why we choose the way we do, we need to look at our motives. You could be walking with the Lord for quite some time and yet some poor choice rears its ugly head. It may be that you have come a long way and are relatively victorious. Yet now, you stumble. This is usually due to fear or a selfish attribute or insecurity. But it is the contrite heart that sees shortcomings and missteps and says "Lord, I am sorry, help me to do better".

December 30

Start With Prayer

"Ask and it will be given to you; seek and you will find; knock and the door will be opened to you." These encouraging words from Matthew 7:7-8 guide us to pursue our aspirations and present our requests. Through prayer and meditation in the Holy Spirit, we gain clear direction and the courage to venture beyond what we can see. We explore new possibilities, using our imagination and fresh ideas. As we seek and co-create with the Creator, we expand our vision of ourselves and unlock our potential to achieve great things.

Most of us find it amazing to be alive, yet life can be brief and pass in the blink of an eye. Therefore, it's wise to start today in envisioning possibilities for greatness in yourself and for those who follow. By focusing on building a lasting impact, we can truly make a difference in our communities and circles, creating a meaningful legacy. A lasting reward.

To see beyond conventional boundaries, tap into the Spirit. This approach helps create a lasting legacy and uncovers unique dreams toward fulfillment. When we begin with prayer, we align ourselves with God's guidance, moving forward to the best possible outcome. Without giving the Lord even a moment of our time or a simple prayer, we limit our vision, protection, and enlightenment. And because the future is uncertain, seeking divine guidance is essential.

Sometimes we seek, ask and knock, and do not get the answers immediately. And there will be times that we don't get what we pray for. So it's good to remember that God knows what is best for us. Nonetheless, as we gradually make steps toward what we think is best, we can seek further direction. The important thing is to not give up. The answers will come.

When we humble ourselves and pray, asking the Lord which door to knock on, we find Grace. This Grace guides us toward positive outcomes. Since all things work together for good, we trust that each step we take aligns with the desires of our hearts. We might begin in one direction only to discover new opportunities that lead us elsewhere. Nevertheless, this guidance reflects God's perfect will for our lives and our true heart's desires.

December 31

A New Day Of Freedom

When one chapter ends, a new one begins. And at the start of the New Year, people generally hope for change. Many make resolutions and begin afresh with their intentions. However, one way to begin a new year, and grow in grace, is to purify your heart.

To have a clean heart means to be clear of all guilt, condemnation and oppression. It is a pure heart of Love that comes from repentance. It requires Truth. So just as you can choose to fast from foods, and purify the body, you can choose to purify the heart.

Psalm 51:10 says, "Create in me a clean heart, O God; and renew a right spirit within me."

This is a beautiful prayer that is a great way to begin the New Year. Now is the time to search within, for concerns that may be holding you from complete freedom in Christ. With Christ as the cornerstone, the negativity in your life has no power. And the enemy is defeated.

Purifying the heart means that we come with a willingness to confront flaws and limitations. It means we are committed to change for the better. We believe in the sacrifice of Christ on the Cross, for the redemption of souls. Here we are washed clean. Every lie is canceled out. And all debts have been paid in full. And in our prayer, we acknowledge and let go of toxic emotions like resentment, anger, and envy. We give all praise to God with gratitude for forgiveness, and compassion, as Christ brings the solution with simplicity. Here and now you can receive complete healing and nurturing at the very core of your being.

And just as precious metals are refined through the purification process, your heart needs constant examination and purification to allow Love's true essence to shine forth. When you prioritize introspection, to better understand your motives and actions, every step, no matter how big or small, contributes to the purification of your heart.

Walking with the freedom that comes from a pure heart brings lasting delight. Would you say that you have a pure heart today? Are there issues that are draining your positive energy? Do you wish to experience more joy? Ultimately, a purified heart leads to a state of peace, where your actions align with your values, fostering harmony within yourself and in the world around you.

Milton Keynes UK
Ingram Content Group UK Ltd.
UKHW021934281024
450365UK00017B/1082

9 798218 520724